Dedication

To Laura who gave an idea wings
and Kelly who lent them lift
and to David who let them soar.

To lovers of natural beauty reaching out with
head and heart in search of things wondrous
To dreamers who see beyond the ordinary
To those yearning to unlock secrets and pass them on
To those seeking discovery in nature and find
themselves discovered
And to the children and the child within,
the simple joy found in the sense of wonder—
wonder in wildflowers…

…and Mother who inspired a lifelong love
of things wild and wonderful.

Blue columbine *(Aquilegia coerulea)*

Colorado's
Best Wildflower Hikes
The Front Range

Symbols in this legend are used in the maps for each hike.

Border	Lake
Trail	○ Point of Interest
Adjoining Trail	**TH** Trailhead
Road	**S** Ranger Station
Dirt Road	**P** Parking
River	
Continental Divide	
35 Wildflower Hike	

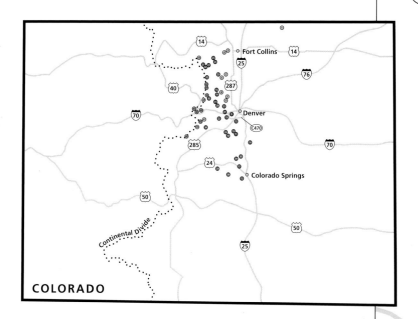

COLORADO

Colorado's
Best Wildflower Hikes
The Front Range

TEXT BY
PAMELA IRWIN

PHOTOGRAPHY BY
DAVID IRWIN

WESTCLIFFE PUBLISHERS

westcliffepublishers.com

ISBN-10: 1-56579-274-2
ISBN-13: 978-1-56579-274-6

TEXT COPYRIGHT: Pamela D. Irwin, 1998. All rights reserved.
PHOTOGRAPHY COPYRIGHT: David Harlan Irwin, 1998. All rights reserved.

PRODUCTION MANAGER: Harlene Finn
EDITORS: Kiki Sayre and Pat Shea
DESIGN AND PRODUCTION: Rebecca Finkel, F + P Graphic Design; Boulder, Colorado

PUBLISHER: Westcliffe Publishers, Inc.
P.O. Box 1261
Englewood, Colorado 80150
westcliffepublishers.com

PRINTED BY: World Print Limited
PRINTED IN: China

LIBRARY OF CONGRESS CATALOGING-IN-PUBLICATION DATA

Irwin, Pamela D., 1942-
    Colorado's best wildflower hikes : the Front Range / by
Pamela D. Irwin : photography by David Harlan Irwin.
        p. cm.
    Includes index.
    ISBN: 1-56579-274-2 (v. 1)
    1. Hiking—Front Range (Colo. and Wyo.)—Guidebooks.
2. Hiking—Colorado—Guidebooks. 3. Wild flowers—
Front Range (Colo. and Wyo.) 4. Wild flowers—Colorado.
5. Front Range (Colo. and Wyo.)—Guidebooks. 6. Colorado
—Guidebooks. I. Title
GV199.42.F86178   1998   97-39213
582.13'09788'6—dc21   CIP

*For more information
about other fine books and
calendars from Westcliffe
Publishers, please contact
your local bookstore, call
us at 1-800-523-3692,
or visit us on the Web at
westcliffepublishers.com*

COVER CAPTION:
Golden banner *(Thermopsis
divaricarpa)*, Roxborough
State Park. Photo by
David Harlan Irwin

PLEASE NOTE:
Risk is always a factor in backcountry and high-mountain travel. Many
of the activities described in this book can be dangerous, especially when
weather is adverse or unpredictable, and when unforeseen events or
conditions create a hazardous situation. The author has done her best to
provide the reader with accurate information about backcountry travel, as
well as to point out some of its potential hazards. It is the responsibility of
the users of this guide to learn the necessary skills for safe backcountry
travel, and to exercise caution in potentially hazardous areas, especially on
glaciers and avalanche-prone terrain. The author and publisher disclaim
any liability for injury or other damage caused by backcountry traveling,
mountain biking, or performing any other activity described in this book.

Acknowledgments

To those who taught me to know and love wildflowers,
my eternal gratitude:

Elizabeth Robinson
Victorine Trammell
Robert Heapes
Panayoti Kelaidis
Andrew Pierce
Bob Robinson
Helen Angel
Carolyn Bredenberg
Members of the Rocky Mountain Chapter of the
American Rock Garden Society and members of
the Windflowers Garden Club.

To those who helped make this book happen, thank you all:

Laura Hagar
Kelly Fitterer
Anne Hobson
Mary Bonnell
Susie Trumble
Tom Sanglier
Deb Nagle
John Fielder
Don Hazlett
and all those who generously gave of their time.

And a deep bow to my dedicated hiking buddies:

Cody Duffney
Pat Whittall
Jan Richings
and the indispensable David.

A salute to copy editor extraordinaire, Pat Shea; talented
designer, Rebecca Finkel; and consulting botanist, Lorraine Yeatts.

And a special salute to my ever-patient editor, Kiki Sayre.

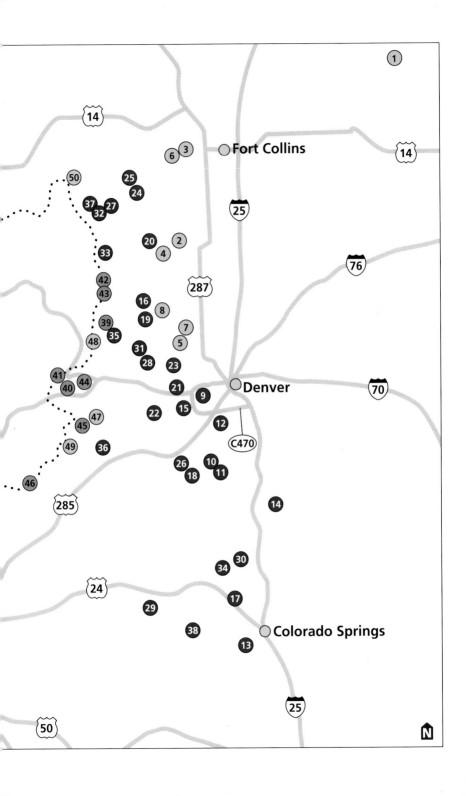

Table of Contents

Wildflower Profiles
(arranged alphabetically)

Introduction

Colorado is famous for its many natural assets. One particular asset attracts outdoor enthusiasts throughout the state: from foothills to fourteeners; from sand dunes to slickrock canyons; from prairie to vast parks. This is our wealth of wildflowers. Within its borders, Colorado has some 2,300 different species of flowering plants and, of that number, almost 700 are exclusive to the eastern slope (the area east of the Continental Divide including the Front Range).

Searching for the best places to experience the wildflower displays could take years—even a lifetime. *Colorado's Best Wildflower Hikes: The Front Range* helps the wildflower aficionado make time-saving choices regarding where to go, when to go, and what there is to see. All of the 50 hikes described in these pages are less than seven miles round trip, and they fit comfortably into the dayhike category. If you're armed with this book, impromptu plans can be as effective and rewarding as long-range plans. Even for those whose main goal is to hike, a landscape filled with wildflowers makes any trail more pleasurable. A number of the hikes are quite short, although wildflower enthusiasts tend to take their time regardless of trail length.

The trails in this book are arranged according to life zone, which includes elevations as well as areas with characteristic flora—typically defined by trees, shrubs, and herbaceous plants. But plants are not completely predictable. Some of them confound us by growing in places and elevations that stretch assumed and arbitrary boundaries.

Colorado life zones and their approximate elevation ranges:

PLAINS: up to 6,000 feet
FOOTHILLS: 6,000 to 8,000 feet
MONTANE: 8,000 to 10,000 feet
SUBALPINE: 10,000 to 11,500 feet
ALPINE: 11,500 feet and above

Scarlet sumac *(Rhus glabra)*, Lair O' the Bear

Broadly speaking, areas in the plains life zone are expected to flower earlier than areas at higher elevations, and so on up through the life zones. The higher you go, the later the flowers bloom. Transition zones are two overlapping life zones, ecologically speaking. Slope, pockets of relative warmth, snowpack, and the vagaries of weather are also determining factors. Wildflower viewing is an inexact science, which lends surprise to any given hike.

Each chapter in this book is organized from trailhead to objective, taking in a selection of blooming plants along the way. (Flowers featured in the hiking directions are set off in bold type.) Species numbers are approximate and determined from counting "showy" wildflowers. Tiny annuals usually didn't make the cut. For those whose interest in wildflowers extends beyond trail-side observations, "Wildflower Profiles" and detailed photographs follow each trail description and provide more information on particular species. Italicized Latin names follow the binomial system of plant nomenclature in which the first part of the name (genus) is a Latin noun, and the second name (specific) is a descriptive adjective.

Be prepared for beauty, but also for the elements. Water, sunblock, maps, sturdy footwear, a waterproof windbreaker, a hat, sunglasses, and a healthy dose of common sense should accompany every hiker.

Colorado's Best Wildflower Hikes: The Front Range offers friendly assistance along a trail to guide enthusiasts in their search for wildflowers in bloom.

— PAM IRWIN

We conserve what we love
We love what we know
We know what we are taught.
—Baba Dioum

The author examining a carpet of sky pilot (*Polemonium viscosum*), and other tundra flowers.

West Pawnee Butte

Wildflower alert: Interesting native wildflowers
include prickly gilia, silky matted pea, and sand dock.

*Pawnee National Grassland is an otherworldly, primal land with
remarkable wildflowers, such as this Rocky Mountain locoweed,
in late May or early June.*

Trail Rating	easy
Trail Length	3.0 miles out and back
Location	Pawnee National Grassland
Elevation	5,420 down to 5,200 feet
Bloom Season	May to June
Peak Bloom	late May to early June
Directions	From Denver, take I-25 north to highway 14. Go east 37 miles to Briggsdale. Turn left on County Road 77, go 15 miles, and then turn right on Road 120 for 6 miles to Grover. Turn right on Road 390, go 6 miles, and take a left on Road 112. At the sign marked Pawnee Buttes, turn right and follow the signs to the trailhead.

One of the most unusual destinations in Colorado for wildflower viewers, as well as history buffs, is a pair of vertical landmarks jutting into the prairie sky just south of the Wyoming-Nebraska border: the Pawnee Buttes. Accessible via the 1.5-mile trail, the buttes take the hiker down into a world of raw beauty and some unusual wildflowers. The route drops hikers into an eroded land, through dry washes (which may gush powerfully in storms), and across a plateau to the base of West Butte. For millenniums, the reportedly 300-foot-high, free-standing sandstone remnants served as points of reference that guided the plains tribesmen who roamed this windswept land.

The shortgrass prairie of the Pawnee National Grassland supports a fascinating variety of flora, some looking decidedly tundra-like with oversized buns and cushions. The sedimentary rock formations create a stark backdrop for grasses, such as buffalo and blue grama, and they are highlighted by intriguing spring wildflowers. A late May or early June trip to Pawnee Buttes is well worth the long drive to walk into an otherworldly, primal land and its remarkable flora.

In addition, Pawnee National Grassland is a great birding area and is home to the lark bunting, Colorado's state bird. You'll also find fleet pronghorn here, along with the short-horned lizard often referred to as the horny toad.

From the trailhead parking area overlooking the buttes, the trail leads down through thin grasses and immediately runs into the cool white stars of **Hood's phlox.** Along the descending track, violet-pink **vetchling,** or **wild sweetpea,** and the golden daisies of **prairie ragwort** join **white evening primrose** and butter yellow **puccoon.** Furry **early white daisy**—or **fleabane**—uncurls its nodding buds, then stands upright upon opening. In contrast,

PRICKLY GILIA
Leptodactylon caespitosum

The common name, prickly gilia, is applied to at least two members of the phlox family growing out on the plains—each about as far off in appearance from the other as it is possible to get. The prickly gilia occurs on the eroded bluffs of the Pawnee Buttes area in northeastern Colorado and Mesa de Maya in the southern part of the state. It grows in a tight mat of tiny, dark, spiky leaves with four-petaled warm-buff trumpets. These firm masses are supported by a knot of tough, woody roots that can be as big around as a wrist. Evening encourages the pointed, tightly twisted floral tubes of tufted (*caespitosum*) prickly gilia to open enough to emit an intriguingly rich scent, leaving the investigator wondering to what the aroma could be compared.

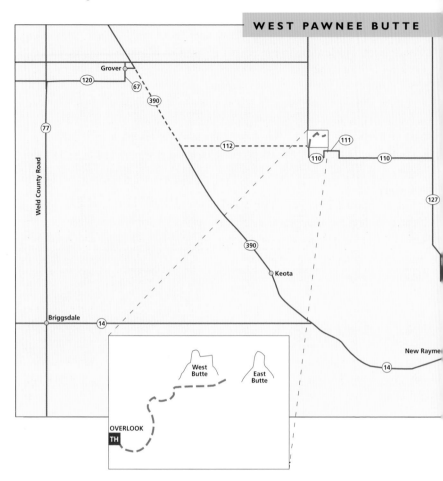

the seal-sleek foliage of **white penstemon** sets off alabaster snapdragon-type flowers.

A large sign along here reminds hikers to observe the importance of golden eagles and prairie falcons. On the right, a small worn outcrop, closer in texture to soil than stone, sprouts woody-rooted buns of **Hooker desert sandwort.** Quite a bit of this member of the **chickweed** family pops up in conspicuously bare places along the trail.

Where the path widens, the disturbed soil supports an expanding colony of **sand dock,** also called **wild begonia** (referring to its showy, salmon-colored bracts). Then, just off the right side of the trail, **sand verbena** or **prairie snow-ball** sprawls on the bank of a shallow ravine. Where the ravine bottoms out, **wild roses** bloom a bit later in the season.

At a narrow gap in the fence, hikers enter an eroded world of sandstone and siltstone so fine it feels like baby powder underfoot. Time-carved cliffs and arroyos, almost fleshtone in hue, demonstrate the thorough job water and the ever-present wind have done. A nearby notice tells hikers Lip Bluffs Trail is closed from March 1 to June 30 to protect nesting raptors who soar above this sere, stark earth. Along this stretch, determined wildflowers cling to the exposed soil. **Stiff stem flax,** in soft orange with reddish petal-base spots, is easily overlooked.

The next section of trail curves down into a fascinatingly raw realm where a number of oddities, such as **prickly gilia** and **silky matted pea,** bloom briefly. Look for two hot-yellow flowers thriving in the weather-worn ground: longer flowering **lavender-leaf evening primrose** and an indigenous parsley *(Aletes)* that has its roots in the same clan as celery.

Familiar **yucca,** interspersed with lavender-blue **narrowleaf penstemon,** guides the narrow track down past tiny-flowered mats. Buff-gold **prickly gilia,** whose pointy flowers sit on a tight-leaved dark mat, has a root that looks like it might belong to a minor tree. In the same vicinity, an *Orophaca* (traditionally connected with the *Astragalus* or milkvetch genus) drapes its minuscule silvery leaves in a flowing cascade over the bare, beige marl. The soft-foliaged mats of **silky orophaca** or **silky matted pea** come to life, typically in the later part of May, with swarms of light purple blossoms. Close scrutiny is required to appreciate the adaptations to life in this xeric land.

Adding tang to the dun earth washing the descending trail is bright yellow **lavender-leaf evening primrose** with

HOOKER DESERT SANDWORT
Eremogone hookeri

So substantial is the look of this plant, it is hard to believe it is a member of the Chickweed family. (The Chickweed family also includes mouse-ear, that ubiquitous spring charmer of the foothills, and those persistent, pesky lawn invaders that tend toward the substance of wilted lettuce.) Hooker sandwort presents spiky, dark-leaved buns—some perfect hemispheres—which rise from tough woody roots in the barest areas imaginable, including several places along the Pawnee Buttes Trail. By mid-June, the buns are covered with perky white flowers with emerald throats.

The genus name *Eremogone,* meaning desert, explains this sandwort's choice of locale while *hookeri* honors Sir Joseph Hooker (1817—1911), director of the Royal Botanic Gardens and visitor to Colorado in 1877.

A cousin, Fendler sandwort (*Eremogone fendleri*) can be found from the foothills to the tundra. It lifts five-petaled white stars high above thin, stiff grasslike leaves. What appear to be red dots on the petals are actually carmine-tipped stamens. Alpine specimens of sandwort, on the other hand, are very compact.

leaves that resemble those of the aromatic lavender plant. Flanked by twisting arroyos, the narrow track is entrenched in soil so tightly textured it appears to have melted rather than eroded. Upon reaching the bottom of a sandy ravine, look for **silky** or **Rocky Mountain locoweed** with its upright banners of sharp-keeled flowers in pinks, soft violet, and cool lavender. Nearby, a few juniper trees offer a touch of precious shade.

The intimate scene widens with West Pawnee Butte ahead and the now road-wide trail levels. Off to the right are the Lip Bluffs, named for fissured stretches of grayish-brown capstone that keep the softer sandstone from rapid erosion. These provide a home for nesting raptors such as prairie falcons.

The trail dips to cross a grassy-bottomed ravine. Here, and occasionally farther on, is what resembles a stout short lupine with a very hairy inflorescence. This is **breadroot scurf pea**—sometimes referred to as **prairie turnip,** a name merited by the thick root once prized by nomadic gatherers.

The two buttes tag the skyline, one behind the other, accenting the endless plains beyond. More frisky yellow clumps of **prairie ragwort** dot the landscape along with cool **white penstemon** (which ages to pale lavender), and long-blooming **Hood's phlox.** As the West Butte grows closer, its 30-story height becomes apparent; to the north the Chalk Bluffs escarpment, of which Pawnee Buttes is a remnant, slopes down from Wyoming.

A few **yellow violets** struggle to grow in the hard gravel surface as the track curves around the south side of the butte. More of those interesting buns and cushions, especially those of **Hooker desert sandwort,** form perfect hemispheres on the butte's uneven south base. West Pawnee Butte's trail description ends at the landmark's east edge. East Pawnee Butte, shaped like the Liberty Bell, is about one-half mile beyond.

An outing to Pawnee Buttes is time well spent for those seeking a unique experience and an appreciative bit of insight into the wildflowers that persevere in this strangely beautiful but harsh country. In many places, the flavor is still wild and free—owned by the wind and wild creatures.

Eagle Wind

Wildflower alert: Myriad spring bloomers highlighted by fuchsia-colored prairie verbena and velvety purple skullcap.

The Eagle Wind Trail east of Lyons offers 60 or more wildflower species and 360-degree views.

easy	**Trail Rating**
3.75-mile loop	**Trail Length**
Rabbit Mountain Open Space/Lyons	**Location**
5,500 to 5,800 feet	**Elevation**
May to June	**Bloom Season**
late May to mid-June	**Peak Bloom**
From Lyons, take highway 66 east to 53rd Street at the Rabbit Mountain sign. Turn north and go 2 miles to the trailhead.	**Directions**

For centuries, hunter-gatherers knew and appreciated Rabbit Mountain. Natural springs, plentiful game, edible plants, and encompassing views for security drew nomadic tribes here. Hikers today can follow in the footsteps of those early Native Americans who found many of the 60 or more wildflower species useful as well as beautiful. In the 1,500 acres of Rabbit Mountain Open Space, Eagle Wind's 3.75-mile loop takes in flowery reaches and four-direction views as it ascends to travel along the west flank of an undulating hogback, crosses a saddle, and then heads north before turning west back to the parking area.

An early-morning hike on Eagle Wind Loop focuses light on the Continental Divide, while a late-afternoon hike throws long ponderosa-spiked shadows out across the plains and may feature the howl of coyotes. Late afternoon is also a time to watch out for approaching thunderstorms. As with many foothills areas, rattlesnakes make their homes here and may be above ground as long as the weather is warm—in fact, Rabbit Mountain was once called Rattlesnake Mountain.

A long, steady climb from the trailhead constitutes much of the elevation gain along Eagle Wind Loop. More than a dozen varieties of wildflowers show up in the first 100 yards. Along the disturbed trail edges, orange-hued **copper mallow** is followed by **prairie verbena**. Also called **Dakota vervain**, tiny fuchsia-colored flowers cluster on this low grower. **Prairie verbena** is beloved of butterflies and bees. Another disturbed soil-dweller here, **purple ground cherry** is a member of the potato or night-shade family and may also be

PRAIRIE VERBENA
Glandularia bipinnatifida

Showy or Dakota vervain, and small-flowered verbena are other names attached to this low-growing perennial with bright pink flowers. Each blossom is shaped a bit like a chain of paper dolls linked by their hands. The floral tubes have five notched, flared lobes centered with four stamens and a four-lobed pistil. The flat clusters of flowers act as landing pads for the butterflies who feed on their nectar. The square stems can root at nodes near the base. This drought-resistant wildflower makes a fine, long-blooming addition to the xeric garden and is often propagated by growers of native plants.

The Latin genus name, *Glandularia*, meaning "acorn," refers to the shape of the seedpod. Another member of the vervain family, blue vervain (*Verbena hastata*), shoots up a yard high and resembles a candelabra decorated with tiny blue flowers. This annual frequents lower elevation wetlands in the region.

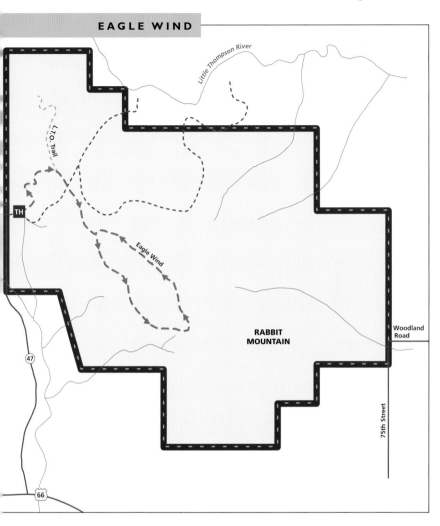

known as purple-blossomed **Chinese lantern of the plains.** The five-paneled calyx of this "lantern" encloses a single fruit. In the same area, square-stemmed **field mint's** pale pink flower clusters sprout in the leaf axils. In June, **yucca** begins blooming, as does **spiderwort** and **blanketflower.**

As the curving trail gains elevation, spring blooming shrubs, such as **boulder raspberry, wax currant, threeleaf sumac, chokecherry,** and **wild plum,** crowd among the rocks. The trail ascends in switchbacks before leveling out to parallel a service road. A signed junction points Little Thompson River Outlook left, while Eagle Wind Trail heads right to cross the service road. There, a sign directs Eagle Wind up to the right. In every opening of the stony slope following the sign, **orchid penstemon, locoweed, leafy cinquefoil, chiming bells, bladder-pod,** and **mouse-ear chickweed** create patchwork color in the hillside rock garden.

The trail continues toward ponderosa pines and comes upon a bench facing a panorama of the Continental Divide to the west. Most of the elevation gain is behind now and a leisurely route curves southeast, revealing **Great Plains paintbrush** or **downy painted cup** and purplish **scorpionweed** with its characteristic coiled flower bundles. Native Americans once gathered this member of the waterleaf family for cooked greens. They also harvested the flavorful **sand onion** with its tight cluster of white flowers. A somewhat similar-looking plant, blooming about the same time, is poisonous **death camas.** It has a conical raceme of rank-smelling, small cream blossoms. Wild onion, on the other hand, smells like nothing other than onion.

At a fork in the trail, Eagle Wind heads right in the vicinity of **wild roses** and **wild geraniums**, both a food source for Native Americans. In addition, the rose hips were used as a pharmaceutical, and the geraniums as a birth control source.

Now on the west side of the hogback, the route grows rockier and heads through mountain mahogany and back into ponderosa pines. Soon a remnant rock wall appears on the right just before a vista looking out on the Boulder Valley and its signature Flatirons to the south.

When the trail opens, look for an erect stand of pale lavender-blue **false pimpernel** or **blue toadflax**— a bit unusual in the region—next to a boulder. Vivid-pink **prairie verbena** grows amid the grasses as the trail continues toward a sign designating the Eagle Wind Trail. Pass an area of blackened vegetation from a recent fire, and then follow a contour leading into pines sheltering **meadow arnica, leafy cinquefoil,** and bi-colored **wild sweet pea.**

Pass the velvet-purple hoods of **skullcap** flanking a rocky service road where deer may appear in the twilight hours. In this transition

SKULLCAP
Scutellaria brittonii

The genus name comes from the Latin *scuttela,* meaning "little shield," while the species name honors an American botanist named Nathaniel Lord Britton.

Royal-purple snapdragon-like flowers sporting velvety hoods identify skullcap. A square stem and a very early bloom-time further distinguish this short mint that is partial to well-drained mineral soils.

Containing an anti-spasmodic (skullcap is *not* to be used for tea), skullcap was once used to calm acute nervous conditions.

Mint cousins in the area include field mint (*Menthe arvensis),* beebalm (*Monarda fistulosa v. menthifolia),* and selfheal or prunella (*Prunella vulgaris).*

zone, both mule and whitetail deer overlap territories. Soon, the loop veers to the right away from the service road and traverses grassy park lands dotted with **purple milkvetch** and **meadow arnica.** Charcoal skeletons of burnt ponderosa pines stand stark against the sky and legions of royal-purple **skullcap,** the earliest-blooming mint, grow among them.

The trail crosses the service road and winds over a saddle to the west side. Eagle Wind Loop finishes at a sign with arrows in both directions. A right here arrives back at the bench. Here, perhaps, is a chance to examine **purple ground cherry,** each of its silky flowers embossed with a dark, five-pointed star. A hand lens reveals tiny crystalline bubbles on the foliage of this weedy, but interesting, wildflower.

Rabbit Mountain is a snappy hike or a leisurely stroll, depending on the goal. In late May, more than 50 wildflower species can be found, while expansive views provide a remarkable backdrop.

Wildflower Hike

Arthur's Rock

3

Wildflower alert: Lupine meadows and hillsides of color.

Hikers who withstand the 1,000-vertical-foot climb on Arthur's Rock Trail, just west of Fort Collins are treated to meadows of silvery lupines.

Trail Rating	moderate
Trail Length	3.4 miles out and back
Location	Lory State Park/Fort Collins
Elevation	5,600 to 6,780 feet
Bloom Season	May to September
Peak Bloom	mid-June
Directions	From Fort Collins, take U.S. 14/287 west and go left on Road 52E (Rist Canyon) to the town of Bellvue. Turn left on Road 23N, and right on Road 25G to Lory State Park. Arthur's Rock trailhead is at the south end of the road. Be prepared to pay the fee.

Located just west of Fort Collins, 2,500-acre Lory State Park has one of the finest wildflower hikes found in the foothill zone. Flowery meadows, colorful rock gardens and outstanding views reward the hiker. Rising more than 1,000 vertical feet in just 1.7 miles, the hike is a challenge worth every step. In mid-June you'll discover about seven dozen kinds of wildflowers blooming along the diverse route—some a grand splash of a single species, including a large expanse of silvery lupine.

Arthur's Rock Trail begins adjacent to handy restrooms and a scattering of picnic tables at the southern end of the park's access road. Immediately ahead is a rocky ravine guarded by legions of butterflies. Some 100 butterfly species have been recorded at Lory State Park. The tight gorge is lined with many flowers, including perfumed **wild rose,** satiny yellow **prickly pear cactus,** and **cinquefoil.**

Climbing through a wooded area, hikers pass into the mouth of the granitic ravine with outcrops decorated in **spiderwort, wild geranium,** and **scorpionweed.** The seasonal creek, hardly a stride wide, has poison ivy near its banks. You can avoid an unpleasant encounter by identifying the plant's trademark: three large glossy leaves.

Farther on where a cliff rises on the left, **cow parsnip** grows in the moist habitat. White-blooming **waxflower** shrubs cling to the cliff. Billows of **ninebark's** rounded blossoms—white when fresh, and soft salmon upon aging—spill over the left side of the track.

A dead end social trail goes a bit farther into the ravine. Where a cottonwood tree grows by the creek, Arthur's Rock Trail takes a left and climbs via a switchback, passing **bluemist penstemon** and the pinkish seedhead plumes of early-blooming **pasqueflower.** Timber risers precede a second switchback, followed by stone steps that lead hikers farther up where the trail levels under ponderosa pines with **whiskbroom parsley, tall pussytoes,** and **common alumroot** at their feet. One more switchback traverses an open area where yellow **stonecrop** and **sulphurflower** have taken root.

The trail then plunges back into pines where clumps of long-blooming **harebell** find a home, and the pathway, built up on timber cribbing, skirts the south edge of the ravine. Early in the season, the steep uphill slope has **snowball saxifrage;** later, **wallflower, larkspur,** and white **wild onion** continue the succession of bloom.

When the trail opens again, a trail sign states: Arthur's Rock 1.3 miles. Midsummer here presents a mass of rosy-lavender **beebalm,** its minty foliage scenting the air. Early-season hikers find **sugarbowls** dangling their burgundy bells, which develop into glistening platinum seedplumes. **American vetch** jostles for a tendril-hold on the meadow grasses along the the trail. A pause here reveals Horsetooth Reservoir and Fort Collins to the east, and the peach-colored bulk of Arthur's Rock to the north.

The trail is gentle through this area, and hikers will encounter golden-yellow **early spring senecio**, creamy **death camas**, white **cutleaf evening primrose**, and wine-red **houndstongue**. Masses of **silvery lupine** fill the meadow in late spring.

Still level, the path wanders through evergreens and Rocky Mountain maple to a small ravine where you'll find **blue columbine** in the filtered shade. **Wild rose, chokecherry,** and **boulder raspberry** close in on the track, along with pillars of pine and towering Douglas firs, to create the hushed ambience of a cathedral.

Ponderosa pines provide room and board for the charcoal Abert squirrel. Sharp claws scrabbling on the pines' bark may be the first clue to a sighting of the elusive tuft-eared squirrel; green-needled branch tips littering the forest floor may be another.

A series of "S" curves carry the hiker up into rocks and a flowery hillside. A trio of signs appears, the one on the right designates the foot-trail to Arthur's Rock. Visible to the east is the dam holding back the waters of Horsetooth Reservoir.

As open skies wash across a south-facing hillside, the lily-like white flowers of the **yucca** bloom on yard-high stalks. The steepening trail takes the hiker into a colorful bed of **spiderwort, wild geranium, lupine, wallflower, locoweed, bush** or **perennial sunflower, orchid penstemon,** and **blanketflower.**

TUFTED EVENING PRIMROSE

Oenothera caespitosa

Tufted evening primrose, also known as stemless evening primrose, produces pure white four-petaled blooms up to a handspan in width, and it is endowed with a lovely fragrance. Its white stage carries over only one night, but it turns a warm pink as it ages through the following morning (its many buds add up to a fairly long bloom time). Though tolerant enough of clay to be nicknamed "gumbo lily," it is often found in well-drained mineral soil.

Many evening primrose cousins frequent the Front Range. Among them are: white cutleaf evening primrose *(Oenothera coronopifolia),* a lavender-leaved evening primrose sometimes called puckered sundrops *(Calylophus lavandulifolius),* and dainty sundrops *(Calylophus serrulatus),* both bright yellow and open during the day. As unlikely as it looks, tufted evening primrose is related to the fuchsia, a native of the Andes. Native Americans found the boiled root nutritious.

ARTHUR'S ROCK

25G

Entrance
Station

*Horsetooth
Reservoir*

Arthur's Rock

**LORY
STATE PARK**

A switchback adds more showy wildflowers to the spectrum. **Tall larkspur** sends its rich blue spikes up two feet, and bristly **miner's candle,** with its small white forget-me-not-type flowers, shoots up almost as tall. Rugged underfoot and assisted by timber risers and convenient rocks, the trail arrives at a saddle where a "T" announces a scenic overlook to the right. A great view from giant boulders attracts hikers for a pause or snack.

Back on the main trail, head north to pass **boulder raspberry,** mountain mahogany, and **waxflower** shrubs; at ground level find **leafy cinquefoil, bluemist penstemon,** and **harebells.** Until now, the view of Horsetooth Reservoir has been partial; here the full 6.5-mile length forms the foreground of a panorama stretching to the horizon.

Along the gently inclined pathway, Arthur's granite massif rises abruptly on the right. Here and there, colorful wildflowers dot the west-facing slope. In the same vicinity, low-growing **buckbrush** is tipped with creamy-white clouds of fragrant flowers. In the pink decomposed granite along here, **wild geranium** and **tufted evening primrose** emerge in spring; later in the season find **standing milkvetch.**

Steadily rising via switchbacks to its high point at the base of Arthur's Rock, the trail requires careful footing up rock ledges before leveling to reach another sensational view. As the trail eases in the shade of pines, **bluemist penstemon,** white **wild onion, sulphurflower, whiskbroom parsley,** and **leafy cinquefoil** present a pleasing combination of color.

Follow the sign to reach the base of Arthur's Rock, a domed mass of pink granite where the flat trail wanders among rough boulders. At the feet of these rocks, tufts of **early blue daisy** and pale lavender **cutleaf daisy** (both fleabanes) bloom early. The trail ends here at the base of Arthur's Rock.

The 1.7-mile trek up to the imposing Arthur's Rock is one of the great wildflower hikes of the Front Range foothills. Wonderful floral displays, grand views, a worthy chunk of granite, and a sense of accomplishment make this trail a winner.

Bitterbrush

Wildflower alert: A spectrum of spring wildflowers, including fleabanes, locoweed, larkspurs, and more.

The Bitterbrush Trail west of Lyons follows a series of "S" curves through ponderosa pine forests on the old Hall Ranch.

easy to moderate	**Trail Rating**
4.0 miles out and back	**Trail Length**
Hall Ranch/Lyons	**Location**
5,550 to 6,210 feet	**Elevation**
May to July	**Bloom Season**
mid-May to mid-June	**Peak Bloom**
From Lyons, turn south on highway 7, and go 1.5 miles to the trailhead on the right.	**Directions**

Hall Ranch Open Space Park is a sprawling old ranch now accessible to outdoor enthusiasts. The trailhead is located just 1.5 miles south of Lyons.

Bitterbrush Trail begins curving around low hills before climbing up via "S" curves through picturesque rocks and ponderosa pines. It levels out at the two-mile mark not far from the middle of the Hall Ranch property where hikers may enjoy the view before returning. Hardy trekkers may choose to continue along the 9.2-mile loop. Diverse ecosystems in this 3,200-plus-acre open space park support a wide variety of wildlife, from black bears to rattlesnakes.

The low elevation allows the wildflower season to start off early here. By mid-May, you'll find close to 30 species in bloom; one month later 50 kinds of wildflowers—including a flurry of white fleabanes—turn up along the first few miles of trail.

From the parking area, Bitterbrush Trail heads west through pasture-land crowded in early spring with various grasses and sporting **yellow violets, wallflower, early pink milkvetch, wavyleaf dandelion, sand lilies,** and **chiming bells** in the proximity of rock outcrops. A search may turn up **green-flowered hedgehog cactus** in late May or early June. In late summer, rosy-purple brushes of **gayfeather** appear.

At the foot of the tilted, red sandstone mesas grows white **Rocky Mountain locoweed.** In mid-June, one month later, the locoweed is an inconspicuous wand of fat pods.

Red-floored washes, flanked by junipers, are dry most of the time. Near these channels look for plush clumps of bright-blue **Geyer larkspur.** Like a garden delphinium, this felted-foliaged larkspur is erect with a stalk of spurred flowers. It is hard to believe this is a xeric wildflower. Look in the same vicinity for **evening primroses,** white when open, worn pink when closed. Also scattered here, large **prickly poppies** with wrinkled-silk blossoms on thistle-like foliage bloom most of the summer.

The ranching past is evident as the track crosses an old stock-pond dam. A full turn here exposes the red of the sandstone bluffs, some of which are being quarried. Another reminder of the past is an old wood building down to the left just before the path wanders up through rocks and junipers into the open.

Follow a sign for the Bitterbrush Trail and cross an old road. Then angle along a warm, sunny slope. The hillside is dotted with **white monarda,** a mint related to beebalm. Another white flower, **white plains larkspur,** is out in late spring. Each delphinium-like flower has a dark purple "bee" in the center. Like its blue cousins, white plains larkspur is toxic.

Along the next mile or so, **prickly pear cactus** unfurls its silky yellow blossoms in June. Also in yellow, but non-native and invasive, is **tall butter 'n**

eggs. Parasitic **naked broomrape** pops up here and there, having tapped into the roots of the fringed sage here to sustain its translucent, flesh-colored tubes.

The trail levels before dropping into a drainage where granite takes over the geologic story. Ponderosa pines now replace the junipers. In an open field look for the hairy **false gromwell,** unremarkable in color, but with interesting flowers formed of closed cones with protruding styles.

Soon, the trail traverses a ravine with a seasonal creek that is hidden by thick vegetation—most notably, pink **wild rose** and **wild geranium.** The route undulates through time-worn granite boulders and pines. Daisy-like white **fleabane** carpets the area. In May, contorted woody trunks of the **bitterbrush,** for which the trail is named, leafs out in distinctive three-toothed foliage resembling long ducks' feet. Small, five-petaled yellow fragrant flowers cover the shrubs. Also called **antelope-brush,** it is a valuable forage plant for wildlife and is especially favored by mule deer. **Spiderworts** tuck into cracks in the rough boulders. Along here, hot yellow **sulphurflower** is present in June, and **bluemist penstemon** is fading. **Spring beauties** and **wild pansies** bloom in early May.

As the trail zigzags up, take time to look back at the view occasionally and compare the layer cake strata of the intense red sandstone with that of the gray granite. The trail passes an old stone wall, and nearby, **harebells** begin their summer-long bloom fairly early in June.

ROCKY MOUNTAIN LOCOWEED
Oxytropis sericea

Showy, silky, and silverleaf loco are other names attached to this attractive member of the pea family. (*Oxytropis splendens* is also called "showy locoweed.") In its pure form, Rocky Mountain locoweed is white. But it likes to hybridize with magenta Lambert loco, resulting in pastels from pale lavender to almost purple, or from shell pink to rose. Erect, long stems lift the plush racemes of pea-type flowers high above silky (*sericea*) silver-green, ladder-like basal leaves.

Locoweed, often referred to as loco, contains toxic alkaloids and is poisonous to livestock. Horses have been known to seek out locoweed, eventually becoming addicted to this selenium-storing pea that brings on the "staggers" and possibly death.

More locoweeds in the region include tufted loco (*Oxytropis multiceps*), showy loco (*Oxytropis splendens*), and Lambert loco (*Oxytropis lambertii*).

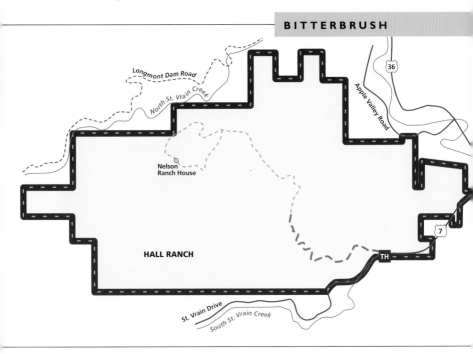

In the British Isles, they are known as the **bluebells of Scotland.**

From here, the trail levels and passes out of the ponderosas to reveal a field of magenta **locoweed, sulphurflower,** and **fleabane daisies.** A fence line defines the completion of this segment of Bitterbrush Trail. In the valley to the northwest is an old ranch house. Hikers wanting to complete the rest of the 9.2-mile loop will continue past the structure. The boulder-studded saddle west of the fence line is an inviting place to enjoy a bite to eat.

Hall Ranch, part of the Boulder County Open Space Park system, is a delightful journey through time and wildflowers in a spacious setting. A hike there offers a sense of both past and present.

South Mesa/ Big Bluestem/Towhee

Wildflower alert: A cornucopia of nearly 80 wildflowers at peak bloom.

Stroll through grasslands, ponderosa pines, and lush meadows on this flower-filled loop in Boulder Open Space just east of Eldorado Springs.

Boulder Open Space parks preserve roughly 27,000 acres for the enjoyment of the outdoor enthusiast. Much of this open space contains hiking trails, such as the popular Mesa Trail. For a leisurely 3.7-mile wildflower hike, follow the South Mesa/Big Bluestem/Towhee loop along the base of the Flatirons. Passing through the transition zone, the three-trail loop may turn up nearly 80 wildflower species at peak bloom.

South Mesa/Big Bluestem/Towhee

Trail Rating	easy to moderate
Trail Length	3.7-mile loop
Location	Boulder
Elevation	5,600 to 6,520 feet
Bloom Season	May to July
Peak Bloom	mid-May to early June
Directions	From Boulder, take highway 93 south to Eldorado Springs Road. Turn right and go 1.6 miles to the trailhead turn-off on the right.

A large parking area on the north side of Eldorado Springs Road is the jumping off place for South Mesa Trail. Immediately after crossing Boulder Creek on a sizable bridge, a cut-stone building appears on the left that was once a gristmill back in the mid-1800s. The existing two-story house rose in 1874. Behind the stone house, the Flatirons—imposing upthrust fins of red sandstone derived from the Ancestral Rockies—dominate the western skyline.

South Mesa Trail takes off to the far right of the stone house through open grasslands studded with rocks, shrubs and spring wildflowers such as **golden banner, leafy cinquefoil, wallflower,** and **houndstongue.**

Along this open part of the trail, look for lavender-pink **orchid penstemons.** The radiant snapdragon-like tubes grow on one side of the stalk of this foothills favorite—the first penstemon to bloom each spring.

The broad path rises slowly as boulders appear, their bases adorned in spring and early summer with the white blossoms of **boulder raspberry.** The road-wide trail then passes through head-high thickets of **smooth sumac** that turn fiery red in autumn.

About one mile into the loop, a sign on the right is labeled Big Bluestem Trail. Follow this fork onto an intimate path. Near some power lines, in an area of additional moisture, orange **meadow arnica** and purple **wild iris** provide complementary color. When the trail forks, continue on Big Bluestem (named for a tall native grass) under the power lines and up beside a rocky ravine filled with spring-blooming shrubs, such as **wild plum, chokecherry,** and **hawthorn**—with an apple tree in the middle of it.

The trail levels a bit upon entering the ponderosa belt. Along here, look for **wallflowers** in yellow, gold, and burnt orange, and keep an eye out for the stout spikes of **miner's candle, lanceleaf chiming bells,** and **many-flowered puccoon.**

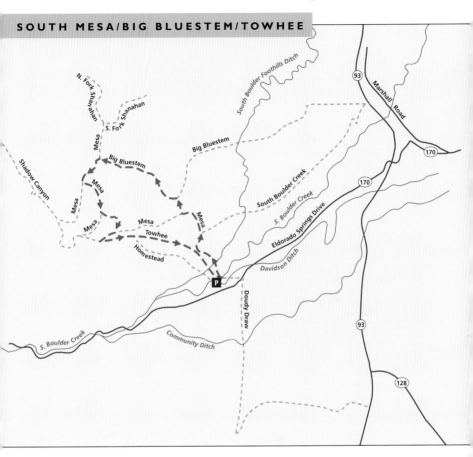

SOUTH MESA/BIG BLUESTEM/TOWHEE

Views of the approaching Flatirons command attention as the trail negotiates another thicket of smooth sumac and three-leaf sumac—or skunkbrush (appropriately named for the scent of its crushed leaves).

An old overgrown stone wall on the right outlines the home of a settler who planted apple trees in this lovely glade. The trail drops into a small drainage where **golden banner** blooms in spring; in midsummer soft purple **beebalm** exudes its fresh minty fragrance.

Rising up the west bank, the track continues in shade. Yellow **common dandelions** bloom early here, followed by scores of **chiming bells.** Nearby, in the shade of conifers, **Canada violets** and **tall scarlet paintbrush**—more of a salmon here—add fresh hues.

Not much farther up the trail, deep pink **shooting stars** gather at a creek in mid-spring. **Cow parsnip** is found here later in the season. Crossing the creek, the trail rises up a few stone steps past wild fruit thickets and into an open area of tall bracken fern and an abundance of **few-flowered false Solomon's seal.**

The next junction rejoins the Mesa Trail. Turn left and soon cross a tiny creek. The path rises higher into the ponderosa belt where a stock tank comes into view. Just east of it, look for a stand of **golden currant** with its clove-scented, red-tinged yellow tubes.

Stay on the Mesa Trail as it curves around the stock tank and rises broadly past a colony of sunny **heartleaf arnica** blooming under sheltering evergreens. The trail traverses rolling ponderosa park land where pools of **wild iris** and **golden banner** prepare the way for a purple sea of summer-blooming **bee-balm.** At a bend in the track, a tumble-down building marks the corner where, just downhill, Towhee Trail takes off sharply left at the next junction. The loop continues adjacent to a hidden waterway on the right. Big-leaved **cow parsnip,** which produces broad flat heads of minute white flowers in late spring, favors the damp aspen copse here. This particular clump of aspens is growing about 1,000 feet below its cousin groves. Cow parsnip favors the aspen understory.

As Towhee Trail angles down, the dry rocky ground provides ideal habitat for **spiderwort,** whose intensely pig-mented blooms last only a day. Here and all along the loop, you'll discover yellow **leafy** and **beauty cinquefoils.** The trail threads down through dense shrubbery before reaching open grass-lands where the walking is easier.

The South Mesa/Big Bluestem/Towhee loop covers habitats from grasslands to forest to riparian, and it offers a scenic escape into the world of wildflowering.

LANCELEAF CHIMING BELLS

Mertensia lanceolata

Though most *Mertensias* appreciate moisture, lanceleaf chiming bells are usually found in drier soil. They are spring-blooming at lower elevations and bloom into summer higher up. Their scallop-edged bells begin as cool-pink buds, maturing into five-lobed powder blue tubes, and eventually fading with age until the bell drops and leaves the style behind. A member of the borage family, which includes forget-me-nots, this foothills and mountain dweller also goes by the name narrow-leaved mertensia and languid ladies. The genus name honors Herr Mertens, a German botanist born in 1764.

Moisture-loving *Mertensias* include greenleaf chiming bells (*Mertensia viridis*) of the high country and tall chiming bells (*Mertensia ciliata*).

Soderberg/ Horsetooth Falls

Wildflower alert: Wild iris in late spring.

Take in Lamberts locoweed and whiskbroom parsley on this colorful trail adjoining Horsetooth Reservoir west of Fort Collins.

easy to moderate	*Trail Rating*
2.75-mile loop	*Trail Length*
Horsetooth Mountain/Loveland/Fort Collins	*Location*
5,760 to 6,000 feet	*Elevation*
May to August	*Bloom Season*
mid-May to mid-June	*Peak Bloom*
From Fort Collins, take College Ave. to Horsetooth Road and turn west. Turn south at Taft Hill Road, and then head west on 38E Road. Continue around the south end of Horsetooth Reservoir to the trailhead on the west side of the road. Be prepared to pay the fee.	*Directions*

Tucked into 2,100 acres just west of Fort Collins and the huge Horsetooth Reservoir, the Soderberg/Horsetooth Falls Loop winds through rugged, forested granite canyons, rounded wildflower-spattered ridges and open grasslands. A wispy waterfall and its attendant riparian habitat sweeten the hike. Along this diverse trail, in late May and early June an abundance of wildflowers is found, notably the royal wild iris.

Despite the good-sized parking area and day use fee, Horsetooth Mountain trailhead fills quickly on spring weekends.

Behind the restrooms and picnic facilities at the trailhead, the Soderberg Trail eases up to the right, along a slope where **locoweed, fleabane, bladderpod,** and **orchid penstemon** get the hike off to a lively start. Not far up, **naked broomrape** thrusts up fleshy tubes (here hosted by fringed sage); a closer look reveals a strangely attractive flower.

The track curves up gently through mountain mahogany shrubs where **wallflower** and **sulphurflower,** both hot yellow, join purplish-blue **lupine, spiderwort,** and **orchid penstemon** spires. Foot-high **tall pussytoes, mouse-ear chickweed,** and **death camas** represent the white flowers.

The trail evens and enters a ravine filled with early-blooming **wild plum,** and (by late May) white-blossomed **hawthorn**—both members of the rose family.

Silky or **Rocky Mountain locoweed** follows across a rounded ridge, along with the more subtle pastels of **Great Plains** or **downycup paintbrush,** and, tucked deep in the grasses, **green-flowered hedgehog cactus.**

NAKED BROOMRAPE

Aphyllon fasciculatum

Strangely attractive, naked or tufted broomrape shoots up fleshy (both in color and texture) scalloped flower tubes on substantial stalks, after tapping into the roots of a host plant, such as fringed sage, an *Artemisia*. Skin-toned naked broomrape was once a food source, eaten either raw or roasted.

Soderberg Trail begins ascending more steeply as it heads east up a rocky slope where **wild geranium** adds pink touches to the route, and **boulder raspberry** accents the outcrops in pure white. The narrow footpath merges into a wide service road as it heads into the ponderosa pine belt.

Crumbling pink granite forms rugged outcrops along the wide track, and maroon **sugarbowls** line the far edge. Youthful ponderosas open up to present a broad swath of fresh grasses studded with purple and lavender **wild iris.** Continuing ahead, you'll find more purple flowers, including **lupine, American vetch** (tendrils), and **purple milkvetch** (no tendrils).

SODERBERG / HORSETOOTH FALLS

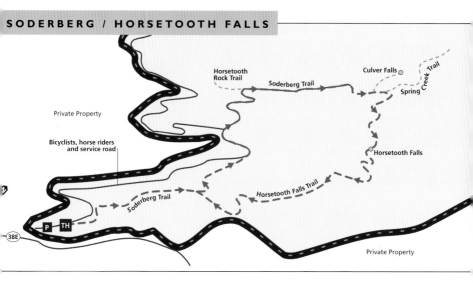

The incline increases as it passes among young pines and sturdy specimens of big-leaved, small-flowered **houndstongue**, its forget-me-not-type blossoms a port-wine color.

The route levels upon reaching another junction—this one to Horsetooth Rock. Ahead, the view opens to canyon slopes and knobby granite stacks as the path passes a towering salmon-pink outcrop. Where one of the ponderosas has bent to conform to the shape of the stone wall, the huge white blossoms of **boulder raspberry** brighten the shady dell.

After the next view of the water, the trail adopts the pink of the rock outcrops as it eases down to overlook a lavish slope of lavender **wild iris** in late May or early June.

The roadway ends rather abruptly as the trail narrows at an "S" curve and descends over some timbered steps. Rocks and roots are part of the trail as the ravine tightens. Here, **sugarbowls** with their leathery purple heads, **few-flowered false Solomon's seal** colonies, and later blooming **ninebark** precede a junction where the loop heads right toward Horsetooth Falls. Along the first few yards of the rugged spur heading left to Culver Falls, **shooting stars** and **golden banner** grow by a tiny creek.

After crossing the waterway on a footbridge and heading south, look for **cow parsnip**, which later bears saucer-sized plates of diminutive white flowers. A tiny pool creates a cool respite. Where the water winds down between lichen-garnished outcrops to a grassy glen, look for **golden banner** in early spring. Stones cross the waterway and soon the scene opens once again to catch the **wild iris** array.

At a fork, go right, up to pothole pools high above Horsetooth Falls. The angle of the waterworn rock makes it slippery and precarious by the pools. An offshoot of the spur climbs roughly above the rock bowls where there is a view down into the pools.

Back on the main route, the trail climbs up to circumvent the top of the narrow falls and zigzags down via steps to a "T." A right turn takes visitors to the base of Horsetooth Falls. The descent to the falls is lined with **wallflower** blooming in lemon yellow, gold, orange, and burnt copper. Huge white blossoms of **tufted evening primrose** cling to the rock ledges. It is cool in the closed-in ravine where Horsetooth Falls squeezes through a narrow gap 30 feet overhead. A bit of coarse sand fans out to accommodate folks, some of which have come up the shorter, but less interesting, Horsetooth Falls Trail. Return to the "T" and continue down, back to the trailhead. The first segment hangs on the canyon wall before dropping quickly to level out along the stream bottom. Then it heads up and out into the open grasslands. The route crosses a ridge of eye-catching **locoweed**. It isn't long before the trail undulates to rejoin the last section of Soderberg Trail leading back to the parking area.

Variety of terrain, habitat, view, and some 80 different kinds of wildflowers makes the Soderberg/Horsetooth Falls loop a winner. Water features and a handy location just west of Fort Collins add to the enticement. Place this destination high on a list of spring wildflower hikes.

WESTERN WALLFLOWER

Erysimum asperum, Erysimum capitatum

A member of the widespread mustard family, this fragrant wallflower is one of the showiest of the spring bloomers, brightening the foothills and mountains with yellow, gold, burnt orange, and coppery red. Western wallflower exhibits the typical cross, formed by opposite petals; these develop into long, slim seedpods, often forming while the terminal raceme is in flower.

The seeds were once a flavoring source, as well as a cure for dysentery. Wallflower may also be known to some as blister cress, as its strong juices helped to heal blisters.

The two Latin species, while each a species on its own, do in fact hybridize, especially in the foothills. *E. asperum* frequents the plains, its seedpods aiming away from the stem; *E. capitatum* routinely shoots its pods upward in different regions from the foothills to the tundra. Its petals are a shade of purple underneath at most elevations; those of the alpine zone are either clear yellow or lilac.

Mustard clan cousins include bladderpod (*Lesquerella montana*), mountain candytuft (*Noccea montana*), and brookcress (*Cardamine cordifolia*).

Marshall Mesa/Greenbelt

Wildflower alert: Drifts of dainty sundrops and buttercups in spring.

Expansive views and meadows of harebell and other wildflowers highlight the Marshall Mesa Trail near Boulder.

easy	**Trail Rating**
3.0 miles out and back	**Trail Length**
Marshall Mesa/Boulder	**Location**
5,800 to 6,100 feet	**Elevation**
April to July	**Bloom Season**
May to June	**Peak Bloom**
From Boulder, take highway 93 south to Marshall Road (#170). Turn left and continue 0.2 mile. Turn right at the stop sign and go 0.6 mile to the trailhead on the right.	**Directions**

Boulder's Open Space acquisitions include historic Marshall Mesa in southern Boulder County. The vegetation has survived in the remains of a coal mining operation active as recently as 50 years ago. The semi-arid grasslands are interspersed with pine. Wildflowers now flourish under open skies where miners once sweated underground.

Marshall Mesa Trail is gentle to its intersection with Greenbelt Trail, and in spring and early summer it's a wonderful wildflower walk highlighted by scattered golden dainty sundrops. Sweeping views of the red-finned Flatirons to the west add a bonus.

YUCCA

Yucca glauca

Yucca's sharp-tipped leaves, which retain their blue-green color all year, give rise to the common name, Spanish bayonet. Generous white bells on a stately spike make yucca prominent when in bloom. The lily-like flowers are pollinated by a single species of moth that lays its eggs in the ovary; the resulting pods provide a food supply for newly hatched larvae—an example of a symbiotic relationship benefitting both organisms. Big pods mature into woody frameworks and are sometimes used in dried arrangements. When ripe, the flat black seeds can be roasted and salted for a wild snack.

Casually referred to as the Indian supermarket, yucca was utilized by Native Americans from flower to root. They ate the new asparagus-like stalks; the buds and petals were served in salads; the dried green seedpods were split and seeded, then steeped for a sweetish drink or enjoyed as an Indian version of fruit leather. The leaves' tough fibers were made into everything from sandals and mats to cordage and paintbrushes. (Even today, traditional Pueblo potters chew the ends of yucca leaves for use in painting incredibly delicate lines on their pots.) The taproot, containing saponin, can be peeled and pounded to lather up for a skin-softening soap or shampoo. Native Americans used this soap year-round by drying and powdering the roots for storage.

From the trailhead parking area, head south to pass **yarrow, blue flax, cinquefoil, lupine,** and **mouse-ear chickweed.** Climb a few log steps past the bridge over the canal-sized Community Ditch dug in the early 1900s. Here, as in many places along the trail, a small bushy plant appears. This member of the evening primrose family, **dainty sundrops,** has lemon-colored blossoms and toothy leaves that account for its other name, **tooth-leaved evening primrose.** The narrow trail follows an almost level plane where another member of the evening primrose family, **scarlet gaura,** lifts fragrant, orchid-like white blooms that age to coral.

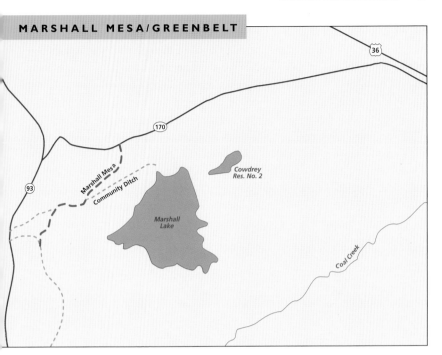

MARSHALL MESA/GREENBELT

Marshall Mesa
Community Ditch
Cowdrey
Res. No. 2
Marshall
Lake
Coal Creek

Turning west toward tall ponderosa pines, the path leaves the bike trail. The grasses here once grew horse-belly high and hid wildflowers such as **copper mallow, sego lily, orchid penstemon**, and **miner's candle**, whose stout "candle" is a mass of prickly foliage and a white forget-me-not-like flower.

Lined by gold **blanketflower** and orange-gold **meadow arnica**, the trail approaches the shade of good-sized ponderosas. Here, an exposed face of soft stone is etched with historical graffiti. At a nearby seep on the right, the trail passes a shallow drainage full of **ninebark** bushes. The five-petaled white flowers cluster on the shrubs' reddish stems. Like apples, ninebark and nearby **serviceberry** are members of the rose family. The slightly twisted white petals of serviceberry's fragrant blooms open early to allow time for blue-black fruits to develop and ripen. Looking like tiny inky apples, the berries were once used for jelly and pemmican (a combination of pounded dried buffalo meat and various berries bound with melted bear fat—a concoction relished by mountain men).

Watch along the north side of the trail for a patch of pale pink **yarrow** with gray-green foliage and flat flower clusters. A close European cousin has offspring in many colors; the yellow varieties are thought to be deer-resistant.

The trail opens to a fine mountain view with a field of blue-purple **silvery lupine** in the foreground. Blooming on the left about the same time is a meadow full of knee-high, off-white **candle anemone**, known too as **thimbleweed** because of its bullet-shaped center cone.

As the trail approaches the first gate, look on the right for a colony of lacquer-yellow **buttercups.** Several extensive colonies of this tall graceful buttercup flourish along the trail in spring runoff.

The trail then rejoins the level Community Ditch path and its cycling enthusiasts. **Dogbane, tall penstemon,** and **wild rose** line the edges of the flat track. Wild roses range from white to dark pink (sometimes striped).

Beyond the bridge the path rises toward an old road passing rapier-leaved **yucca.** Stately and striking when in bloom, yucca's huge white blossoms are a food source for mule deer. The trail soon meets the Greenbelt Trail; turn left and hike up the abandoned road to reach a great vista of the plateau from the top. If taking photographs, look around the nearby pine groves for a colony of **harebells** to use for foreground with the grand view the of the Flatirons and Longs Peak behind.

Marshall Mesa to Greenbelt Trail is a fine hike for views and wildflowers. In mid-June, more than 50 flower species adorn the gentle Marshall Mesa Trail, and you can enjoy the trail year-round.

Chautauqua/ Bluebell Mesa

Wildflower alert: A riot of pink and white wild sweet peas in July.

In June, wild sweet peas come out in a colorful profusion along this loop at Boulder's Chautauqua Park.

easy	*Trail Rating*
1.5-mile loop	*Trail Length*
Chautauqua Park/Boulder	*Location*
5,800 to 6,240 feet	*Elevation*
May to August	*Bloom Season*
June	*Peak Bloom*
From Boulder, take Baseline west to just past 9th. Then turn left into the parking lot.	*Directions*

On the western outskirts of Boulder, historic Chautauqua Auditorium and resort complex rests nostalgically by a vast meadow. Boulder Mountain Parks oversees this open space where a network of trails include the short loop featured here. Beginning at the Ranger's Cottage, the trail slopes up toward the Flatirons' sandstone slabs and returns down a pine-covered mesa. In spring, some five dozen wildflower species accompany the Chautauqua/Bluebell-Baird/Bluebell Mesa trails that make up the loop. In July, a riot of wild sweet peas scramble among the lengthening grasses near the loop's start.

PURPLE SALSIFY AND
Tragopogon porrifolius

YELLOW SALSIFY
Tragopogon dubius ssp. major

Tragopogon sounds like a species of dinosaur, but actually it's Latin for "goatsbeard," another common name for salsify. Actually Greek in origin, *tragos,* meaning "goat," and *pogon,* meaning "beard," make up the genus name. This purple import, although considered somewhat of a weed in this country, is still cultivated in the Mediterranean region as it has been for 2,000 years. There, it is known as oyster plant.

Yellow salsify (*Tragopogon dubius ssp. major*) grows in the vicinity and hybridizes with its purple relative as verified by wine-colored salsify specimens. The softball-sized seedheads resemble dusty-looking billy goat beards—hence, the name goatsbeard.

Salsify's coagulated milky sap was once chewed to solve indigestion problems.

Before starting out on the loop, check out the Ranger Cottage garden planted with native wildflowers. Then peruse the descriptions of the various trails on the locator map on the building's veranda. The parking lot fills quickly, especially on weekends.

The scenic trail starts southwest up through many spring-blooming flowers familiar to foothills hikers, such as **blue flax, yarrow, chiming bells,** and **yellow salsify.** In early June, one of the tallest and richest-colored flowers is **purple salsify.** Nearby, wine-colored versions of purple salsify display their habit of hybridizing with yellow salsify. Around the Fourth of July, enjoy the dazzling display of **wild sweet peas,** from white through every shade of pink and into violet-rose. In this area as fall approaches, colonies of big bluestem grass gain attention by turning soft salmon.

CHAUTAUQUA/BLUEBELL MESA

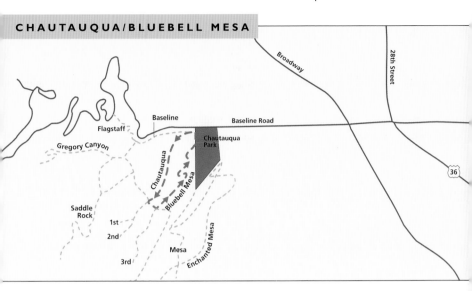

Also adding late season color are **asters, goldenrod,** and the vivid red hips of **wild rose.**

Chautauqua Trail rises steadily on a broad track past **houndstongue** and its furry-leaved cousin **false gromwell,** its closed-cone shaped flowers spitting out a single style. The unique **gromwell** blooms develop into seeds so hard that another name for the tidy-foliaged plant is **marbleseed.** When the path reaches a group of rocks, pause and turn around to view the Boulder Valley and the red-roofed buildings of the University of Colorado below.

Resuming the uphill trail, stay straight ahead on the gravel surface as a spur materializes to the right. Just beyond, a barrier fence introduces upcoming patches of perfumed **wild rose** growing on both sides of the trail.

As the track proceeds into areas of shorter grasses, look on the south side for the fragrant lavender globes of **purple milkvetch.** Just up the trail as it enters the ponderosa pine belt, **tall scarlet paintbrush** rises above the neighboring vegetation. In the company of sturdy pines, wildflowers such as **wild iris** and **wild geranium** bloom in intensified hues.

Chautauqua Trail has risen almost 400 vertical feet since the start, making pauses a pleasure. Look for the small, reddish paws of **pink pussytoes** in the grasses, or **many-flowered puccoon** with its golden-tubed clusters on generously foliaged clumps.

Just before entering a conifer forest, look for thickets of **wild plum.** Plush patches of poison ivy abound here, so be careful. Still climbing, the trail leads up stone steps toward the First Flatiron. Evergreens offer shade as more steps—these log—lead up to a junction where a sign points left to the Bluebell-Baird Trail. Long-blooming **harebells** and **common alumroot** grow tall in the filtered shade along this short section of trail. Soon the loop takes a left on Bluebell Mesa Trail. The 450-foot elevation gain to this point will be lost as the trail eases down Bluebell Mesa.

The large pines are far enough apart along this trail segment to qualify as a ponderosa parkland. The track is a bit rough as it descends slowly, passing colonies of **bluemist penstemon, Oregon grapeholly,** and **leafy cinquefoil.** Halfway down the slanting mesa top, grasses grow more thickly, and among them, a stand of **American hawksbeard** appears left of the path under a ponderosa.

Continuing on Bluebell Mesa Trail where it heads left at a junction, the route begins to drop off the mesa passing more **many-flowered puccoon** and **bluemist penstemon.**

Later in the season, **harebells** appear near yet another junction where the loop takes a right. Close by this intersection, look for the pink bells and pointed drooping leaves of **dogbane.**

Continuing downward, Bluebell Mesa Trail passes between specimens of **buckbrush,** which may be covered with fragrant white flower clusters. This low-growing, tight-branched shrub sports a liberal collection of thorn-like branchlets.

Much of Boulder spreads itself into an impressive vista as the trail continues to descend. The last section traverses a north-facing slope where wildflowers, such as **blue flax, wild rose, cinquefoil,** and **lupine,** add color in their season.

Though the Chautauqua/Bluebell-Baird/Bluebell Mesa loop is not long (name excepted), it is very scenic.

Hayden/Green Mountain

Wildflower Hike

9

Wildflower alert: Open hillsides colored by wildflowers in spring.

The Hayden/Green Mountain Trail arrives at a vantage point with views of Denver and the Front Range.

moderate to easy	**Trail Rating**
3.3-mile loop	**Trail Length**
Green Mountain/Lakewood	**Location**
6,080 to 6,770 feet	**Elevation**
May to July	**Bloom Season**
mid-May to June	**Peak Bloom**
From west Denver, take C-470 south to Morrison Road. Turn east and go 2.2 miles to Bear Creek Blvd. Turn left and go 2.2 miles straight ahead (the road becomes Alameda Parkway East). Turn left at the Florida Trailhead lot.	**Directions**

Hayden/Green Mountain Open Space Park on the outskirts of Lakewood is awash with colorful flowers in spring and early summer. Green Mountain's gentle slopes, especially those north and east, are a wildflower enthusiast's dream come true. Typically, mid-May to late June is the optimum window of bloom.

The Hayden/Green Mountain Trail sets out by climbing along old roads to gain most of the elevation before arriving at the trail's high point where hikers enjoy a 360-degree view of Denver, the Dakota Hogback, and three fourteeners beyond the foothills of the Front Range. It then changes direction to traverse back down.

The sign in the large parking area indicates the beginning of the Hayden/Green Mountain Trail. Pick up a handy trail map here.

In early summer, the slope immediately adjacent to the trailhead parking lot is dotted with electric **blue penstemon**. Partial to gravelly soil and drought-tolerant, this eye-popping wildflower is a rare true blue, especially when the blossoms are fresh.

The Hayden Trail leaves from the far end of the parking area and climbs an old jeep road. **Lupine, blue flax, orange paintbrush,** and **spiderwort** provide a colorful start.

Continuing up past road banks, look for the large blooms of **tufted evening primrose** that change from youthful white to aging pink in just one day. Another plant fond of disturbed soil, **prickly poppy,** has big silky-white blooms throughout the summer. In the same arid earth grows a sandpaper-foliaged wildflower that blooms beautifully late in the afternoon: **white evening star.** Later in the summer, yellow-flowered **prickly pear cactus** and **bush sunflower** stand out on the hillsides along this part of the trail.

Heading toward a radio tower, the trail rises quickly past **orange paintbrush,** magenta **Lambert locoweed,** and blue-flowered **silvery lupine.** In midsummer, **Mexican hat** or **prairie coneflower** blooms near the tower.

As the trail crests, **locoweed's** bright magenta racemes stand out in front of snow-capped Mount Evans. Not far from here, **tall butter 'n eggs** blooms a bit later. Stand for a moment and pick out the tallest mountains from the south to the northwest: Pikes Peak, Mount Evans, and Longs Peak, each rising over 14,000 feet.

Continuing north a short way, look for well-defined Hayden Trail angling sharply left and back, aiming for Mount Evans on the skyline. This junction begins the downhill leg of the loop through a wealth of wildflowers. Yellows paint the north and west-facing slopes with **blanketflower, arnica, stonecrop, cinquefoil, sulphurflower,** and **whiskbroom parsley. Blue flax,** purple flea-banes, **orange paintbrush** (which may vary from salmon to scarlet), and pink **wild geraniums** fill the palette.

HAYDEN/GREEN MOUNTAIN

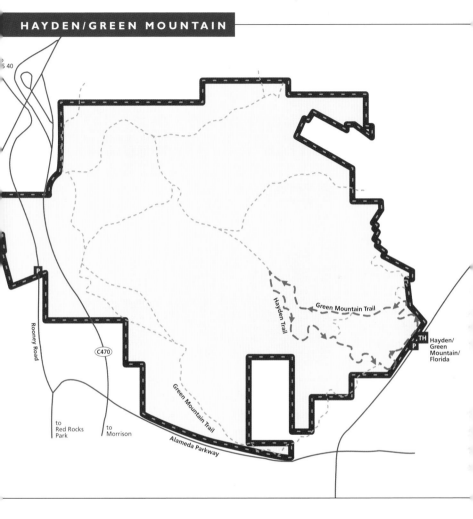

Pass spikes of **white plains larkspur** and blue **tall larkspur** as the track meanders down. Like most of their delphinium relations, these two larkspurs exhibit the porpoise-shaped buds that inspired their genus name *Delphinium,* derived from the Latin for "dolphin."

With Pikes Peak straight ahead, more muted yellow **blanketflowers** or **gaillardia** stand tall in the waving grasses. Sharp-lobed ray petals surround a center of minute red disk flowers; each of these florets becomes a seed.

The trail heads down leisurely through **wild roses** and sprawling patches of **wild sweet pea**. This bi-colored member of the legume or pea family crawls through and over neighboring vegetation. Later along this section of trail, deep apricot **copper mallow** blooms. Distinctive for its singular color, this relative of cotton and okra claims the common name, **cowboy's delight.**

Farther down the trail in small ravines, **chokecherry** and **hawthorn** shelter **showy townsendia**, a pale, lavender-white "daisy." Next, you'll see **white gilia's** long slim trumpets spatter the slope, each perfectly designed for humming-birds and the coil-tongued hawkmoth.

Following the trail map, zigzag down in a southerly direction. Then bear east and finally north up a short incline back to the parking area.

The City of Lakewood and Jefferson County have preserved an entire mountain in its midst for the hiker, biker, horseman, and wildflower enthusiast. It is a challenge to count the species blooming on each visit to Green Mountain. Each year is different with varying levels of moisture, viable seed, and other germination and survival factors.

WHITE EVENING STAR
Nuttallia nuda

Plains evening star and blazing star are an additional pair of romantic common names for white evening star, but its others, stickweed and stickleaf, are anything but romantic. Its foliage is scraggly and sandpaper-like. But like viewing time-lapse photography, close observers can watch its pointed-petaled flowers open in late afternoon or on dark, clouded days. The satiny flowers are also quite fragrant. (Try to catch the flowering show between 5 and 7 p.m.)

The two-foot high plant's stems were once pounded for their yellow juice, which was boiled and then applied externally to reduce fevers. It is also considered to be a honey plant.

White evening star's genus name honors an acclaimed English botanist, Thomas Nuttall, who ventured west in the early 1800s. A taller cousin, giant evening star *(Nuttallia decapetala)*, has 10 petals and about 100 stamens. Its larger flowers are open evenings and mornings. It blooms about one month later than white evening star.

Fountain Valley

Wildflower alert: A wet meadow filled with golden wintercress and, later, golden banner.

The 2.2-mile Fountain Valley Loop in Roxborough State Park passes through a lush basin flanked by fins of red sandstone.

easy	***Trail Rating***
2.2-mile loop (plus a 0.5-mile spur to Lyons Overlook)	***Trail Length***
Roxborough State Park/Littleton	***Location***
6,200 down to 6,050 feet	***Elevation***
May to September	***Bloom Season***
late May to mid-July	***Peak Bloom***
From west Denver, take C-470 south to Wadsworth. Then turn south and continue to Waterton Canyon. Turn left and continue to Rampart Range Road. Turn right and follow the signs to Roxborough Park Road. Turn left, and then right onto the entrance road. Be prepared to pay the fee.	***Directions***

Located adjacent to Pike National Forest, Roxborough State Park nestles at the base of the Front Range foothills southwest of Denver. The Fountain Valley Loop, once an old ranch road, allows companionable side-by-side travel. The 2.2-mile loop ambles down a grassy valley to a historic stone house and returns through a lush basin flanked by upthrust fins of red sandstone. Options include two spur trails: a brief one to an overlook of the park's unique geology, and a second one to an observation deck with a grand view.

The wildflower scene features golden wintercress in a moist meadow in the spring. The wildflower roster changes weekly. Before starting out on the Fountain Valley Trail, consider picking up an interpretive guide at the visitor center, which correlates to numbered posts along the trail. The center's rock garden is especially colorful in spring and early summer.

NARROW-LEAVED PUCCOON

Lithospermum incisum

Named puccoon by Native Americans, the roots of this drought-resistant plant could be eaten or could be used to make a reddish-purple dye. In addition, a tea made of the seeds once served as a method of birth control.

With rather scrawny foliage, puccoon has five frilly-edged petals forming a bugle. These butter-yellow flowers form rock-hard white seeds, which are the source of the genus name, *Lithospermum. Lithos,* meaning "stone," and *sperma,* meaning "seed," are of Greek origin.

A later blooming cousin, many-flowered puccoon (*Lithospermum multiflorum*) flaunts lush clumps with loose clusters of gold tubes.

The gravel roadway leading north from the flagstone patio provides a surface geared for people of all hiking abilities. At the start, a low sign on the left offers sage advice: "Leaves of three, leave them be." Poison ivy surrounds it.

Between the first two numbered posts is **prickly gooseberry**, white tubes dangling between the thorns, that develop into tasty fruit when ripe. By the next signpost on the right, **chokecherry** yields drooping racemes of white flowers, resembling bunches of miniature grapes when in bud. Chokecherries are an important source of food for wildlife in late summer and fall. Nearby on the left of the track, small trees of pervasively perfumed **wild plum** bloom before they leaf out—unlike chokecherry, which leafs out before blooming. Bears

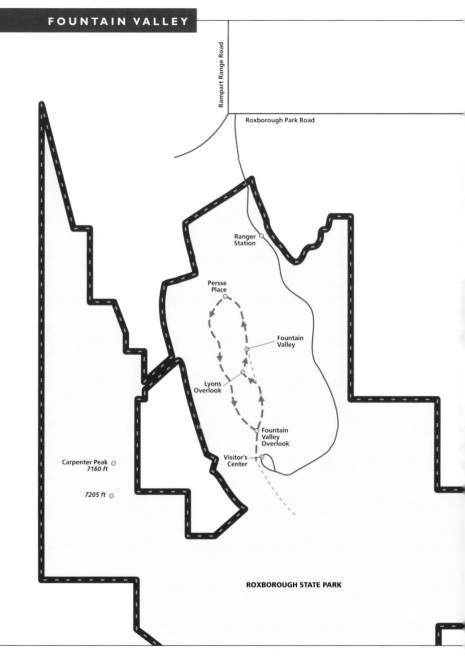

and coyotes enjoy the astringent dusty-purple plums that ripen late in the autumn.

The brief spur to Fountain Valley Overlook soon appears on the left. Along it, the pink stars of **spring beauties** may be found as early as February, but more often in March. Blooming soon after, **biscuitroot** is also known by a more descriptive common name, **salt and pepper.** By May, a thick stand of **golden banner** appears with showy racemes of yellow, pea-type flowers.

The spur ends at a pair of convenient back-to-back benches. Look west to 7,160-foot Carpenter Peak's 1.6 billion-year-old granite top; then look northwest at the 300-million-year-old iron-oxide stained Fountain Formation. To the north is the buff-banded Lyons Formation, and to the east is the younger Dakota Hogback.

Back on the main trail, continue past an embankment of bluish-purple **silvery lupine.** Like many members of the legume family, lupines have nodules on the roots that store nitrogen to enrich the soil. On the left is a large copse of scrub oak sheltering **spring beauties** and a comfortable bench. The loop forks here. Take the right fork for an easier hike.

The trail passes white-blooming **yucca** and **yarrow,** and yellow-flowering **mullein** and **narrow-leafed puccoon.** This soft yellow member of the borage family is also known as **fringed gromwell.**

Along the grassy bank on the left, June produces big white heads of **showy townsendia.** This jaunty daisy-like wildflower is a late riser compared to its March- or April-blooming cousin, **Easter daisy.** In the same vicinity, when the soil is still cold, a member of the pea family, **early pink milkvetch,** is worth seeking. On the other end of the flowering season, look for vivid rosy-lavender brushes of **gayfeather** blooming among the mountain mahogany shrubs in late summer.

The trail approaches a spur on the left to Lyons Overlook. Follow the spur signs up to a splendid vista at the top of the petrified sand dunes that comprise the Lyons Formation. Along the way, scrub oak shelters myriad blue-purple spikes of **early larkspur.** As the trail levels at the top the Lyons Formation, pause near a shaded bench on the left to inhale an elusive aroma. On warm days the crevices in the bark of mature ponderosa pines smell like vanilla. The odor is said to discourage insect appetites.

The spur winds down through decomposing sandstone dotted with **kinnikinnick** and **yellow stonecrop** to a railed deck. From the front rail, view Carpenter Peak ahead and the red-finned Fountain Formation; to the north, Longs Peak is just visible in the distance.

Heading back down the spur trail, go straight ahead at the first fork to rejoin the main trail. The added mileage of the Lyons Overlook to the Fountain Valley loop is 0.5 mile. Follow the roadway as it descends, passing **beebalm, snowberry, lupine,** and deadly **poison hemlock** to the historic Persse Place. Built around 1900, the restored stone house was once owned by Henry Persse, who entertained hopes of turning the Roxborough area into an upscale resort.

As the loop curves west from the historic house, look over the trees at the distinctive rock formation straight ahead. This area was once called Washington Park because the rock's profile resembles our nation's first president.

Passing Little Willow Creek and thickets of **hawthorn, wild plum,** and **wild licorice,** the trail enters a wet meadow area bordered on the west by red sandstone fins and on the east by the uniquely eroded Lyons Formation. Pause at the frog signpost by the second creek crossing. In April and May, the sound of male chorus frogs, one of which fits comfortably on a dime, may be heard. In spring, this wet meadow is blanketed with bright yellow **wintercress.** In the same vicinity, buttercup-yellow **cinque-foil** blooms as wintercress fades. Later, in midsummer, tall **blue vervain** stretches three feet high, its branches ending in bluish-purple blossoms—quite ambitious for an annual.

Up the trail, signpost #17 is engraved with an aspen leaf motif. The extensive grove of aspens at the base of the Fountain Formation is all one male organism. The grove thrives 1,300 feet below its typical elevation. Near this sign, look for the rosy-lavender flowers of **beebalm,** a member of the mint family.

The trail curves to pass the Sentinel, a towering pillar of eroded red sandstone colloquially referred to as a "hoo-doo" in parts of the West. Note the taller scrub oak along the trail now. These trees are half a millennium old; they may have been seedlings when Columbus landed in America. Along here, showy violet-pink **tall penstemon** blooms about the same time as **sego lilies** in mid-June.

The redrock-rimmed valley widens and the path winds north past a bench shaded by mature scrub oak that serve as homes for woodpeckers. Just before arriving at the string portion of the balloon-shaped loop, another bench

SHOWY TOWNSENDIA
Townsendia grandiflora

Showy Townsendia's grooved, whitish ray petals tend to be suffused with subdued pink or purple. This summer bloomer is fond of open fields. Its hairy stems are long compared with early Easter daisies, or Townsendias' stemless appearance.

The Latin species name *grandiflora* means "big flowered." Showy Townsendia's blossoms are larger than its early-blooming (sometimes blooming before the grasses green up) cousins, Hooker townsendia (*Townsendia hookeri,* also referred to as Easter daisy) and Easter townsendia (*Townsendia exscapa).* The genus name honors David Townsend, an American botanist born in 1787.

huddles in a scrub-oak copse, the perfect habitat for early-blooming pink **spring beauties.** Ahead, the O'Malley Visitor Center signals completion of the loop.

Roxborough State Park, in the transition zone between the plains and the foothills, has been designated a National Natural Landmark and a Colorado Natural Area. Just a brief drive from the Denver metro area, it is a park for all seasons. In spring and early summer, wildflowers share star billing with the spectacular rock formations. And in autumn—typically the first two weeks of October—the scrub oak displays warm pigments.

South Rim / Willow Creek

Wildflower alert: Wildflowers found in the plains/foothills transition zone, including larkspur, paintbrush, and scarlet gilia.

Roxborough State Park's South Rim Trail is a 2.7-mile loop through a changing display of wildflowers, such as these golden banners.

easy	*Trail Rating*
2.7-mile loop	*Trail Length*
Roxborough State Park/Littleton	*Location*
6,100 to 6,300 feet	*Elevation*
May to September	*Bloom Season*
June	*Peak Bloom*

Directions

From west Denver, take C-470 south to Wadsworth. Then turn south and continue to Waterton Canyon. Turn left and continue to Rampart Range Road. Turn right and follow the signs to North Roxborough Park Road. Turn left, and then right onto the entrance road. Be prepared to pay the fee.

Inspiring Roxborough State Park is in the transition zone between the plains and the foothills. Plants from the two life zones overlap here, creating an area rich in wildflower species. The park's approximately 3,400 acres are anchored by an intriguing series of rock formations, including the Fountain Formation's imposing red fins; the petrified sand dunes of the Lyons Formation; the sharp-ridged Dakota Hogback, and the dinosaur-footprinted shale of the Morrison Formation. The park's high point, Carpenter Peak, is granite.

The South Rim Trail can be accessed from the visitor center or, for a shorter loop, from the east trailhead located just after passing through the Dakota Hogback where a parking area on the left has room for a few vehicles. The 2.7-mile loop of South Rim takes the hiker through a changing parade of seasonal wildflowers by heading leisurely upslope to reach a view from the ridge. The trail then traverses a shady stretch before returning along open ground.

Even before reaching the small east trailhead parking area, and just prior to the gap in the hogback, watch the roadside for the cherry red **poppy mallow** on the east shoulder near the speedbumps. This eye-catching long-bloomer is outstanding in the xeric garden. Poppy mallow tolerates hot exposures, and even clay.

South Rim loop starts out between skunkbrush, **snowberry**, and willow. Just before the sturdy bridge crossing tiny Willow Creek, look left for the sleek shrubs of **golden currant**, an upright bush with clove-scented blossoms. **Clovebush** is an appropriate name too. Just beyond the bridge, **Canada violet** begins appearing under the scrub oak. In the company of **early larkspur** and **golden banner,** this cool-loving violet blooms in spring and early summer. Also in the shelter of scrub oak, although it seeds rampantly in disturbed exposed soil too, **poison hemlock** *(Conium maculatum)* is noteworthy for several things: it is the first bright green of spring; its ferny leaves mimic those of carrot; and, as its name implies, it is deadly. By summer, the ferny rosette shoots up a tall, hollow, purple-splotched stalk with a wide umbel of tiny white flowers at the top. The stalks fade to white in winter.

The trail reaches an open slope that, in early summer, is filled with a profusion of colorful wildflowers. One of the showiest is **orchid penstemon,** its spires of lavender-pink blossoms contrast with waxy blue-green foliage.

The South Rim Trail heads up the left fork at a junction with Willow Creek Trail, where a bench offers views of the red-finned Fountain Formation, golden-buff Lyons Formation, and the granite-studded summit of Carpenter Peak. The trail follows a warm southwest-facing slope dotted with yellow-blooming **creeping** or **Oregon grapeholly.** This subshrub's evergreen leaves—which often turn wine-red in winter—are prickly, like that of holly. Native Americans used it for food, dye, and medicine.

SOUTH RIM/WILLOW CREEK

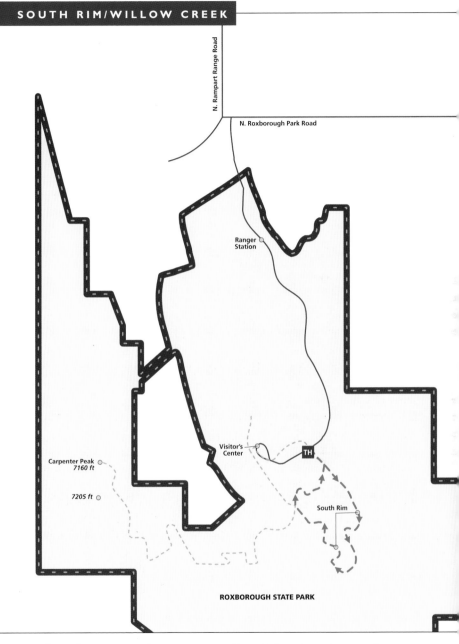

Early in the season in the same area, **yellow violets, American vetch,** and **cinquefoil** join milk-white **Drummond milkvetch.** On the dry slope here are **sulphurflower** and **golden aster.** Golden aster is not really an aster, but a member of the prolific sunflower family that comprises one-fifth of all Rocky Mountain wildflowers. Alabaster-white **sego lilies** bloom along here in mid-June, as do **orange paintbrush, scarlet gaura, white gilia,** and, later, **prairie cone-flower** and **copper mallow.** An unusual orange sherbet color defines copper mallow. It is also known in the vernacular as **cowboy's delight.**

The next bench site, shaded by scrub oak, is a nice rest stop before continuing up the gradual incline. After winding up a few switchbacks, passing both **purple** and **white prairie clover,** the trail levels and arrives at an overlook with a sweeping view of the rock formations and a cityscape beyond.

As the trail follows the ridge, it passes an unmarked spur on the left leading to an east-facing, shaded bench. This looks out at the pine-rimmed escarpment of Daniels Park in the distance.

SCARLET GILIA

Ipomopsis aggregata

In summer, scarlet gilia adds dashes of red along Roxborough trails. This biennial member of the phlox family forms a basal rosette of off-putting odored leaves that look like green-edged snowflakes; a tall stalk shoots up the following season, spiked with slender scarlet trumpets and pointy buds. Poetically called sky rocket or fairy trumpet, the starburst tubes bloom most of the summer and are a favorite of hummingbirds.

Also found in Roxborough Park is white gilia (*Ipomopsis aggregata ssp. candida*). In other places, a third color, that of soft apricot, is found and thought by some to be a hybrid of white and scarlet gilia.

In summer, biennial **scarlet gilia,** a favorite of hummingbirds, adds dashes of red along Roxborough trails. When the trail slopes down, the keen eye may discern **tall scarlet paintbrush** under the shelter of scrub oak along north-facing sections of South Rim Trail.

The trail, now reddish decomposed sandstone, heads down through evergreens and taller scrub oak. A large, rounded boulder marks the turn where a spur soon appears on the right, leading to a bench shaded by a stately Douglas fir.

Back on the main trail, pink **spring beauties** may bloom as early as February. The scrub oak gives way to open grasslands where masses of **silvery lupine** bloom in early summer. Continuing on, the path travels along the top of an old stockpond dam, crosses a footbridge, and winds up through thick grasses. Pass a bench shaded by an old cottonwood before the loop takes a right at the intersection with the Carpenter Peak Trail.

Head right again at the next junction on Willow Creek Trail, which crosses an open meadow to reach a small footbridge spanning tiny Willow Creek, soon after which the May hiker might find the locally uncommon **birdfoot violet** in bloom. Traveling in the open, watch for substantial **green gentian** and fragrant **purple milkvetch** before the path rejoins the South Rim Trail. As the loop draws to a close, retrace the steps returning to the parking area.

In June, some 70 species of wildflowers may bloom along the 2.7-mile length of South Rim Trail loop. A grand collection of rock formations and a wide variety of wildflowers awaits the appreciative eye. The unique visitor center has a good selection of books and a supportive staff to help enhance the nature enthusiast's knowledge of Roxborough State Park and the transition zone.

Meadowlark/Plymouth

Wildflower alert: A chance to discover the locally uncommon, piquant prairie starflower.

Tall butter 'n eggs highlight sections of trail along the Meadowlark/Plymouth loop southwest of Denver.

Trail Rating	easy to moderate
Trail Length	3.5-mile loop
Location	Deer Creek Canyon Park/Littleton
Elevation	6,100 to 6,550 feet
Bloom Season	May to September
Peak Bloom	June
Directions	From west Denver, take C470 south to Wadsworth. Turn south on Wadsworth and go 0.25 mile. Then turn right on Deer Creek Canyon Road. Turn left on Grizzly Drive at the sign for Deer Creek Canyon Park. Turn right into the parking lot.

Deer Creek Canyon Park is another of Jefferson County Open Space's fine foothill parks. Conveniently close for Denver metro visitors, it offers nearly 10 miles of trail through diverse habitats. In June, more than 60 wildflower species compete for attention with views of the red sandstone Fountain Formation and the distant Denver cityscape. Unique to this hike is the prairie starflower.

While this is a varied-use park, several of the trails are for hikers only, including much of this loop. In its 3.5 miles, Meadowlark/Plymouth trail travels through open grasslands, scrub oak, Douglas fir, and rocky riparian ecosystems. The Meadowlark Trail portion of the loop is for foot traffic only until it joins the Plymouth Trail at 2.2 miles. The last 1.3 mile leg, which drops fairly quickly, is used by mountain bikers as well as hikers.

Before setting out, pick up a trail-marked park brochure from the information kiosk. Begin hiking west. Crusher-fines (minced rock) cover the gently rising trail as it heads past widely spaced picnic shelters sited with commanding views.

In early spring, yellow and white wildflowers dominate the open grassy areas flanking the first part of Meadowlark Trail. Tucked in the grasses are sweet-smelling **sand lilies.** Their waxy, white stars and leathery leaves disappear underground with the onset of summer's heat. Lingering longer is **mouse-ear chickweed**, occurring from the foothills to the alpine zones. By early June, the red-tinged buff flowers of **nipple cactus** bloom briefly on half-buried globes. Look by the gravel

STAR SAXIFRAGE
Lithophragma parviflorum

This wildflower's common names are as charming as the flower itself: star saxifrage, prairie starflower, and fringecup. In early spring, white blooms dance on the ends of foot-high, thin stems, their petals cut into three points like teeth on a comb. Though usually found farther north in Rocky Mountain National Park, or to the east, this delightful member of the saxifrage family, while not common locally, has made itself at home in Deer Creek Canyon Open Space Park. The Latin *Saxifraga,* meaning "rock-breaker," could be applied from the family's habit of growing in rock crevices and creating soil pockets with its decayed foliage. But more likely the term is due to ancient medicinal theory: old herbal guides claimed saxifrages were useful in breaking up kidney stones.

Other saxifrages in the region include spotted saxifrage (*Ciliaria austromontana*), snowball saxifrage (*Micranthes rhomboidea*), and brook saxifrage (*Micranthes odontoloma*).

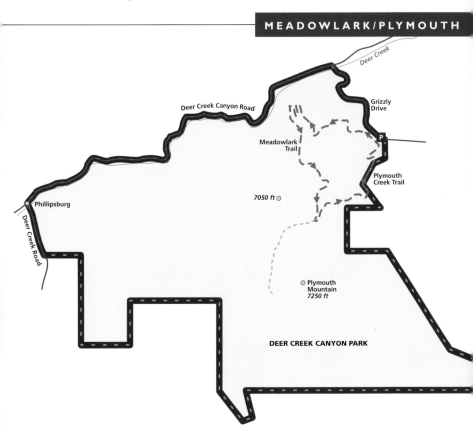

trail near the picnic shelters for the descriptively named **nipple cactus.**

The track then traverses an east-facing slope dotted with mountain mahogany and juniper. Along here a wildflower uncommon to the region is found on the lower slopes of Deer Creek Canyon Park: **prairie starflower** or **star saxifrage.** This split-petaled wildflower sits high on a bare stem.

By June, these meadowed shrub lands are colored with purple **spiderworts** and white **sego lilies.** Blooming about the same time, yellow **prickly pear cactus** appear inviting to the touch, but are protected by vengeful spines. The big spines seem bad enough, but it is the small ones that are the most painful to remove.

As the trail follows a small drainage, the soil is perfect for delicate pink **spring beauties, Canada violets,** and unobtrusive, soft-leaved colonies of **Fendler waterleaf.** Just before the path arrives at the drainage's apex, look for the off-white plumes of the **rock spirea** shrub.

The trail then heads for its first switchback where sunny **yellow violets, golden banner, wallflower,** and **early spring senecio** catch the hiker's eye.

There are more than 2,000 species of senecios around the globe, including some in Africa that reach tree-size proportions.

A pause here offers views of the Fountain Formation, the same ancient red sandstone found at Roxborough State Park and Garden of the Gods. Gambel oak or scrub oak shelters rich purple-blue **early larkspur,** white **mouse-ear, snowball saxifrage,** and golden **senecio.**

The trail levels amongst dry grasses to expose a native of Greece, **tall butter 'n eggs** or **Dalmatian toadflax.** It spreads underground, casting seeds flagrantly to fill yet another landscape next season, putting it on the Native Plant Society's "most unwanted" list.

Open slopes and wide views are interrupted by a big Douglas fir that provides cool shade by a ravine which, in late May and early June, fills with golden **arnica** and **prairie starflowers,** and **tall pussytoes** add white accents.

As Meadowlark Trail heads west on a south-facing slope, plumed seed-heads of **pasqueflower** and fresh clumps of long-blooming **harebell** nestle under the scrub oak. The delicate-appearing **harebell** is as tough as nails, long-bloomed, and drought-resistant.

Douglas firs fill in the way as the single-track trail descends to join Plymouth Creek Trail at a footbridge. Just before the bridge, watch butterflies land on the bright coppery heads of **orange agoseris.** Also called **burnt orange dandelion,** they grow tall in the foothills but hug the earth at alpine altitudes.

After crossing Plymouth Creek, turn left and head down the wide road, which passes through land first homesteaded by a man from Plymouth, England.

Find a ponderosa-topped outcrop on the left, then edge over to the creek as it begins dropping off rock shelves. There, among emerald cushions of moss, find fuchsia-colored **shooting star.** Many species of butterflies frequent the lusher vegetation along Plymouth Creek. In fact, Colorado has more species of butterflies than any other state. Along the rocky road, wildflowers such as **lupine** (including a subspecies of silvery lupine: pure **white silvery lupine**), **wild plum, wild raspberry,** and a patch of **thimbleberry** may be in bloom.

Follow the road down into decomposed red sandstone soil where the creamy white flowers of poisonous **death camas** emit an unpleasant odor. Other common names for it are **lonely lily** and **wand lily.**

As the road turns back into trail, look for more **star saxifrage** or **prairie starflower.** This welcome wildflower seems to be increasing here.

Deer Creek Canyon Park, just minutes off C-470, makes a fine after-work or last-minute destination for the Denver metro area visitor. While its 1,700-plus acres can be hiked most of the year, the best wildflower season, as is true for most of the foothills zone, is spring and early summer.

Coyote Gulch via Creek Bottom and Mountain Scrub

Wildflower alert: Many shades of early pasqueflower and brilliant fuchsia orchid penstemon.

Yucca punctuate this colorful mesa on a loop trail in Bear Creek Regional Park within the Colorado Springs city limits.

Trail Rating	easy
Trail Length	2.0-mile loop
Location	Colorado Springs
Elevation	6,330 to 6,440 feet
Bloom Season	mid-May to August
Peak Bloom	early June
Directions	From Colorado Springs, go west on highway 24 and south on 26th St. (Cimmaron). Continue for 2 miles to Bear Creek Nature Center.

Colorado Springs has preserved a bit of wild within its busy borders with the Bear Creek Regional Park complex. Several trails radiate from the outstanding center. One leisurely trail, the Coyote Gulch Loop, is passable even after a rain, thanks to gravel pathways. It begins on Creek Bottom Trail, climbs briefly to link up with Coyote Gulch Trail, and returns down Mountain Scrub Trail. A handy map is posted at the starting point. After traveling west in the cool shade along Bear Creek, the loop rises to a sloping mesa top amongst scrub oak. It then follows a gentle ravine back toward the creek and visitor center. Along Coyote Loop, typically in May, the lovely pasqueflower blooms. In early June, blue, lavender-pink, and magenta penstemons fill the sunny parts of the leisurely trail. Between 50 and 60 wildflower species can be spotted at peak bloom.

A good way to learn about the area is to visit the Bear Creek Nature Center (open Tuesday through Saturday). Inside, the first rate staff can provide visitors with trail maps and a helpful list of local wildflowers.

The center's landscaped patio is the starting point for a network of loops. These foot-trails are accessible every day of the week.

From the nature center courtyard, take the concrete walk south to a junction. Head right and cross Bear Creek on a wood bridge, following Creek Bottom Trail as it passes a wall of stacked timbers. In the rich, shaded soil above the wood, look for spikes of **kittentails** in May. By June this member of the figwort family (which includes penstemons and paintbrushes) resembles the tail of a lazy, green armadillo more than that of a kitten. Where the decomposed granite path levels, **dogbane** stands under the scrub oak, its long leaves pointing earthward. A member of a mostly subtropical clan, including the rubber tree, oleanders, and frangipani, **dogbane** thrives in temperate climes like that of the Eastern Slope of Colorado. It features delicate, lightly scented bells.

Creek Bottom Trail heads right passing a bench on the left. Continue over a footbridge to reach another bench near Bear Creek and some **wild roses**. Again, cross the creek and climb timber risers up a brief, steep section past a woody ravine with hanging **dainty western clematis**. Where the route levels it opens and passes through shrubs, such as threeleaf sumac and mountain mahogany. Underneath, look for June-blooming **wavyleaf dandelion** and **actinea**, an upright yellow daisy sometimes called **perky Sue**. Actinea's flowers, broad tri-toothed ray petals, and a waxy disk sit atop long bare stalks. **Bluemist penstemon** and bushy **Drummond milkvetch** coexist with **sandwort**—its stars suspended from the grasslike leaves—and **early pink milkvetch**, with its violet-pink tubes. Very early season walks here turn up **pasqueflowers**, from palest lavender to soft purple, and **lanceleaf chiming bells**, pink-budded and blue-flowered. By June, the pasqueflower sepals are gone, leaving feathery pinkish plumes in their place.

To the right, the wide landscape funnels into a canyon where Gold Camp Road winds up to its lookout. At the next junction the loop heads right across open grasslands on Coyote Gulch Loop where Cheyenne Mountain materializes ahead. Spiked **yucca** dominates the grasses with **orange paintbrush**, blue **narrowleaved** or **skyblue penstemon**, yellow **wallflower**, and **orchid penstemon**.

ORCHID PENSTEMON

Penstemon secundiflorus

This showy foothills favorite, also called sidebells or one-sided penstemon, echoes its Latin (but Greek in origin) binomial. In the binomial system of plant nomenclature, the first part of the name (genus) is a Latin noun, the second name (specific) is a descriptive adjective. The two together (sometimes with added subspecies designation) comprise a plant's scientific name, unique to that plant alone. The radiant snap-

dragon-like flowers of orchid penstemon have five stamens: four working stamens, along with one fuzzy sterile stamen; its Latin genus name, *Penstemon,* can be broken down into *pente,* meaning "five" and *stemon,* meaning "stamen." The specific name, *secundiflorus,* derives from *secunda,* meaning "facing one side," and *flora* meaning "flower" or "flowered." So, employing Latin, literally in this case, *Penstemon secundiflorus* becomes "one-side flowered penstemon." The blossoms do grow on one side of the stalk.

Since orchid penstemon typically prefers a warm exposure and gravelly soil on the xeric side, it often grows in habitats favored by rattlesnakes. Navajos often applied the plant's wet, pounded leaves to rattlesnake bites.

More than 250 penstemon species are found in the western hemisphere, 150 of which inhabit the Rocky Mountains. Some likely to be met include bluemist penstemon (*Penstemon virens*), littleflower penstemon (*P. confertus ssp. procerus*), Whipple's or dusky penstemon (*P. whippleanus*), and tall penstemon (*P. virgatus ssp. asagrayi*).

Continuing around the loop, pass a social trail heading toward a residential area: Coyote Gulch Loop goes left here. A grand view of Colorado Springs fans out eastward. Descending gently, the pink gravel path enters oak and pines. Along here, the plentiful **orchid penstemon** is brilliant fuchsia.

In the shelter of Douglas firs and scrub oak, look for deer in the shallow gulch. The track then winds up and around, opening to a distant view to the north where the red Garden of the Gods rock formations point skyward. Pass a field of **yucca** before

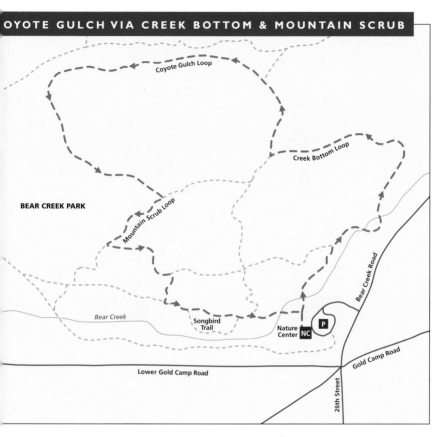

COYOTE GULCH VIA CREEK BOTTOM & MOUNTAIN SCRUB

Coyote Gulch Loop

Creek Bottom Loop

BEAR CREEK PARK

Mountain Scrub Loop

Bear Creek

Songbird Trail

Nature Center NC   P

Bear Creek Road

Gold Camp Road

Lower Gold Camp Road

26th Street

descending to meet Mountain Scrub Loop. Here, turn right and pass a bench before winding down to another intersection. Take a left and zigzag to yet another bench preceding a "T"; a left here comes out on a wide concrete walk. Continue on past the exit of wheelchair-accessible Songbird Loop, where gold **many-flowered puccoon** and **few-flowered false Solomon's seal** bloom in the shade. At the entrance, look for grapefruit-sized **ball nipple cactus**—the name describes everything but the rosy-pink bursts crowning it in late May or early June. The walkway crosses Bear Creek on a footbridge and returns to the starting point. The nature center is just to the right.

The combined Creek Bottom, Coyote Gulch, and Mountain Scrub trails form a satisfying loop through a pleasant diversity of plant communities and changing casts of wildflowers. Take advantage of the Bear Creek Nature Center's peninsula of tamed wilderness on the west edge of Colorado Springs.

Wildflower Hike

14

Lake Gulch/Inner Canyon

Wildflower alert: Spring flowers, beginning with orange paintbrush.

Hikers stroll along Cherry Creek, then hike out of the canyon's rock walls on this loop trail at Castlewood Canyon State Park.

Trail Rating	easy
Trail Length	2.0-mile loop
Location	Castlewood Canyon State Park/Franktown
Elevation	6,600 down to 6,400 feet
Bloom Season	mid-May to July
Peak Bloom	June
Directions	From south Denver, take I-25 south to Castle Rock. Go east on highway 86 to highway 83. Turn south and continue for 5 miles to the park entrance on the right.

Located in eastern Douglas County, Castlewood Canyon is an unexpected surprise in the rolling plains of the region. Where Cherry Creek carved an interesting fissure in the prairie, ponderosa pines and Douglas fir dominate Castlewood Canyon.

Lake Gulch/Inner Canyon loop offers the wildflower seeker more than 50 species throughout a variety of ecosystems from sunny riparian to deep-shaded Douglas fir, and from scrub oak to shallow-soiled shelf rock. It takes the hiker down a warm southern exposure to arrive at Cherry Creek, then turns east along the stream until it recrosses and rises quickly to complete the loop.

A visitor center has a labeled native plant garden, a fine slide show, and a helpful staff. A broad wheelchair-friendly concrete walk called Canyon View Nature Trail extends for 0.8 mile.

Lake Gulch Trail begins at the northernmost parking lot. The wide path heads northwest past picnic shelters and out through open grasslands punctuated by vivid bracts of **orange paintbrush**. White **yarrow** and **Drummond milkvetch**, violet-blue **American vetch**, orange **cowboy's delight**, yellow **cinquefoil**, and magenta **locoweed** thrive along with various grasses and **limbervetch**. An agile mini-flowered member of the pea family, **limbervetch** climbs over everything in sight.

As the trail starts down through ponderosa pines, look along the shelves of rock for the bright stars of **yellow stonecrop**. Found in virtually all the life zones from plains to alpine, this plump-

ORANGE PAINTBRUSH
Castilleja integra

Named for Spanish botanist Don Castillejo, orange paintbrush has bracts of flaming hues from fluorescent orange to scarlet. Also called broadbract and plains or foothills paintbrush, this figwort family member is semi-parasitic. A few growers have begun offering infant paintbrush, hosted by native bunch grass, such as blue grama, in pots. It is worth experimenting with in a xeriscape plan; the colored bracts last a long time.

More regional paintbrush species include Great Plains paintbrush (*Castilleja sessiliflora*) in lower elevations, narrow-leaved paintbrush (*Castilleja linariifolia*), and tall mountain or scarlet paintbrush (*Castilleja miniata*) in middle elevations. In the high country, find western yellow paintbrush (*Castilleja occidentalis*), and rosy paintbrush (*Castilleja rhexifolia*).

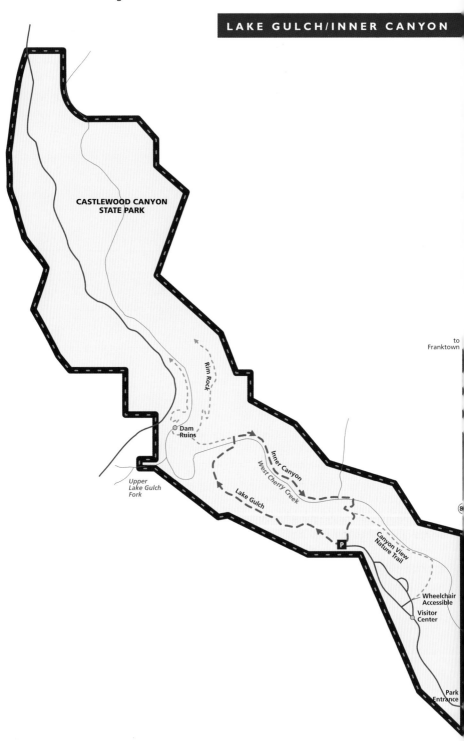

CASTLEWOOD CANYON
STATE PARK

to
Franktown

Rim Rock

Dam
Ruins

Upper
Lake Gulch
Fork

Inner Canyon

West Cherry Creek

Lake Gulch

P

Canyon View
Nature Trail

Wheelchair
Accessible

Visitor
Center

Park
Entrance

leaved succulent prefers rocky ground. Stonecrop is so drought-tolerant it can be left out of the ground and still continue growing.

Several types of rock appear along the trail and some plants, such as **clovers** and **lupine,** manage to grow in the rock-bound strata, enriching the thin soil. **Silvery lupine** adds the compost of its foliage to the soil each season, and its roots have nitrogen-fixing nodules (as do many members of the pea family). Lupine seeds, if frozen, can germinate years later.

A bit farther on the descent, in spring, watch for the yellow blossoms of **prickly pear cactus** and waist-high spikes of **tall penstemon,** a rosy-violet here. As the trail curves down, pause to look south: the open valley of ranchland was once a lake when Cherry Creek was dammed here in the late 1800s. Today's stream hardly resembles the pent-up waters that took two lives and caused $1 million worth of damage to Denver in 1933 when the stone dam gave way.

The path widens and heads down through brome grass to view the dam's remains. After crossing a small footbridge over West Cherry Creek, Inner Gulch Trail turns right. The creekbed is habitat for **cow parsnip, wintercress,** and **white campion.** The minuscule yellow flowers of wintercress bloom early. In the same vicinity, white campion, a encroaching import, has begun spreading through the foothills landscape.

The trail climbs through the rocks and **prickly pear cactus** before it levels in the shade of evergreens and oak. In addition to **early larkspur** and **pussytoes,** three-leafed poison ivy advances close to the trail in places.

Recrossing Cherry Creek on another footbridge, the trail climbs a series of steps. In early summer along this trail segment, a few peeling-barked bushes of **ninebark** bloom in delicate white flowers alongside gray-barked **waxflower** shrubs with opaque-white blossoms. Emerging through shrubs at the top of the canyon, the trail meets a concrete walk where the loop heads straight south. Along this brief leg back to the parking area, a few gold **meadow arnicas** may be blooming. The trail ends, as it began, surrounded by grasses.

Castlewood Canyon State Park is a great destination that offers year-round recreation, including naturalist-led activities. Varied habitats and a scenic canyon make for interesting hiking.

Bruin Bluff

Wildflower Hike

15

Wildflower alert: Thousands of purple pasqueflowers in April; June features buttercups.

The Bruin Bluff Loop begins along the banks of Bear Creek. In mid-June, its banks are lined with yellow Macoun buttercups.

Trail Rating	easy
Trail Length	2.0-mile loop
Location	Lair O' the Bear/Morrison
Elevation	6,520 to 6,780 feet
Bloom Season	April to July
Peak Bloom	mid-June
Directions	From west Denver, take C-470 south, then go west on highway 74 through Morrison, continuing on 5.4 miles to Lair O' the Bear Open Space Park.

Lair O' the Bear, a Jefferson County Open Space Park, nestles in an east-west canyon through which fair-sized Bear Creek flows. The Bruin Bluff Loop covers a variety of habitats from riparian to rocky outcrop and from conifer forest to dry shrub land in its two-mile length.

The loop begins evenly along the creek and rises after a bridge crossing. Leaving the open, the route enters a conifer-dominated segment, followed by rocky outcrops, before dropping back down to creek level.

A bounty of at least six dozen kinds of wildflowers may be blooming, including a splendid display of pasqueflowers in April. In mid-June, the banks of Bear Creek near Dipper Bridge turn bright yellow with Macoun buttercup.

In early summer, the open meadow in front of the huge parking area is strewn with the violet-pink spires of **tall penstemon.** The Creekside Trail heads straight to a fishing deck on the river, makes a right turn, and follows the water. Watch for patches of yellow **Macoun buttercup.** Close by, in mid-May, one of the area's apple trees blooms. At the junction with Brittlefern Trail, head left. A nearby copse of **sand cherry** trees, when in bloom, is covered with white blossoms.

The Bruin Bluff Trail heads left at the Dipper Bridge, named for the American dipper, a slate-colored bird also called the water ouzel. At the next junction, turn right and follow the yellow **Macoun buttercups** lining the streambanks. Down the path, a bench on the left faces the vibrant buttercup display on the north shore of the creek.

Heading west, Bruin Bluff Trail climbs a rocky slope dotted with mountain mahogany shrubs, under which grows yellow **Oregon grapeholly** and **yellow violet.** While most violets prefer moist, shaded areas, yellow violet thrives in hot, dry conditions. Extremely early to bloom, **biscuitroot,** or **salt and pepper,** is well-camouflaged among the lichen-speckled rocks. Named by pioneers who learned of the powdered root's value from Native Americans, they likened the taste of biscuitroot's flour to that of stale biscuits.

In the same terrain, voluptuous globes of **mountain ball cactus** erupt in pink starburst blooms with an elusive scent—some say of old roses. In the dry rocky earth, **early pink milkvetch's** elongated, violet-pink tubes provide some of the earliest color in the foothills. Another early bloomer along the Bruin Bluff Trail, **mountain candytuft** survives from the foothills to the alpine zone. Enjoying the same dry mineral soil, **fiddleleaf bladderpod's** light yellow flowers develop into rubbery seedpods. Bladderpod's root was once used as a remedy for snake bites.

The trail continues on the south side of Bear Creek Canyon leveling along a north-facing exposure. Conifers appear, and with them early-blooming flowers such as **spring beauty** and soft-purple **pasqueflower.** Here on the Bruin Bluff trail, the tulip-like pasqueflowers congregate in the hundreds.

Benches are strategically placed along the trail as it follows the contours of the hillside. Heading into one ravine, the hiker is treated to a mass of flowering **ninebark.** Along a rugged part of the trail, hikers may spot **mountain ball cactus** in bloom in a ragged rock outcrop. Later, **harebells, stonecrop,** and **prickly pear cactus** bloom in this rock garden.

PASQUEFLOWER
Pulsatilla patens ssp. multifida

The tulip-like goblets of pasqueflower bloom, typically, in April, reiterating the root of its common name, Pasque— French for Easter. The appearance of the downy flower buds, promising a lavender-purple blossom, is a harbinger of spring. Also known as anemones, windflowers, wild crocus, and lion's beard, pasqueflowers are members of the buttercup family.

Pasqueflowers are great plants for gentle color among spring bulbs and the plumed "manes" of the seedheads are attractive, too. A warm-amethyst-colored Eurasian cousin, *Pulsatilla vulgaris* (*vulgaris* is Latin for common), also defies capricious spring weather. It tends to seed about the home garden, generally flowering about the same time as early daffodils.

Pioneers used the purple sepals of pasqueflower for dyeing Easter eggs.

The trail switchbacks down from the outcrop past **biscuitroot.** Here too, plain-foliaged **ninebark** becomes adorned with clusters of white flower in late spring, which turn to salmon as they mature. The foliage of ninebark turns red and orange in autumn. In the same vicinity, **waxflower** exhibits porcelain-like white flowers, blush-pink buds, and strongly veined matte green leaves. Leaf fossils show this member of the hydrangea family to be of ancient origin.

After descending to the Cutoff junction, stay right to continue on Bruin Bluff Trail. Near the cool shade of a ponderosa with a bench below it, in mid-May look for a member of the bellwort family with pairs of split bells and zigzag stalks: **wartberry fairybell.**

The trail approaches Bear Creek again, passing cottonwoods, boxelders, willows, and **wild raspberry.** Bear left toward a streamside bench overlooking the water next to the Ouzel Bridge. Over the bridge and left (past some picnic sites) sits yet another bench below a **wild rose.**

A clump of tall **golden currant** shrubs flourish by the trail as it returns to the parking area. Its smooth leathery leaves and yellow flowers make it a handsome native landscaping plant. Autumn turns the leaves of golden currant to red. The lobed tubes smell like cloves, giving it the common name, **clovebush.** The edible currants make a fine jelly, too.

On the east end of Lair O' the Bear Park, a sizable slope of **smooth sumac** turns fire-engine red in fall. Also called **scarlet sumac,** cone-shaped clusters of nondescript flowers mature into rusty-red, velvety pyramids of acidic fruits. These persist through the winter unless cropped by hungry mule deer.

Lair O' the Bear is a wonderful park for all seasons. Abundant pasque-flowers, a wide variety of wildflower species, a stunning autumn display of red smooth sumac, and an inviting creek make this open space park a special destination.

Pines to Peak

Wildflower alert: A duet of pink phlox
and white mouse-ear chickweed.

*Bald Mountain,
a Boulder Open
Space park in
Sunshine Canyo,
features dozens
of wildflower
species sheltered
by towering
ponderosa pines.*

Just a few miles west of Boulder is a delightful destination for a short
wildflower walk. The one-mile Pines to Peak Trail loops Bald Mountain and
tops out at a sturdy bench offering views east to the plains and west to the
Continental Divide. The walk traverses ancient Boulder Creek grandiorite,
now decomposed granite, but molten material 1.7 billion years ago.

Bald Mountain is home to ponderosa pines and a variety of shrubs
and wildflowers. Especially appealing is the June-inspired duo of Rocky
Mountain phlox and mouse-ear chickweed.

Trail Rating	easy
Trail Length	1.0-mile loop
Location	Bald Mountain/Boulder
Elevation	6,860 to 7,160 feet
Bloom Season	late May to July
Peak Bloom	June
Directions	From Boulder, take Mapleton Ave. west (which becomes Sunshine Canyon). Go 5 miles up the canyon to the Bald Mountain parking lot on the left.

The Pines to Peak Trail begins on the west side of the parking area and passes generously spaced picnic tables shaded by big ponderosa pines. Follow the trail under the pines and through grasses where, in spring, the first 50 yards introduces a dozen wild-flower species, including earth-hugging drifts of fragrant **Rocky Mountain phlox.** Along the way, in late summer, columns of rosy-purple **gayfeather** attract attention. By autumn, salmon-colored patches of colonizing big bluestem, a valuable native grass, stand up to five feet high.

The trail rises to the right where it meets a fork pointing out "Summit." Keep

GREEN-FLOWERED HEDGEHOG CACTUS
Echinocereus viridiflorus

Hen and chickens is another common name—which is more often applied to a popular garden succulent—but hedgehog (*echinos*) cactus dons a ring of chartreuse (*viridis*) flowers (*florus*) in early summer. Vertical rows of long spines cover the prickly spheres, which, like icebergs, are largely under the surface. This ball cactus will later retract its globe until it is nearly impossible to find, perhaps for protection from sharp animal hooves and winter. It takes a keen eye to spot this well-camouflaged cactus when not in bloom.

Another round cactus, mountain ball cactus (*Pediocactus simpsonii v. minor*) is similar looking to hen and chickens when not in flower. It has earlier-blooming fragrant pink flowers on top and spirals of prickles. It too retracts into the earth.

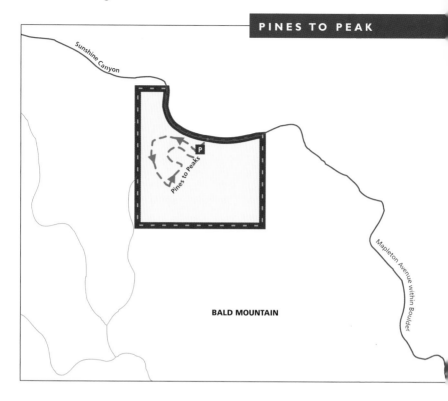

right on the Pines to Peak Trail to encounter white **mouse-ear chickweed** and pink **Rocky Mountain phlox**. Early in the season, pale-purple **pasqueflowers** are in bloom ahead of the other flowers.

Shaded by conifers scattered beside the gently rising trail, another of the earliest wildflowers to bloom, pink-colored **spring beauty,** appears too fragile to survive springtime in the Rockies. But it is incredibly hardy. Its five pink-veined petals and fleshy dark leaves disappear when summer heats up.

The trail now enters a stand of young ponderosas where a bench overlooks rolling forested hills. Along here, bright **wallflower** thrives in yellow, gold, and an occasional burnt orange. Mats of yellow **sulphurflower** help avert erosion on the trail cutbanks.

Cross an area of young pines to note low-growing **buckbrush**, its minuscule ivory flowers bloom over gray-green foliage in early summer. The path then travels back among larger pines where a short social spur, unsigned but well-worn, leads to a pile of boulders with a pleasant view.

Another bench with a view appears on the right as Pines to Peak Trail continues up around Bald Mountain. As the pines thin, cacti, such as **prickly pear** and **green-flowered hedgehog cactus**, claim the open grassland.

Heading up toward the summit, the trail grows steeper and rockier as it passes through a dry stony meadow dotted with the hedgehog cactus, also called **hen and chickens**. This is not the familiar garden succulent, but a cactus that dons a ring of chartreuse blossoms in early summer. Another round cactus, **mountain ball cactus**, earlier blooming and pink-flowered, likes this type of habitat.

Pines to Peak Trail crests at a sturdy pine-shaded bench just 300 feet higher than the trailhead. This is a grand place to study the view. Nearby, butterflies flit among **blanketflower, narrow-leaved puccoon, cinquefoil, locoweed, milkvetch,** and the curiously-named **miner's candle.**

Just below the top, on the left under ponderosas, look for an Easter daisy cousin, **showy townsendia.** Another daisy-type wildflower in the vicinity is **cutleaf fleabane** or **daisy;** its lavender-blue flowers sit on mounds of pale-green foliage.

As the path winds back down, it introduces good examples of two similar members of the parsley family. Both are yellow-flowered and grow to 18-inches tall; there the comparison ends. **Whiskbroom parsley** has foliage as thin as piano wire and and minute flowers arranged umbrella (umbel) fashion. Compare them to the denser, more curved umbels of **mountain parsley,** which produces broader but nonetheless deeply cut foliage. Additionally, mountain parsley likes a higher elevation than its cousin.

The trail drops through shady pines as it loops back, meandering past **phlox** and **mouse-ear,** retracing the steps to the parking area.

Where once cattle grazed and miners prospected for precious minerals, this 108-acre park is now preserved for the outdoor enthusiast. Bald Mountain Open Space Park offers a gratifying wildflower walk along the Pines to Peak Trail and is a special treat when Rocky Mountain phlox is in bloom in late spring or early summer.

Waldo Canyon

Wildflower alert: An abundance of bluemist penstemon
and the northern limit for scarlet bugler penstemon.

*Orange paint-
brush light up
a stretch of the
Waldo Canyon
Trail. Colorado
Springs resi-
dents have easy
access to this
close-in hike.*

Waldo Canyon is a surprise. Its stimulating loop trail takes the hiker far from
the hectic metropolis and into a world of soaring mountain vistas, tranquil
streams, and wonderful wildflowers. A luminous bluemist penstemon show,
accented by scarlet bugler penstemon and upwards of 80 wildflower species, is
a rite of spring in Waldo Canyon. This fairly long day hike leads the hiker up
and along, then over and down through an amazing collection of ecosystems.
The views of Pikes Peak alone inspire hikers to take on the 6.8-mile loop.
During peak bloom in the last half of June the scenery gets even better.

Trail Rating	moderate
Trail Length	6.8-mile loop
Location	Manitou Springs
Elevation	7,000 to 8,000 feet
Bloom Season	May to August
Peak Bloom	mid-June to early July
Directions	From Colorado Springs, take U.S. 24 west 2.2 miles past the Manitou Springs/Cave of the Winds exit to the trailhead parking lot on the right.

Like many trailheads close to a city and adjacent to a busy highway, Waldo Canyon's parking lot, though sizable, fills on weekends.

Waldo Canyon Trail ascends quickly from the parking area on timber risers. Near the trail register and thereafter, the racemes of **rock spirea**, cream-colored when fresh and sienna when aged, bloom on spare shrubs trailside. Here, it is known as **mountain spray**, while on the coast it is called **ocean spray**. The over-sized flowers of white **tufted evening primrose** and **spiderwort's** tri-petaled purplish-blue blooms spark up the mountain mahogany and scrub oak along the pink granite trail. **Bluemist penstemon**, with its dark glossy leaves and radiant trumpets, is so impressive on this hike it could well be called Bluemist Trail. The miniaturized apple blossoms of **ninebark,** unfolding white and aging to salmon, complement the clumps of bluemist. Lavender-pink **orchid penstemon** also glows along the way.

A sign illustrates the geology of the trail's course from limestone and sandstone to billion-year-old Pikes Peak granite over which much of the trail travels. Long-blooming **orange paintbrush** and more **spiderwort**, some violet-pink, join the display along the south-facing trail headed into a ravine. Living farther north than is usual, **scarlet bugler penstemon** grows in the swiftly draining mineral slopes of Waldo Canyon. Up to three-feet tall with slim scarlet tubes, this southwest native is a find here.

Turning onto a west exposure, the decomposed granite trail rises through pines and Douglas fir before it opens and encounters two oddities: **naked broomrape** and **antelope horns.** The first, flesh-colored, resembles a cluster of scalloped periscopes; the second is a cluster of small green cups with a maroon pinwheel in the center.

White blossomed **chokecherry** and **boulder raspberry** shrubs close in on the trail and lead to a distant mountain view where the trail passes **prickly pear cactus** with its silky yellow flowers.

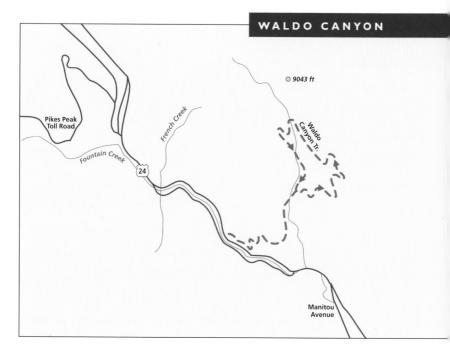

Along the descending slope here, another odd-looking plant, **kittentails,**
pops out of the gravelly soil under conifers. The east-facing slope drops into an
unexpected grassy glen accented by **bluemist penstemon, boulder raspberry,**
and **leafy cinquefoil.** By midsummer, beebalm adds a rosy tint to the forest.

A sign stating: "Waldo Canyon Loop 3.5 miles" appears. The best way
to hike the loop is to turn right, cross the creek, and head up the west face of
a pink granite slope. The minute yellow heads of **twisted pod draba** grow out
of the mineral soil under the evergreens.

A view of Pikes Peak opens at a switchback—one of a number of switchbacks offering sweeping panoramas of the commanding fourteener. Pikes Peak,
14,110 feet, is named for explorer Zebulon Pike, and was made famous by the
"Pikes Peak or Bust" slogan emblazoned on covered wagons. The trail continues
to climb, passing **scarlet gilia, bluemist penstemon, tufted evening primrose,
wild rose,** and the porcelain-like blossoms of **waxflower.**

Another switchback series tops out on a flat area where **orange paintbrush,
orchid penstemon, wallflower,** and **senecio,** accompanied by **bluemist penstemon,** lead to a sign at the 2.5-mile point. A sign describes the shaping of this
land from 500 million years ago to the present.

Descending gently, the faces of **bush** or **perennial sunflower** light up the
trail a little later in the season. The trail's pink granite is replaced by burnt red
Sawatch Sandstone, and stairsteps up. The ancient sandstone is home to the
golden daisies of **perky Sue** or **actinea. Rocky Mountain locoweed** hugs the

Waldo Canyon Trail on the way to the 3.0-mile marker. The footing becomes rough on the sandstone trail before it passes a wall of **waxflower** and a view over the Broadmoor area of Colorado Springs and the plains beyond.

After alternating between red and white rock, the trail climbs into ponderosa pines and out again to reach a junction where Waldo Canyon Loop heads left. Along the next segment, spatterings of **Drummond** and **early pink** and **standing milkvetches** line the incline.

Patches of **wild iris** flourish in the shelter of Douglas fir and scrub oak as the ridge eases up to a saddle. The trail orientation changes from east to west, exposing Pikes Peak again. Along the descent, **scarlet bugler penstemon** leads toward the 4.0 mile point. Hanging rock gardens along the decomposed granite trail drop through boulders crowded with **boulder raspberry**. Steep flowery slopes and the sound of running water lead hikers to a small stream where **shooting stars** may be in bloom.

Follow switchbacks down through huge boulders shaded by an old Douglas fir; there ivory-belled **Hall's alumroot**—endemic to the Pikes Peak region—tucks into rough crevices.

Continuing on, the trail crosses the creek. Brilliant pink **shooting stars** and **blue columbine** line the way between creek crossings. A pleasant park land area features **tall scarlet paintbrush** off to the side, and the path levels as it approaches the loop's conclusion and retraces the route back to the trailhead.

Waldo Canyon Trail is an invigorating and rewarding hike into a foothills elevation that is montane in ambience. Not far west of Colorado Springs, the loop offers variety in its terrain and vegetation.

GREEN ANTELOPE HORNS
Asclepias asperula

Also called creeping milkweed and spider antelope horn, green antelope horn's curved pale-green petals on each flower cluster form a sphere. They can be popped open by deft fingers to reveal a pinwheel of dark burgundy hoods and knob-tipped stamens, called a corona. These interesting blooms develop into curved pods that split into "horns," hence the common name, antelope horns. Bristle-like hairs cloak the foliage, which could account for the Latin *asperula,* meaning "rough." Then, too, the dried pod is the epitome of rough.

A common, stronger-hued cousin, showy milkweed (*Asclepias speciosa),* forms erect clumps of large-leaved plants with globes of dusty-rose flowers. The genus name harkens back to the Greek god of medicine, *Asclepius.* Milkweeds are named for their thick white juices, evident when a stem is severed. The mature pods release silky parachute-like seeds that drift on the breeze.

Oxen Draw/Eagle's View/Raven's Roost

Wildflower alert: The unusual spurless columbine and streamside pockets of shooting stars.

Uphill sections of this 3-plus-mile loop are shaded by blue spruce and Douglas fir trees— some lined with blue columbine.

Reynolds Park is a good example of a transition zone where the foothills meets the montane zone. South-facing dry slopes, typical in the foothill zone, and cool north-faces of Colorado blue spruce and Douglas fir, with the feel of montane elevations, are contained within the park's 1,200-plus acres.

Trail Rating	moderate
Trail Length	3.4-mile loop with spur
Location	Reynolds Park/Conifer
Elevation	7,200 to 8,100 feet
Bloom Season	mid-May to July
Peak Bloom	late June
Directions	From southwest Denver, take highway 285 south, and turn left on highway 97 (Kennedy Gulch). Go 5 miles and park on the right at Reynolds Park.

Riparian habitats range from the tiny creek running through Oxen Draw to the cottonwood-flanked stream flowing down Kennedy Gulch that divides the park. All this adds up to a great diversity in wildflowers and habitats. In mid-June on the Oxen Draw/Eagle's View/Raven's Roost loop, more than 70 species of wildflowers may be encountered, highlighted by spurless columbine, a variation of the famed Colorado state flower the blue columbine, and, near many of several creek crossings, shooting stars. The Eagle's View spur trail is well worth the extra effort—the panorama of distant Pikes Peak with wildflowers in the foreground is inspiring. Excluding the spur, the loop is about two miles long. The trail starts gently and increases in incline before following an old road back to the starting point.

Reynolds Park maps are available from a metal box west of the parking area by Kennedy Gulch Creek. Note the Oxen Draw shortcut on the map; this begins the loop at a trail sign near the restrooms.

The first creek crossing along the Oxen Draw Trail is not far from the trailhead. Take the first left after crossing the creek and before long, you'll reach a second creek crossing where **tall chiming bells** flourish in the shaded waterway. This plush plant is a favorite food of elk (Reynolds Park is an important wintering ground for both elk and deer).

At a junction marked by signpost #9, take a right. Nearby, look for **purple rock clematis** climbing around rocks, over shrubs, and even up trees. Also called blue virgin's bower, it blooms along the forest floor in spring and deserves a look inside its graceful bells at the many "clappers." Like others of its kind, the seedheads are feathery plumes.

Soon, the loop heads left following Oxen Draw Trail, which now labors uphill under the cool shade of Colorado blue spruce and Douglas fir. Beautiful

blue columbine shares the shade with **mountain blue violets** and **wild raspberry.** Bright yellow daisy-like **senecios,** or **groundsels,** light up intermittent openings in the forest.

Near the next two creek crossings, look for the rich-pink arrows of **shooting stars.** In the same area, later in the season, **fireweed,** another showy pink flower, blooms here. Named after its affinity for burned-over areas, fireweed is a good honey plant that was once eagerly sought for spring greens and, in the fall, for a tea rich in vitamin C.

Listen for the sound of water cascading among rocks on the left before starting up a steep rock fall area on the right. The path is rougher and rockier now.

A small causeway forms the next creek crossing where alders, Rocky Mountain maples, and blue spruce line the rocky waterway. Just before another creek crossing, look for **spurless blue columbine** in mid- to late-June, a fascinating variation of the famous Colorado blue columbine. The typical swept-back spurs are absent in open-faced spurless columbine. This group is single-colored; bi-colored specimens appear farther up the trail.

After a couple more stride-wide creek crossings, Oxen Draw Trail reaches the Eagle's View Spur Trail. This shady side-trail is well worth the trip, as it leads to a panoramic view of Pikes Peak. As an added incentive, **calypso orchids** sometimes make an appearance in late May. Start looking for these orchids about one-third of the way up Eagle's View Spur on the right bank (behind a broken off stump). Along the way, be on the watch for clumps of **early blue daisy,** at home in the mineral soil of the forest.

SPURLESS COLUMBINE

Aquilegia coerulea form: daileyae

Spurless blue columbine displays wide open purple-blue sepals radiating from a cluster of yellow stamens. The usual long spurs typical of *Aquilegias* are absent. The latinized form name, *daileyae,* honors a woman named Dailey. The lovely spurless columbine was collected by Miss Anna Dailey in the Evergreen area in the late 1800s.

The elegant columbines in the region are also represented by the state flower, the famed Colorado blue columbine (*Aquilegia coerulea*) found from the foothills to alpine zones. Dr. Edwin James discovered the blue columbine in 1820 near Palmer Lake northeast of Pikes Peak. The notable red columbine (*Aquilegia elegantula*) typically grows east of the Continental Divide; and the elfin and uncommon dwarf columbine (*Aquilegia saximontana*) can be found if the hiker has a keen eye and is lucky.

OXEN DRAW/EAGLE'S VIEW/RAVEN'S ROOST

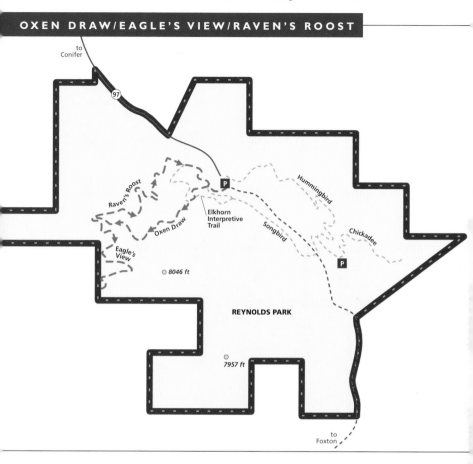

On top, enjoy a view of Pikes Peak to the south. This fourteener is often snow-covered when vivid magenta **Lambert locoweed, bluemist penstemon,** yellow **senecios, orange paintbrush,** and softer-colored **Rocky Mountain locoweed** (which hybridizes happily with **Lambert locoweed**) bloom in the foreground.

Back at the spur junction, take Raven's Roost Trail to continue the loop. Cross over the creek to reach a fairly easy trail segment that traverses a warm south-facing slope. **Prickly pear cactus** bloom among ponderosa pine on the arid hillside.

Ravens Roost Trail runs into an old roadway and swings left as it drops steadily before joining Elkhorn Trail. You'll find a bench placed in a small saddle on the way down that makes a nice stop.

Where the trail levels briefly, delicately flowered **ninebark** shrubs appear and then give way to switchbacks as the trail descends to the next level. The switchback area is short, but it displays **orchid penstemons, orange paintbrush,** and **locoweed.** At the bottom, not far from the banks of Kennedy Gulch Creek, several species of **penstemon** may be compared within a few hundred feet of each other.

Just ahead are the restrooms, and beyond them, the picnic area and a pump that gushes refreshingly cool water. Reynolds Park is an hour from the Denver metro area, but it's worlds apart. It offers a fine diversity in hiking and wildflower viewing experiences. The Oxen Draw/Eagle's View/Raven's Roost loop may turn up five or six dozen wildflower species.

SHOOTING STAR
Dodecatheon pulchellum

Many common names, such as Indian chiefs, roosterheads, and birdsbills, are applied to the moisture-loving shooting star, a member of the primrose family. High on a bare stem above smooth basal leaves, the hot pink arrows point down prior to pollination and turn up following fertilization. In dry years they may not flower at all.

Relatives of the lovely cyclamens of Greece, shooting stars were given their botanical name by the author of Historica Naturalis, Pliny the Elder, in first-century Rome. He assigned *dodeca,* which is 12, and *theon,* which means gods, to honor the pantheon of deities of his time. Native Americans roasted the roots and ate the young leaves of shooting stars.

Meyer Homestead

Wildflower alert: A mosaic of wildflowers
that glow at sunset.

*Tall penstemon, blanketflower, and silvery lupine bloom along
the Meyer Homestead Trail up Boulder's Flagstaff Road.*

easy	**Trail Rating**
5.0 miles out and back	**Trail Length**
Walker Ranch Open Space/Boulder	**Location**
7,350 to 8,050 feet	**Elevation**
June to August	**Bloom Season**
late June to early July	**Peak Bloom**
From Boulder, take Baseline west up Flagstaff Mountain to the Walker Ranch/Meyer Homestead trailhead on the right.	**Directions**

The Meyer Homestead Trail on Walker Ranch is an array of color at peak bloom. About five dozen wildflower species add their bright color to the floral still life along an easy-going 2.5-mile trail through rolling meadowlands—once choice homestead holdings.

Listed as a "historic cultural landscape" on the National Register of Historic Places, Walker Ranch has a cluster of time-worn wood buildings from the early 1880s. A picnic area adjoins the parking spaces near the trailhead. Expect company on weekends, and a wholesome dose of solitude during the week.

SEGO LILY

Calochortus gunnisonii

Also called mariposa lily, meaning "butterfly" in Spanish, this elegant wildflower—typically white, but shading from lilac-pink to lavender-blue—stands out in grasslands. Deep inside the chalice-shaped cups of some specimens is a purple band; others lack the encircling ribbon, but all have showy golden fringes near the inner base of the three petals. Star tulip is another name.

With such beauty, it is surprising that sego lily bulbs are edible. Native Americans generously taught starving Mormon pioneers the secret of the sego lily—not only were the roasted bulbs sustaining, but they could be dried and made into flour for bread.

The genus name of the Latin binomial, *Calochortus,* comes from the Greek *callos,* meaning "beautiful," and *chortus,* meaning "grass." The specific name honors Captain John Gunnison, an explorer of the West who was ambushed there in 1853.

From the trailhead, the hike sets out northwest along a wide fire road traveling through an expansive ponderosa park land. The flower display begins with June-blooming **wild iris** and **houndstongues'** wine-colored flowers. Later, the yellows of **sulphurflower, blanketflower, golden aster,** and **aspen sunflower** dominate, setting off the strong pinks of **tall penstemon, wild geranium,** and bold **locoweed.**

Curving into an isolated valley 0.5 mile from the trailhead, the trail overlooks an old sawmill resting off to the left in a broad meadow. Straight ahead on the main trail, note blue **mountain** or **alpine penstemon** joining daisy-like **showy townsendia** and **yellow stonecrop** —all flourishing along the road cutbanks. **Sego lilies** are apparent here, too.

A riparian habitat takes over where **cow parsnip** and morning-blooming **blue flax** keep damp-footed company with **tall chiming bells** and **false forget-me-not.** In the

same area, cousins **tall coneflower** and **black-eyed Susan** stand over yellow **bur avens**, a big-leaved, small-flowered member of the rose family. **Beebalm's** rosy-purple heads appear here in midsummer.

Rising, the red-colored road highlights the ultramarine intensity of **mountain** or **alpine penstemon**. Shrubby **buckbrush**—creamy white when blooming—thrives by granite outcrops. The same mineral soil is home to mat-forming **kinnikinnick.**

Wildflowers appear in the dappled shade of small aspens on the right, while **wild rose** and **meadow anemone** are found on the left. Continuing up the easy-going gradient, you'll reach an outcrop that marks the arrival of a seep inhabited by **shooting stars.**

The ascending trail curves up into aspens sheltering **tall scarlet paintbrush**, **lupine**, and **harebells.** Leveling out, the road passes stately **tall**

penstemons, their colors varying from violet-pink to blue. Just as butterflies like flat—or cabochon-shaped—flowers, hummingbirds are partial to tubular blossoms. In addition to the long-tubed **penstemons,** such as **bluemist, tall** and **mountain,** both **white** and peach-**pink gilias,** or **fairy trumpets,** attract the hummingbirds at Walker Ranch.

Wildflower-filled meadows stretch out to the north. Homesteaders once grazed livestock here, but little is left of their tenancy. The exclusion of cattle has given wildflowers the ability to increase in kind and number. Each blooming season exhibits more color.

Rocky now, the fire road climbs onto a ridge dominated by ponderosa pines and coarse granite, interspersed with several species of yellow **cinquefoil.** The trail ends abruptly, overlooking Boulder Canyon.

One after another, colorful mosaics of wildflowers spread across the wide open spaces of Walker Ranch along the Meyer Homestead Trail. A walk here, especially when the setting sun lights up the flowery fields, is a visually rewarding experience. Boulder County Parks and Open Space has preserved this tranquil place so that those who come here may leave refreshed.

Lion Gulch

Wildflower alert: A "century" trail that features more than 100 species at peak bloom, including the rare wood lily.

The lush gulch leads up to an open, flower-filled meadow with remnants of old homesteads in this "century" wildflower hike west of Lyons.

easy to moderate	*Trail Rating*
6.0 miles out and back	*Trail Length*
Lyons	*Location*
7,360 to 8,400 feet	*Elevation*
June to August	*Bloom Season*
late June to July	*Peak Bloom*
From Lyons, take highway 36 west to milepost 8. Park on the left at the trailhead.	*Directions*

Though Lion Gulch Trail actually begins in the foothills life zone, the entire hike's ambiance is characteristic of the montane zone, in which it eventually arrives. Located between Lyons and Estes Park, Lion Gulch is a highly floristic trek to a broad valley homesteaded in the late 1800s.

The route rises steadily, with a few brief segments stony and steep. The trail never strays too far from the water, and it travels in and out of shade before opening into a wide valley at the head of Lion Gulch.

As is true throughout the Rockies, timing is important. By mid-June, wildflower species may number around 50, while one month later yields upwards of 100 species, qualifying Lion Gulch as a "century" trail. The uncommon (and uncommonly beautiful) wood lily blooms here in early July, while hikers may find the distinctive calypso orchid in June. If your hike is perfectly timed, they may both be in bloom.

The trailhead sign is located down the hill west of the large parking area. A dozen species common to the foothills, such as **sulphurflower, harebell, wild geranium, stonecrop,** and **blanketflower,** may be found between the parking area and the sign.

Switchbacking down to a bridge crossing Lion Creek, the trail is well trod by both hikers and horseback riders. On the creekbanks near the bridge, **cow parsnip, tall coneflower,** and its shorter cousin, **black-eyed Susan,** thrive. A level trail segment follows, passing an outcrop hung with **bracted alumroot.**

A series of switchbacks carry the hiker up under ponderosa pines until the trail levels and drops to cross a stream on a footbridge. Rocky now, the trail travels up a steep, but brief, pitch before leveling on decomposed granite. Look along here for **tufted evening primrose** in early white or second-day pink, **prickly pear cactus,** and **silvery cinquefoil,** as well as the pinkish **hoary umbrellawort,** a four o'clock family member.

The sound of running water replaces highway noises as the trail approaches a grassy swale with **beebalm** and its attendant butterflies.

Sandy now, the trail passes through a grove of aspens where **white geranium,** showy **aspen daisy,** and **black-eyed Susan** flourish. Next, a sturdy bridge spans a creek lined with alder and river birch. Aspens on the far side shade a colony of **pearly everlasting.**

The trail starts up a rocky pitch through evergreens. Scrambling over rocks, bushes, and up an occasional tree, **purple rock clematis** appears along here in tints from pale lavender to purple. A few pink **calypso** or **fairy slipper orchids** may be blooming in the forest duff.

Still rising, the trail widens as it arrives at a massive ponderosa where, in early summer, the lovely **wood lily** blooms in the filtered shade.

For every rocky incline along Lion Gulch trail there appears a sandy moderate section. Following one of these sandy segments, a glance down to

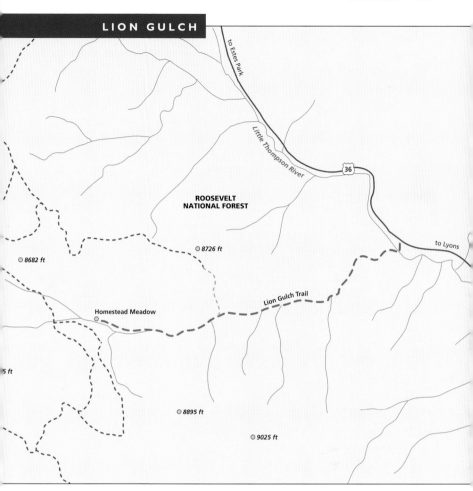

the creek reveals **tall chiming bells** and very tall **twisted stalk** with its dangling bells. As the path once again takes an upward tack, a few more **wood lilies** linger in the shade.

Continuing on, the trail follows the creek, passing under blue spruce and aspen where **tall larkspur's** deep blue-purple spikes reach almost head-high. A log spans a feeder creek, near which a claw-marked aspen records the passage of a black bear. A bit further, **wild roses'** sweet fragrance mingles with **beebalm's** minty aroma.

The climb continues as the route bridges the creek several times through lush vegetation punctuated with **tall coneflower, bur avens,** and **cinquefoils.**

The trail then leaves the water and climbs steeply through a rugged, rocky portion while gaining altitude. Look for white flowering **false Solomon's seal** and **spotted saxifrage** in the vicinity. Later in the season, magenta **fireweed** blooms here.

The incline finally levels out after crossing the creek over stones. Sun lovers **fleabane** and **sego lily** flank a gentle gradient along what may have been an old wagon road. On the high side of the roadway, hybrid colors of **locoweeds** and pink **tiny trumpets** add splashes of color.

Wildflowers flourish in a wide, grassy valley studded with relic homesteads. Interpretive signs note that this verdant valley, in accordance with the Homestead Act of 1862, was once available for $1.25 per acre. Grazed in the past by domestic livestock, the meadows today provide forage for deer and elk. **Paintbrushes, cinquefoils, penstemons, anemones, and bistort** sway in the grasses.

A flowery "century" hike arrives at an open point where vistas and history expand the Lion Gulch experience. This choice hike is time and effort well spent.

WOOD LILY

Lilium philadelphicum

The elegant wood lily, with scarlet-orange, purple-spotted tepals, is generally found east of the Continental Divide in the foothills and montane zones. Also known as Rocky Mountain red lily, glade lily, and flame lily, this brightly colored flower is a real find. Unfortunately, due to thoughtless picking and heavy grazing, it is also rarely found. In late June or early July, wood lily's satiny red tepals (petals and sepals—in this case three of each) are indistinguishable from one another. The tepals flare atop a two-foot stalk. Parallel-veined lanceolate leaves whorl around the sturdy stalk like spokes of a wheel.

While *Lilium philadelphicum* is the only species in its genus, there are several lily family members of note in the region, such as sand lily (*Leucocrinum montanum*), glacier or avalanche lily (*Erythronium grandiflorum*), and alplily (*Lloydia serotina*)—the latter two are denizens of the high country.

Stapleton Nature Trail

(featuring braille explanations)

Wildflower alert: Purple rock clematis blooms
on the shaded, north-facing banks.

Beebalm and butterflies are featured on this trail west of Denver along I-70.

easy	*Trail Rating*
0.6-mile loop	*Trail Length*
Genessee	*Location*
7,400 down to 7,200 feet	*Elevation*
late May to September	*Bloom Season*
mid-June	*Peak Bloom*
From Denver, take I-70 west to exit 253 (Chief Hosa). Turn right on Stapleton Dr. (gravel) and go 1.1 miles to the trailhead.	*Directions*

Conifer trees dominate the short informative Stapleton-Braille Nature Trail. Denver Parks and Recreation's Mountain Parks system manages the unique loop that flanks a small spring-fed creek and features a plastic-covered guidance cable. Thirty-one interpretive signs in both print and braille make for an informative hike. For the sight-impaired, a careful descent is advised; a clockwise hike might be considered as the gentler west side gradient of the loop makes descending smoother. This description, however, travels counterclockwise, dropping 190 vertical feet in 0.3 miles on the south-southwest-facing slope and returning up the cooler, well-graded north-facing bank.

Though the Stapleton-Braille loop is just 0.6 miles round trip, it offers the chance to compare flora on opposing exposures. Between the two, hikers shift from a pine-dominated descent to a Douglas fir-dominated ascent, with a chance to view the 50 or so flower species growing on either side.

PURPLE ROCK CLEMATIS
Atragene occidentalis

Also known as purple virgin's bower or western blue clematis, this thin woody vine produces white specimens too. It climbs over rocks and shrubs, and even up trees. Its flowers consist of four, two-inch long purple sepals that form translucent split bells. Also called ruebell or blue virgin's bower, it blooms along the forest floor in spring and deserves a close look. Like others of its kind, the seedheads are showy feathery plumes.

Far less widespread than purple rock clematis is a refined cousin: dainty western clematis (*Atragene columbiana*). Look for it in filtered shade on decomposed Pikes Peak granite.

Begin the loop on the right with an interpretive sign explaining the formation of the Rocky Mountains. Wildflowers dot the area, including **chiming bells, blue flax, wallflower, bluemist penstemon,** and moisture-loving **meadow anemone** with clear white sepals surrounding a burst of yellow stamens. Bluemist penstemon is as happy in the dry shade of ponderosa pines as on the open hillside. **Leafy cinquefoil** grows on this warm slope as well as on the cooler north bank.

A broad bench on the right offers a partial view of the distant Continental Divide. The sign preceding it explains the significance of the dividing of the waters—west toward the Pacific Ocean and east to the Gulf of Mexico.

Footing is uneven and the track narrows as it continues its descent. Look for two prickly, red-stemmed

STAPLETON NATURE TRAIL

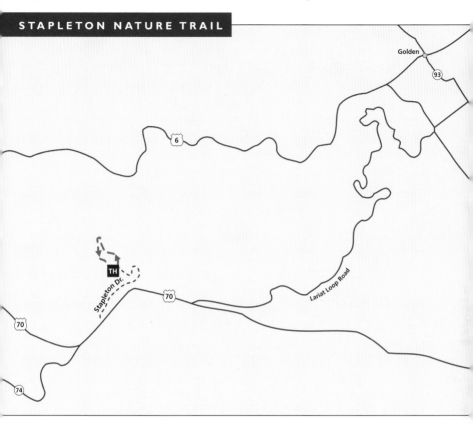

plants, perfumed **wild rose,** which has scarlet hips in autumn, and a **wild raspberry** that yields red fruits in late summer. Another vivid red in fall is sometimes found in **wild geranium** leaves; during the bloom season, the flowers are a showy pink. On the drier slopes, look for tall bristling spires of **miner's candle:** the sweet white flowers resemble those of forget-me-nots while the foliage is reminiscent of shredded steel wool.

At the interpretive sign for ponderosa pine, turn to the tree and take a deep whiff of the crevices in the reddish-orange bark. The surprising aroma usually calls for a second sniff: some say vanilla, others say butterscotch.

As the track continues downward, mats of gray-leafed **pussytoes** cling to the gravelly soil. When they first flower in spring, before the bracts get too papery, touch the cool softness of kitten's paws. Native Americans ate the seeds and chewed the stems for gum.

An old logging road bisects the path and the guidance cable for a few feet just above a small open meadow. The aspen-dotted area has a west-facing bench upon which you can relax before the uphill return. The colorful meadow is full of **wild roses, smooth goldenrod, silvery lupine,** and **beebalm.** Well-named, rosy-purple beebalm is a favorite of bees, butterflies, and hummingbirds.

At the bottom of the trail is a level area with a few picnic tables and an outhouse. **Yarrow** grows abundantly near the tables.

Uneven stepping stones challenge the hiker as the trail approaches a footbridge before turning left where the cable resumes. The loop advances in the shade of tall evergreens where cool-colored wildflowers such as **blue columbine, Canada** and **mountain blue violets,** and **purple rock clematis** bloom. Purple rock clematis, ranging from white to lavender to mauve, clings to rocky slopes in the forest. Occasionally, one manages to climb a tree, making it easier for the observer to peer inside the bells at the collection of yellow stamens.

Another fan of shaded, dry, mineral soil is evergreen **kinnikinnick,** which roots its creeping mats in the ponderosa pine belt. The petite, urn-shaped pink and white flowers are a real find in spring; small red berries follow, which are a food source for wildlife. The small leathery leaves were smoked by mountain men who called it Larb, claiming it warded off malaria, and by Indian peoples from whom the trappers and pioneers learned its use as a tobacco.

Continuing up in the shade, the path arrives at a wood bench built out over the tiny spring-fed creek. It provides a perfect spot to sit and listen to the trickling water before completing the loop.

In mid-June, some 50 flowering species may be encountered on the short and pleasant Stapleton Nature Trail; those responsible for this unusual loop are to be commended.

Bluebird/Ponderosa/Brother

Wildflower alert: A sea of wild iris in June, changing to waves of gold meadow arnica in July.

Wild iris fill the meadow along the first stretch of this loop trail in a Jefferson County Open Space Park outside the town of Evergreen.

easy to moderate	*Trail Rating*
2.7-mile loop	*Trail Length*
Alderfer-Three Sisters Park/Evergreen	*Location*
7,400 to 7,800 feet	*Elevation*
late May to September	*Bloom Season*
June	*Peak Bloom*

Directions

From the Front Range, take I-70 west to the Evergreen exit. Follow highway 74 south to Evergreen. Turn right on highway 73 and wind around to Buffalo Park Road. Turn right and stay on the winding main road for 1.3 miles to the westernmost trailhead where hikers head off to the right.

West of Evergreen, Alderfer-Three Sisters, another great Jefferson County Open Space Park, has several trails in its 770 acres. June holds a special treat for wildflower enthusiasts at Alderfer-Three Sisters Park. Then, the meadows come alive with color, first filled with lavender wild iris. July follows with golden pools of meadow arnica.

The Bluebird/Ponderosa/Brother Loop meanders through meadows, conifer forests, and aspen groves. Craggy rock outcroppings and bright wildflowers punctuate its 2.7-mile length. The loop turns a number of directions in its gentle circuit and includes one strong uphill segment that accesses the top of "The Brother" outcrop via a short spur. There, views materialize in every direction.

Homesteaded in 1873, this scenic former ranch is full of wildlife and wildflowers today. The large level parking area on the park's west boundary is adjacent to some ranch buildings.

Head east on Bluebird Meadow Trail, portions of which may be awash with early spring runoff. In June, the meadow will be a sea of lavender as thousands of **wild iris** bloom. Later in the season, when the iris have receded, a golden wave of **meadow arnica** flows in.

Bluebird Trail runs into Silver Fox/Ponderosa Trail where the loop heads right. Near this junction, dusky-purple **sugarbowls** bloom. Take a peek inside at the intense color. Then compare it to the outside, which is frosted by silvery hairs. The four lavish tepals (when petals and sepals are not differentiated) gather into heads described by other common names: **leatherflower, old maid's bonnet, vaseflower,** and **lions beard.** The last is descriptive of the silvery plumed seedheads that were once used as a handy source of portable tinder.

WILD IRIS
Iris missouriensis

Wild iris, also called western blue flag, is easy to identify; it is the only species of iris native to the Rocky Mountains. Beautiful veined petals and sepals—three of each—mark the striking lavender blooms. Some specimens are light purple, others white, and some are a true purple.

Wild iris' Latin binomial *Iris,* means "rainbow," and *missouriensis* refers not to the state, but to the headwaters of the Missouri River in Montana where wild iris was first noted.

It is said that Native Americans once made a poison for their arrow points by combining raw iris roots with rotted deer liver. Deer and cattle know to avoid wild iris.

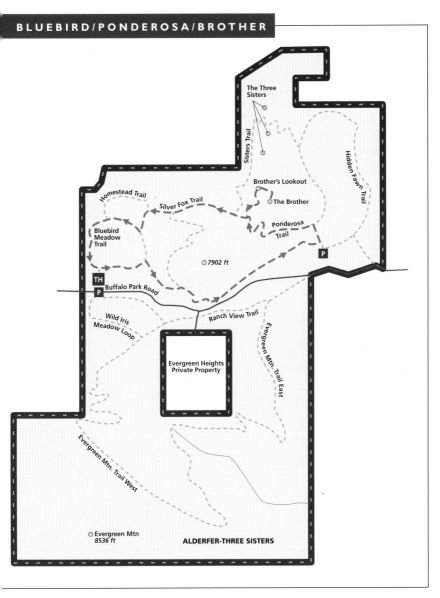

Boulder raspberry is abundant along the trail. Pure white petals surround golden pistils and stamens, called a "boss."

Ponderosa Trail wanders beneath its namesake pines with the yellows of **senecios, arnica,** and **golden banner** in the sunlit openings. Mats of **pussytoes** present velvety new heads. Scrub-oak and mountain mahogany dominate the forest as the trail continues along a southern exposure. **Tufted evening primrose** may be in bloom nearby. **Wallflower, mountain candytuft, stonecrop,** and **yarrow** thrive here as they do everywhere from the foothills to the fourteeners.

Head left up a short leg of the Sisters Trail to rejoin Ponderosa Trail; a left here takes the trail up 0.3 mile to the spur trail leading to the rounded rock formation called "The Brother." Lavender **fleabanes** and gold **many-flowered puccoon** are found along the way.

Not all the way up the gravelly spur, a **waxflower** bush flowers in June, bearing pink buds and waxy white flowers. The trail continues to climb toward the Brother's broad summit. Along the way, clumps of **bluemist penstemon** nestle in the decomposed granite. Other common names for this eastern slope denizen are **foothills** and **greenleaf penstemon.**

Once on top, head to the west side of the stone summit for an encompassing view of snow-capped Mount Evans and the meadowed valleys before it.

MEADOW ARNICA
Arnica fulgens

A member of the composite or sunflower family, which comprises one-fifth of all Rocky Mountain wildflowers, meadow arnica is a golden spring-bloomer. Also called orange arnica, its brightly-rayed flowers—occasionally creamy-yellow—top rough-foliaged sticky stems. The hairy leaves of this colonizing arnica are strong-smelling when crushed.

Cousins in the region include heartleaf arnica (*Arnica cordifolia*), rayless or Parry arnica (*Arnica parryi*), and subalpine or woolly arnica (*Arnica mollis*).

Return down the rocky spur to the main trail and veer right by some small aspens. Just before the intersection, look next to the grove of young aspens for **early blue daisies.** This cool-lavender dwarf fleabane prefers gravelly soil in dry meadow areas. Nearby is another fleabane, less showy **cutleaf fleabane.**

Along the next part of the trail, conifers quickly succeed the aspens. Look for mats of ground-hugging **kinnikinnick.** In spring, this member of the heath family produces a few tiny white bells edged in pink. A common name is **bearberry,** but the hard red berries are likely enjoyed more by chipmunks than bears. Native Americans made use of **kinnikinnick's** tannin content to cure pelts; they also brewed a concentrate of the leaves for urinary problems.

A bit further, in the dry shade of evergreens, watch for the tall, reddish-brown stalks of **pinedrops** that emerge as fleshy asparagus-like sprouts. Upon maturing, the hanging whitish bells will dry the same dark rust as the rest of this plant which, lacking chlorophyll, is dependent on decaying plant material such as rotting wood.

In the open now, the trail heads toward distant Mount Evans. Where ponderosa pines thin, look for **pasqueflower** and **snowball saxifrage** to bloom in early spring. The pathway soon rejoins Bluebird Meadow Trail.

Back at the iris-flooded meadow, take a right on the Bluebird Meadow Trail. Circling the meadow may be risking wet feet, but it is worth it. More **sugarbowls** and **pink plumes** add to the display.

Alderfer-Three Sisters Open Space Park offers a fine montane experience at a foothills-zone elevation. Among the 100-plus wildflowers found in the park, about half are typically in bloom in mid-June. Peak bloom depends on snowpack melt and warming days. Calling the helpful staff at the Jefferson County Nature Center may help determine the best time for peak iris viewing.

Wildflower Hike 23

Rawhide/Wrangler

Wildflower alert: Purple beebalm dominates
the midsummer scenery.

*Outcroppings create the setting for colorful rock gardens in sections
of this loop in White Ranch Open Space Park above Golden.*

Trail Rating	moderate
Trail Length	2.3-mile loop
Location	White Ranch/Golden
Elevation	7,450 down to 7,120 feet
Bloom Season	late May to mid-August
Peak Bloom	June to July
Directions	From Golden, take highway 93 north and turn west on Golden Gate Canyon Road. Turn right on Crawford Gulch Road and continue on before turning right on Belcher Hill Road. Follow the gravel road east to the farthest parking lot.

When warm days mark the beginning of summer at White Ranch Open Space Park, great patches of rosy-purple beebalm accent the 2.3-mile Rawhide/Wrangler Loop.

Diverse habitats here, from ponderosa park lands to wet, riparian meadows, were once the property of the ranching White family. Ranches like this one kept the land in one piece; the 3,000-acre historic White Ranch, maintained by Jefferson County, even has pack-in backcountry campsites.

Rawhide Trail drops steeply before meeting level Wrangler Trail. Then it resumes the name Rawhide as it climbs gently back to the parking area. Along the way, hikers are treated to a variety of wildflowers in different stages of bloom from late May until August.

From the northeast corner of the main parking area, Rawhide Trail heads left through a level area where a medley of familiar foothills wildflowers are found in the grasses.

Not far from a pair of facing benches, Rawhide Trail heads north toward a distant redrock formation. Along here, late-blooming **yellow owl clover** may pop up. Not actually a clover, it is an annual member of the **figwort** family characterized by **paintbrushes** and **penstemons. Yellow owl clover** is notable for its fresh bright green foliage when most vegetation is drying up.

Before Rawhide Trail enters the pines, white **sego lily, orange paintbrush,** and the yellows of **goldenrod, stonecrop,** and **sulphurflower** appear in an area of rocky soil. **Smooth golden-rod** has tiny bright-gold thready flowers. A myth exists that golden-rod causes hayfever. The real source is the nondescript ragweed.

BEEBALM
Monarda fistulosa var. menthifolia

Also known as monarda, wild bergamot, purple horsemint, and Oswego tea, bee-balm retains its minty fragrance even when dried. The rosy-lavender flowers are hooded, with two lips and a protruding pistil. Like many members of the mint family, aromatic beebalm forms large patches by spreading underground, and like all of the mint clan, it has a square stem. Hummingbirds and butterflies are always attracted to the wild garden planted with this midsummer bloomer.

Some species of *Monarda* contain thymol, an effective antiseptic. Native Americans boiled beebalm leaves to heal sore throats, skin problems, and headaches.

Another square-stemmed monarda, white horsemint or whorled monarda (*Monarda pectinata*) is also a midsummer bloomer. Monardas honor Señor Nicolas Monardes, a 16th-century Spanish doctor, writer, and botanist who recorded New World medicinal plants.

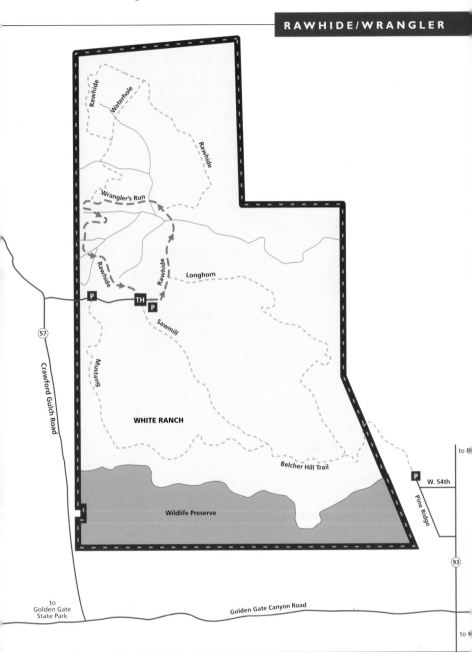

Sulphurflower sports full heads of hot yellow flowers held in an umbel. In autumn, the leathery leaves of this member of the buckwheat family turn brick-red. Its slow spread makes it choice for the xeriscape garden.

Along the descending trail, lavender-blue **harebell** flowers a bit later. The long-blooming clumps expand rather quickly in the home garden, offering their nodding flowers all summer; a few diehards hanging on until frost.

The trail now heads down steeply through ponderosa pines. A series of waterbars helps slow the hiker and spring runoff. **Blanketflower,** which figures in many foothills hikes, flourishes in sun or light shade along the trail. Very drought-tolerant, gold **blanketflower** is a stately perennial for the xeric garden.

As the trail continues down, a bounty of **beebalm** appears in warm-purple drifts. The flowers sport two lips and a protruding pistil.

At the bottom of Rawhide Trail's 300-foot descent, a junction points the loop left on Wrangler's Run. Near a small creek, moisture-loving **creamy cinquefoil** stands tall. This rose family member grows up to three-feet high and is also called sticky cinquefoil, due to a tacky substance in its foliage.

The trail levels for the next half mile. Where a creek runs south of the path, **cow parsnip,** with its large white heads of myriad tiny flowers, grows along the waterway. In contrast to cow parsnip's plate-sized heads, look among the grasses for the few-flowered clusters of blue **tall polemonium,** also called **leafy** or **tall Jacob's ladder.**

A bit farther, the vegetation grows more sparse and **whorled** or **white monarda,** a beebalm cousin, blooms in midsummer. Preferring sandy soil, this member of the square-stemmed mint family has bristly tiers supporting lavender-tinged white flowers encircling the stems

Wrangler's Run ends where it again meets the Rawhide Trail. The loop gently regains the 300 feet it lost along an old ranch road. It winds its way up past pines and rocky outcrops where **evening primrose, blue flax,** and **fireweed** bloom. Farther up, a sloping meadow of **beebalm** blooms in hues from pale lavender to purple-rose.

DOTTED GAYFEATHER
Liatris punctata

Made up of plumed florets, the rosy-violet brushes of gayfeather bloom in late summer. Open grassy areas are the site of choice for this showy member of the composite or sunflower family. Also called blazing star, the crowded florets bloom from the top down. Tough, narrow leaves with translucent dots (*punctata,* meaning "dotted") line the sturdy flower spike that is a beacon for butterflies.

While gayfeather's root was once utilized as a nutritious food source, it is said to taste awful; the corms were fed to horses for endurance.

An uncommon cousin, *Liatris ligulistylis* is a rather rare, tall gayfeather with even brighter rose flowers. It is a find in middle elevation wetlands, which are quickly disappearing.

A few buildings off to the side signal the loop is almost completed. After reaching the parking area, take in views of Denver and the plains from some picnic tables. In the drying grasses of August, **dotted gayfeather** decorates the picnic area. While most flower spikes bloom from the bottom up, those of vivid-rose gayfeather open from the top down. Another common name is blazing star.

While multi-use White Ranch has 18 miles of trails from which to choose, the 2.3-mile Rawhide/Wrangler Loop usually has at least 50 wildflower species in bloom during the height of the season. Like most foothills hikes, you can enjoy a different selection of wildflowers if you space your visits about a month apart.

Gem Lake

Wildflower alert: Check out hot pink telesonix tucked into Gem's granite crevices in July.

Small, picturesque Gem Lake is tucked into a granite bowl in a section of Rocky Mountain National Park called "Lumpy Ridge."

moderate	**Trail Rating**
4.0 miles out and back	**Trail Length**
Lumpy Ridge/Rocky Mountain National Park	**Location**
7,740 to 8,830 feet	**Elevation**
June to August	**Bloom Season**
mid-June to late July	**Peak Bloom**
From the east end of Estes Park, take the U.S. 34 bypass north, and turn right on MacGregor Avenue (this becomes Devil's Gulch Road). The trailhead parking is about 2 miles north and across the road from North Lane.	**Directions**

Though Rocky Mountain National Park could, as a whole, be called a gem, the small lake found in a granite bowl on Lumpy Ridge is aptly called Gem Lake. Not only is it an interesting hike geologically, but an extraordinary saxifrage, called telesonix, blooms here in July. This pink flower found here (and on Pikes Peak) tucks itself into crevices in the mounded granite surrounding Gem Lake.

Devil's Gulch Road (which began as MacGregor Avenue) has trailhead parking for about 20 vehicles, and it pays to arrive early or to wait until late afternoon. The close proximity to Estes Park makes Gem Lake easily accessible. The route rises more than 1,000 feet in just two miles, making it a good workout, albeit with views, character, and a fine finale.

TELESONIX

Telesonix jamesii

If telesonix sounds uninspiring, try boykinia or James' saxifrage. Telesonix comes from the Greek, *teleos,* meaning "perfect," and *onyx,* meaning "claws." The deep-pink petals narrow into claws that issue from a reddish cupped calyx, leaving wide spaces in between each one. Within the cup is a burst of yellow stamens.

Many saxifrage cousins have substantial leaves; the toothy basal leaves of telesonix are flimsy by comparison. Nonetheless, this is an interesting plant to seek out. It also thrives at Windy Point along the Pikes Peak Cog Railway.

A number of Rocky Mountain wildflowers carry the name James, or *Jamesia,* or *jamesii.* In 1820, the Stephen Long Expedition explored the Platte River environs. Dr. Edwin James, the expedition's young surgeon, collected many plants in the area, including the blue columbine. He is also said to be the first white man to climb 14,110-foot Pikes Peak. Although his boss ended up with his name on a fourteener, hikers can visit James Peak— a mere 13,294 feet.

A few hundred feet up the fenced corridor west of the parking area, a Rocky Mountain National Park sign counsels hikers on the rules of the trail, including no pets. The trail passes flowered pastureland with showy **tall penstemon, blanketflower, black-eyed Susans,** and about two dozen other kinds of wildflowers mixed within the grasses. Early-season hikers enjoy **wild iris** along here. The route angles right, toward the granite domes of Lumpy Ridge.

The wide trail edges up to an elk-gnawed grove of aspen and golden granite. The lichen-encrusted granite is crumbling into the decomposed mineral

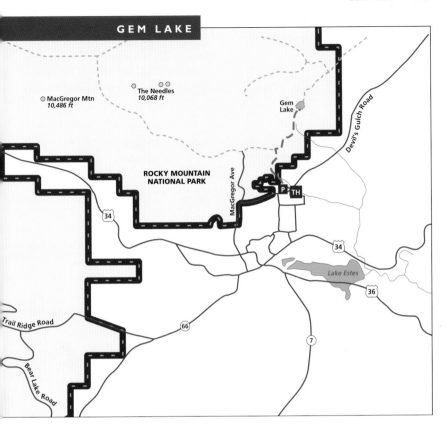

material that serves well as the trail surface. Soon, an outcrop appears with **waxflower** shrubs around its base. This relict shrub, a member of the hydrangea family, has been around for millions of years. Its fossils have turned up at Florissant National Monument west of Colorado Springs.

The trail climbs in the shade of conifers, steepening as it goes. It switchbacks through a canyon flanked by granite walls. After you pass a sign that says, "Entering Rocky Mountain National Park," the trail enters a ravine lined by **brackenfern**. Soon another sign points the trail right, toward Gem Lake. Ponderosa pines soon frame a view of the Estes Park valley to the south.

Pasqueflower and mounded **cutleaf daisy** bloom early along here. The open ridge section of trail turns and heads back onto the firm granite of Lumpy Ridge. Flat rock forms the trail now. Longs Peak, the only fourteener in the park, becomes a handy 14,255-foot landmark.

The trail continues up into a copse of aspen, then levels as it passes in and out of aspen glades. The dramatic view of the softly rounded granite turrets off to the north opens up as the trail comes off a saddle.

The trail now heads down amid a weathered-stone ravine, then up past more **waxflower** and **boulder raspberry**. A creeklet on the right, hardly more than a trickle, provides a home for early summer-blooming **shooting stars, tall chiming bells,** and nearby **purple rock clematis.** On the left, the trail hugs a rough wall with a fine stand of midsummer-blooming **fireweed** at its base.

The trail then travels up to a mossy outcrop with clumps of **bracted alumroot,** its stalks of subtle bells rising from dark basal leaves. The plants survive wedged in crevices and on ledges. Narrowing, the track switchbacks in and out of rocks on built-up walls. **Leafy cinquefoil** and **wild geranium** survive here. More switchbacks, some on stone steps blasted out of solid rock, cross through blooming **spotted saxifrage,** with its red dotted petals and moss-like mats, and **bracted alumroot,** whose clumps often contain last year's rusty leaves.

Along the staircase of core-drilled rock, stop and look at Longs Peak and its signature keyhole off to the south. One of the most interestingly sited outhouses around is coming up.

Log risers, a rocky tread, and a switchback lead the trail up just a bit farther to Gem Lake. Along the small lake is a beach and plenty of shoreline seating. For the wildflower enthusiast, the best is yet to come if it is July. Just up from the north shore of this rock-girt bowl, pressed into the towering granite, is the intriguing deep pink **telesonix.**

Along with more than 60 wildflower species along the Gem Lake Trail, discover the lake's July-blooming secret. The tiny lake is a great find even when the **telesonix** is not flowering. It is one more gem in the Rocky Mountain National Park treasure box.

Bridal Veil Falls/ Cow Creek

Wildflower alert: More than 80 wildflower species make for a colorful excursion.

The trail to Bridal Veil Falls winds through groves of aspen trees—their trunks scarred by elk who scrape away the bark with their teeth.

While the spectacular main body of Rocky Mountain National Park is justifiably famed, the park has several corners worth investigating. Bridal Veil Falls on Cow Creek is one. Located north of Estes Park in the eastern sector of Rocky Mountain National Park, Bridal Veil Falls Trail is a 3-mile, flowery trek to a 20-plus-foot-high waterfall plunging over a dark rock face. Most of the route is quite gentle, but the last segment is a steep rocky pitch to the base of the falls.

Trail Rating	easy to moderate
Trail Length	6.4 miles out and back
Location	Estes Park/Rocky Mountain National Park
Elevation	7,840 to 8,840 feet
Bloom Season	late May to September
Peak Bloom	June to July
Directions	From the east end of Estes Park, go north on the U.S. 34 bypass, then turn right on MacGregor Avenue (this becomes Devil's Gulch Road). Bear left after 4 miles onto McGraw Ranch Road and go 2.2 miles to the trailhead.

Parking is limited to the side of the access road at the historic McGraw Ranch where the Cow Creek trailhead is located. Late weekend arrivals may find parking some distance up on the roadside.

After crossing the Cow Creek culvert, the trail originates along the east side of the McGraw Ranch complex, taking the hiker through lush grasses punctuated early in the season with **golden banner.** It then skirts the wooden structures along an old road. Near the ranch outbuildings, about two dozen wildflowers bloom, including tall, grayish-green **prairie cinquefoil,** and its woolly-leafed cousin, **silvery cinquefoil.** Along the wide, level trail, you'll find **wild geranium, lupine, yarrow, penstemons, blanketflower, paintbrush,** and richly colored **mountain** or **alpine penstemon.**

With the prominent granite knobs of Lumpy Ridge rising on the left, a junction soon appears with the Cow Creek Trail continuing straight ahead through a beautiful broad valley. Along the casual roadway, bright stands of **fireweed** grow in midsummer. Soon the trail narrows to a single track that rises over roots and waterbars. Elk-scarred aspens shelter **black-eyed Susans, harebells,** and **beebalm. Yellow owl clover,** with diminutive beaked flowers, may also be present. It's really not a clover at all, but is related to paintbrush and penstemon.

Tall granite stacks line the south wall of the valley. Another junction comes up at 1.2 miles, sending Gem Lake Trail left; Cow Creek Trail to Bridal Veil Falls continues straight ahead. Light pink bells of **nodding onion** grow along the decomposed granite trail before it reaches ponderosa pines and spruce.

Rising somewhat, the trail passes straight-stalked **Rocky Mountain locoweed**—pure white in its original form, but here it has hybridized with

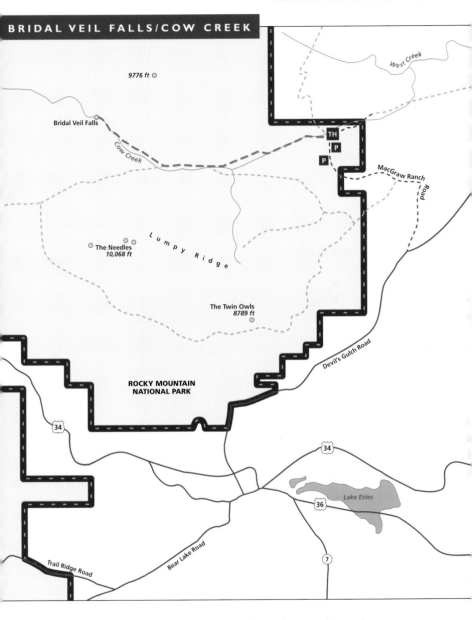

BRIDAL VEIL FALLS/COW CREEK

9776 ft

Bridal Veil Falls

Cow Creek

West Creek

TH
P
P

MacGraw Ranch Road

The Needles
10,068 ft

L u m p y   R i d g e

The Twin Owls
8789 ft

ROCKY MOUNTAIN
NATIONAL PARK

Devil's Gulch Road

34

34

36   Lake Estes

Trail Ridge Road

Bear Lake Road

7

startling magenta **Lambert locoweed**, and the result is a palette of eye-catching pastels.

The trail is rougher underfoot where the valley starts closing in to hug Cow Creek. Flowers flourish under elktooth-scraped aspens, evidence of Rocky Mountain National Park's large population of Wapiti. A bull elk can weigh 750 pounds—his antlers may account for 25 of those pounds—all of which translates to a big appetite (bad news for young aspens).

Above the cascading stream, the trail climbs to overlook a slope of rosy-purple **beebalm** scenting the air with mint. An open grassy area sports **white aster** in late summer. A sign then sends Bridal Veil Falls Trail right among **nodding onion, harebell, sulphurflower, owl clover,** and **limbervetch.** It ascends past **prairie cinquefoil** to arrive in a meadow of timothy, a non-native grass grown for hay. Aspens line the way to a log crossing; then the trail enters ponderosa pines with mats of evergreen **kinnikinnick** in the undergrowth.

Granite boulders line an incline before the trail drops through **ninebark** shrubs interspersed with **wild strawberry.** A ripe berry the size of a fingernail is packed with flavor. The evergreens are larger where the trail crosses the creek again over a split-log bridge. **Tall chiming bells, arrowleaf senecio,** and **twisted stalk** grow in the moist environment. Confined in a tight drainage now, the stream curves through rocks and lush vegetation, such as **tall coneflower.**

Another split-log bridge takes the hiker over the creek just before a sign states, "No horses beyond this point." The route grows more rugged as it ascends, first over water-polished granite where the trail is not obvious, next up stone steps climbing over rugged terrain, followed by a steep rocky section. The creek is gaining momentum down the rugged gorge with the falls not far now. The trail

PRAIRIE CINQUEFOIL
Potentilla pensylvanica

Despite its confining name, prairie cinquefoil grows from the plains to subalpine heights. Gray-green feathered leaves, hairy stems, and yellow five-petaled flowers are familiar features of this cinquefoil. This wildflower blooms up to 20 inches tall, even in dry soil.

The common name cinquefoil can be divided into two parts: *cinque,* meaning "five," and *foil,* meaning "leaf" in French. Some cinquefoil species do have five-part leaves shaped like the palm of a hand and are referred to as "palmate." The genus name *potentilla,* meaning "little potent one" in the medicinal sense is especially apt in silver cinquefoil (*Potentilla anserina*). The typically yellow flowers have five petals, as do many members of the rose family, of which the cinquefoils are a part.

A very common cousin is leafy cinquefoil, also known as "wood beauty" (*Drymocallis fissa*), the leaves and petals of which may be laid in hiking boots to prevent blisters. They were once brewed as a healing sun tea for saddle sores on horses.

skirts an overhanging outcrop harboring ferns, **waxflower** shrubs, and **bracted alumroot** tucked into cliff ledges.

Just above is Bridal Veil Falls, a 20-foot cascade falling into a shallow pool. The constant moisture along the edges of the falls provides a setting for **yellow monkeyflower** and pink **shooting star**.

There is a little room for a picnic here among the rocks, but don't be surprised if the resident golden mantle squirrel watches closely. Wildlife-wise hikers know not to feed the bold rodent the strange stuff lugged up in their packs.

An excursion up Cow Creek to Bridal Veil Falls is a fine trek to introduce the hiker to another facet of magnificent Rocky Mountain National Park.

Wildflower Hike
26

Owl Perch/Lodge Pole Loop

Wildflower alert: A flower-filled meadow at the start and columbine along the way.

Meyer Ranch Park's beautiful wildflower-packed meadow features blue columbine, mouse-ear chickweed, whiskbroom parsley, and more.

Trail Rating	easy
Trail Length	2.0-mile loop
Location	Meyer Ranch/Aspen Park
Elevation	7,875 to 8,175 feet
Bloom Season	June to August
Peak Bloom	mid-June to late June
Directions	From southwest Denver, take highway 285 south, almost to Aspen Park, and angle back left on South Turkey Creek Road. The trailhead is immediately on the right.

Located on the north-facing slope of a beautiful meadowed valley, Meyer Ranch Park is just 30 minutes west of metro Denver. Once a working ranch and ski hill, the park's nearly 400 montane acres have been designated as open space by Jefferson County.

Owl Perch Trail meanders up to meet Lodge Pole Loop, which rambles through field and forest, descending quickly on the return.

Within sight of the fenced trailhead parking area (where trail maps are available) is a lush meadow full of surprising wildflowers. The visitor need not walk far to count a few dozen species.

For the wildflower enthusiast, the adventure begins with the first step onto the "string" of Owl Perch/Lodge Pole Loop. South Turkey Creek flows through an exuberant meadow full of blooming flowers, hardly noticed by traffic whizzing past on the adjacent highway.

The broad trail is elevated above the meadow where waving white **bistort, little pink elephants, shooting stars,** and **wild iris** prevail. Joining them are **tall chiming bells, golden banner,** and **pink plumes.**

The wide trail turns where leathery-textured **sugarbowls** and **pink plumes,** also called **prairie smoke** and **old man's beard,** accent the corner. Pink plumes are members of the rose family, and their trios of dusty-pink urns later develop into feathery seedheads of the same color.

The roadway rises gradually, passing a well-drained bank on the south side carpeted with **lupine, mouse-ear chickweed, lanceleaf chiming bells,** and **pussytoes.** Along here, just a bit later in the season, **stonecrop** and **sulphur-flower** display cheery yellow blossoms. The trail's north side yields both **white geranium** and pink **wild geranium** and stunning clumps of **blue columbine.** Pink pussytoes, shrubby potentilla, and **early spring senecio** are the next to add to the count.

At the restroom facilities, the trail has gained about 75 feet in elevation and passed at least three dozen species of wildflowers. South of the facilities the trail divides. Go right past a stand of **wild iris** and **American speedwell's** delicate blue blossoms. At a second junction, the loop heads right again to reach a split-log bench shaded by aspens. Near it grow **shooting stars, bistort,** and **wild onion.**

The pathway meanders up under good-sized ponderosa pines—the favorite habitat of tuft-eared Abert squirrels, often charcoal black here. Some sun reaches the forest floor here to allow **bluemist penstemon, tall scarlet paintbrush, leafy cinquefoil,** and fragrant **wild roses** to thrive.

Where pines give way to aspens, a right turn at the next junction takes the hiker onto Lodge Pole Loop where the sign states simply: "Trail." A covered bench looks out over a scene—accented by boulders—composed of **paint-brush, penstemon, cinquefoil,** and **columbine.** The level path enters a mixed

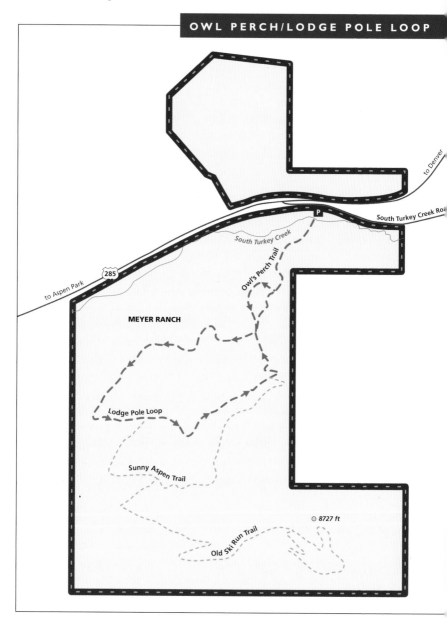

conifer forest and passes a sunny plot of flowers before turning to dense
shade. Next, a small drainage yields **tall chiming bells, shooting stars,** and
the ubiquitous **wild geranium;** the upper side, shaded by big blue spruce,
produces **waterleaf** and sparse, but widespread colonies of **heartleaf arnica**
with its bright yellow flowers. Where the forest provides deep shade little
grows in it, not only for lack of sun, but because the soil is generally
nutrient-poor.

The trail climbs slightly to a level section, passing more **columbine** and **geraniums.** At an opening in the pines look for **lupine, golden banner,** and **paintbrush.**

Where a service road crosses the trail, stay to the right and continue on Lodge Pole Loop. A bit farther, a fine stand of interesting **bracted lousewort** lifts its creamy yellow beaks on stout stalks above ferny foliage. A switchback leads up to an area on the left studded with old stumps where the keen eye may detect spotted **coralroot** sprouting.

About halfway into the hike at a junction near the high point, continue straight ahead on Lodge Pole Loop; Sunny Aspen Trail climbs off to the right.

The track levels along here and the mineral soil is excellent habitat for violet-blue **mountain penstemon.** At a bridged culvert, look for tall **twisted stalk** flourishing in the ravine along with shade-loving **bunchberry,** infrequent in this area and the regional pride of the dogwood family. Up to the right, you might find more **blue columbine.**

Out in the sun now, the trail curves into a small meadow featuring **wild roses.** Soon after, a trail sign points the hiker straight ahead to a sturdy split-log bench in the midst of **columbine, roses, cinquefoil,** and aspen trees with black

SPOTTED CORALROOT
Corallorhiza maculata

While orchids are usually associated with the tropics, an impressive number of species are indigenous to the Rocky Mountain area, one of which is spotted, or mottled, coralroot. The perfectly formed miniature orchids have a white lower lip petal freckled with purple dots, while the other petals and similar sepals are reddish-purple with brown overtones. This fleshy, leafless plant cannot manufacture chlorophyll, so it is dependent on mycorrhizal fungi in the soil of evergreen forests to feed it.

The name coralroot is descriptive of the blunt branching roots that spread underground, resembling saltwater coral formations. The Latin genus name, *corallorhiza,* is quite literally "coral root." This dainty-flowered orchid is best appreciated under a hand lens. An uncommon cousin is striped coralroot (*Corallorhiza striata*) with parallel lines decorating this reddish orchid.

Other members of the orchid family likely to be seen on regional hikes include the calypso or fairy slipper orchid (*Calypso bulbosa*), twin-pronged twayblade (*Listera sp.*), fragrant white bog orchid (*Limnorchis diliata ssp. albiflora*), and lady's tresses (*Spiranthes romanzoffiana*) with its tiny white orchid blossoms as coiled as a French braid.

scabs where elk have scraped the bark away. A bit farther, **fireweed** blooms in midsummer. A view of a rugged mountain opens on the left, followed by more **columbine.**

Lodge Pole Loop heads left at the next trail intersection and descends via a switchback where **spotted coralroot** displays tiny orchid flowers. More easy-going switchbacks lead the trail down into an opening where **mountain blue violets** bloom. **Wild roses** flank the path as it rejoins Owl Perch Trail cruising down the east side of the picnic area. Just south of the water pump, look for a colony of pink **Geyer onion.**

One of the best parts of this loop is retracing the way back through the dense wildflower meadow to the parking lot. Meyer Ranch Park is a treasure of flowers and easy to reach from the nearby metro area.

Cub Lake/The Pool

Wildflower alert: Pockets of wood lily
and a lake of yellow pond lilies.

*A bridge crossing on the Big Thompson River starts out
this scenic loop trail in Rocky Mountain National Park.*

easy to moderate	**Trail Rating**
6.2-mile loop	**Trail Length**
Rocky Mountain National Park/Estes Park	**Location**
8,080 to 8,620 feet	**Elevation**
June to September	**Bloom Season**
July	**Peak Bloom**
From Estes Park, enter Rocky Mountain National Park, and take Bear Lake Road to Moraine Park Road. Just south of Moraine Museum, go right to the trailhead. Be prepared to pay the fee or show your park pass.	**Directions**

In addition to the many superlatives for Rocky Mountain National Park—spectacular, impressive, memorable—"rewarding" should join the list for the Cub Lake/The Pool Loop. Diversity lies at the heart of this fine hike. The 6.2-mile loop at montane elevation travels through a number of interesting habitats populated with well over 80 wildflower species.

From a level beginning, the trail climbs with most of the elevation gain accumulated as the trail nears Cub Lake. From there, it rambles down to The Pool, returning on a fairly flat track along the Big Thompson River.

A shorter out and back hike to Cub Lake covers 4.6 miles. However, hikers will miss some of the ambience and interesting flowers if they don't complete the entire loop. At different times of the bloom season hikers may come across calypso orchids in late June (one-quarter mile east of The Pool); wood lilies not far from the beaver ponds in early July; yellow pond lilies on Cub Lake in July; and prince's pine on the downhill run from the lake to The Pool in late July.

Several possible parking areas at the west end of Moraine Park serve the Cub Lake/The Pool Loop. Each requires a walk down a portion of the level dirt road ending at The Pool/Fern Lake Trailhead. The second parking area driving west has restrooms and is a good place for starting the loop.

From the parking lot with the restrooms, walk back down the access road (east) to the Cub Lake Trailhead on the south side of the road and cross the Big Thompson River on a bridge. Another water-crossing has **shrubby potentilla** or **cinquefoil** nearby, as well as two members of the bellflower family within comparing distance: nodding common **harebell** and less common, upfacing **Parry harebell.** Before narrowing and rising on peeled logs, the level pathway reveals small, flowery meadows with **black-eyed Susans** and a few rare **wood lilies,** too. Before narrowing and rising, the trail edges around knobby granite where **bluemist penstemon** blooms early. Down the track is an area of **tall coneflower** and **fireweed,** and the vista stretches across a broad meadow to the South Lateral Moraine, a reminder of the intense glacial action that was so instrumental in the formation of this spectacular national park.

A well-worn social trail on the left meets the Cub Lake Trail as it continues on, a bit rockily, then leveling among **chokecherry** bushes with displays of cool pink **nodding onion** and **narrowleaf paintbrush.** Beavers have left their mark here in silty-bottomed ponds that will eventually fill in to create new meadows. **Wild roses** exude an enticing fragrance in early summer along here. Later, **beebalm** and **goldenrod** bloom as the vegetation closes in. The sound of running water to the left marks where **white checkermallow** flowers bloom a bit later in the season. A hand lens reveals blue-tipped stamens rising from the fragile white petals of this tall plant also known as **modest mallow.** It looks like an anemic hollyhock and is related to the marshmallow of Europe, whose

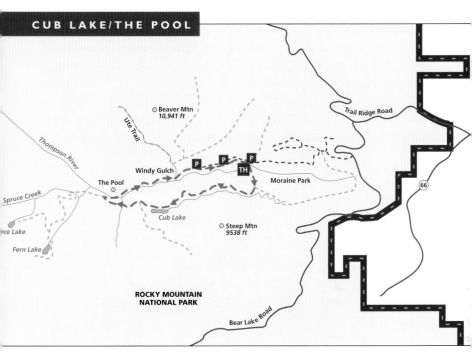

root supplied the gooey substance that once made marshmallow candy stick together. Another white flower in the vicinity is **meadow anemone,** appearing in colonies.

After passing another beaver pond, a turn of the path brings one of the glories of July into view: the spectacular **wood lily.** On the left, set in a grassy glade sheltered by Rocky Mountain maple, is a scarlet-orange troupe of the uncommon lily also colorfully called **flame lily.** Once a fairly common sight, the striking wood lily is now a "find;" unfortunately, its beauty has endangered its existence.

Worn granite domes dominate the landscape on the right; on the left willows and bog birch cover the area before the trail enters evergreens. Look for **tassel-flower's** ivory fringe and **pinedrop's** reddish spires among the trees. Open areas sport brackenfern, **red-berried elder,** and the widespread **wax currant.**

The trail comes up on a south-facing slope and the last half-mile to the lake becomes steeper and rockier. Along a small creek, a jungle of verdant vegetation full of **cow parsnip, tall chiming bells,** and more **tall coneflower** follows the trail up into aspens. In their rustling shade, rich-purple **monks-hood** thrive where the rocky trail ascends to a switchback and steepens.

At last the trail levels upon reaching a backcountry campsite sign in an aspen grove. After climbing a few peeled-log risers, another sign proclaims "privy."

Cub Lake is just ahead. The maintained trail rises along the north bank that overlooks the dark waters reflecting conifer-covered slopes. A few inviting boulders make handy places to relax and watch for ducks weaving among the floating pond lily pads. Mallards with their fluffy babies are often active here at this time of year. In July, about the same time the wood lily blooms, big gold blossoms of **yellow pond lily** add brightness to the dominant greenery. The usual contingent of wildlife, such as golden mantle squirrels and jays, come begging for goodies; hikers should refrain from supporting their habit.

PRINCE'S PINE OR PIPSISSEWA

Chimaphila umbellata

Low on the reddish stalk of prince's pine twists a whorl of toothed, dark leaves, complementing the rich pink of the flowers. Round rosy buds develop into a five-petaled hanging flower centered with a stout green pistil. Keen eyes notice a familial connection in the blossoms of prince's pine and shy wood nymph, both in the wintergreen family.

The Greek genus name, *chimaphila,* can be broken into two parts: *cheima,* meaning "winter," and *philos* meaning "loving;" the species name, *umbellata,* means "umbrella-shaped." Pipsissewa comes from an Indian name that means "to break into bits," referring to the plant's ancient medicinal use in shattering kidney stones.

Also in the wintergreen family, pink pyrola (*Pyrola rotundifolia ssp. asarifolia*) is a tall, showy wildflower with a three-part Latin name, and a number of other common names, such as bog wintergreen and shinleaf. Another member of this family also has multiple common names: shy wood nymph, a one-flowered wintergreen, is also called single delight and shy maiden, but it has one botanical Latin moniker: *Moneses uniflora.*

Continuing after a lake break, the trail inclines slightly, passes Cub Lake's inlet, and follows a ridge where **wild rose, dogbane,** and **narrowleaf paintbrush** (Wyoming's state flower) bask in the sun. The sandy trail evens out as it enters evergreens to arrive at a junction where Mill Creek Basin Trail takes off to the left and The Pool is one mile farther on to the right.

July brings an enchantment of less-encountered wildflowers along the north-facing slope of the descending trail: **prince's pine** or **pipsissewa, pink pyrola, rattlesnake plantain,** and **twinflower.** Examine the fascinating pink faces of Indian-named **pipsissewa.** Prominent paired stamens and a drum-shaped green ovary hold the center of this nodding pink flower. Not far away is an uncommon species of orchid. Usually, orchids crave moist habitats, but **rattlesnake plantain** favors this drier forest location. While its greenish-white flowers aren't very eye-catching, its forest-floor-hugging basal leaves display an unmistakable white midrib and veining.

Still dropping, the uneven trail passes rock and moss gardens of **one-sided wintergreen** and **prince's pine**. As you approach the sound of falling water, the cool, rocky terrain yields mats of **twinflower,** each forked stalk dangling a pair of dainty bells. Also dainty in fragrance, twinflower loves the shaded shelter of north-facing places.

Baneberry specimens come in both glassy red and opaque white along the next section of The Pool Trail. Both color berries develop from conical racemes of tiny creamy flowers. Tipped with a tiny black dot, the shiny white variety also carries the old name of doll's eyes—innocuous sounding, but the berries are poisonous.

A mossy boulder on the left shoulders a mantle of **twinflower** and **heartleaf arnica.** The trail approaches a moist area populated with **green bog orchids** and **pink pyrola,** followed by carpets of **twinflower.** A sudden opening reveals towering stone cliffs reminiscent of Yosemite. Soon, a sturdy log bridge crosses a small falls where white **brook saxifrage** and the scarlet-orange berries of **twisted stalk** heighten the scene. Lovely **blue columbine** and rock-loving, well-named **waxflower** bushes accent the way to a mossy cascade and the path traverses peeled logs. A rockfall follows the trail down to an aspen grove carpeted with showy lavender **aspen daisies.** Some years, the daisies desert this spot—wildflowers can be fickle.

The hefty bridge crossing the Big Thompson River calls for a pause. Look upstream into a time-worn, water-carved bowl called simply, The Pool. The west side of The Pool's bowl is an inviting spot for hikers to relax.

After a right turn from the north end of the bridge, the trail is a cruise. Big Thompson River parallels the nearly flat trail most of the way back. Gigantic boulders, called Arched Rocks, line the path through mixed forest. **Pinedrops** sprout from the forest duff. Pass great granite cliffs and small creeks before coming to the parking lot farthest west. From there, hike down the level dirt road to return to where the loop began.

While Rocky Mountain National Park is full of wonderful hiking trails, each with an individual character, Cub Lake/The Pool Loop in the montane zone is one of the best for those who love water, stimulating scenery, and of course, sensational wildflowers.

Wildflower Hike 28

Horseshoe to Frazer Meadow

Wildflower alert: Wildflower meadows of color and variety.

Mount Tremont rises beyond the tall grass- and wildflower-filled Frazer Meadow of Golden Gate State Park.

Trail Rating	easy to moderate
Trail Length	3.6 miles out and back
Location	Golden Gate Canyon State Park/Golden
Elevation	8,160 to 9,080 feet
Bloom Season	June to August
Peak Bloom	July
Directions	From Golden, take highway 93 north to Golden Gate Canyon Road. Turn left and go 15 miles to the visitor center. Turn right on Crawford Gulch Road to the trailhead on the left. Be prepared to pay the fee.

Less than one hour's drive from the Denver metro area is a beautiful state park with roughly 22 square miles of scenic terrain to explore. With 35 miles of trail, ranging from foothill to subalpine zones, Golden Gate Canyon State Park is a magnet for hikers and wildflower viewers.

The 1.8-mile Horseshoe Trail to Frazer Meadow is a gradual uphill trail that follows a flower-filled creek drainage and rambles past flowery aspen-dotted meadows to a historic log building sagging in open grassland. From early July to early August, in a kind-weather year, about six dozen species of wildflowers bloom along the way.

Pick up a map and purchase a pass at the visitor center near the junction of Golden Gate Canyon Road and Crawford Gulch Road.

Not far from the map-posted trailhead, the trail crosses a tiny creek flowing through cool aspen. Look nearby for closely-related sunflower family members: **tall coneflower** (also known as **cutleaf coneflower** or **goldenglow,** growing up to six feet high) and **black-eyed Susan** at half the height.

Also along here, **wild rose, blanketflower, nodding onion, meadow anemone, orange agoseris,** midsummer-blooming **fireweed,** and late-summer-blooming **smooth goldenrod** add to the amazing variety of species.

As the trail continues its ascent, lichen-speckled rock outcroppings punctuate the sloping drainage. Watch for a smooth pair of boulders on the right that angle in together to form a pocket where a colony of

COW PARSNIP
Heracleum sphondylium ssp. montanum

Stream bank and damp aspen grove habitats are the places to look for the frisbee-sized white heads, each made up of countless minute white flowers. The cow parsnip's leaves are also notable from their size. Spanning up to one-foot wide, they look like huge, coarse maple leaves.

This Herculean member of the parsley family is a valuable food source for wildlife, attracting deer, elk, and even bear, for the salt content found in the hollow base. Butterflies find them convenient landing pads, and birds eat the seeds that develop.

Sometimes listed under names such as bear weed and cow cabbage, strong-smelling cow parsnip has long been reputed to remedy everything from toothaches to arthritis to sore throats, but it is thought by some to have a degree of toxicity.

Smaller cousins include subalpine lovage (*Ligusticum tenuifloium*), biscuitroot or salt and pepper (*Lomatium orientale*), and the dainty cowbane (*Oxypolis fendleri*).

bracted alumroot crowds the crevice. Short spikes with pale greenish-tinged yellow bells rise above toothed and scalloped basal leaves. **Bracted alumroot** is related to showy red coralbells of garden fame.

Up the trail a bit further, a concave boulder framed with **chokecherry** provides a point of reference to locate a patch of **selfheal** or **prunella.** Its rich pink, two-lipped tubular flowers wrap around a stout square stalk—the shape associated with the mint family. People once brewed **selfheal,** a mint-flavored tea said to be medicinally beneficial. While dodging butterflies in the area, look for another square-stemmed mint, **beebalm,** whose unique rosy-purple flowers are butterfly magnets.

Cross a small bridge, head up past evergreen mats of **kinnikinnick,** and negotiate a steep, rocky switchbacked segment before Horseshoe Trail resumes its gentle incline. At the junction stay left on Horseshoe Trail. Continue on past a flowery meadow area studded with small aspens. The best is yet to come.

In the deep shade along the stream, look for white **monkshood** and the minuscule creamy white flower clusters of **baneberry.** A bush-like plant, **baneberry's** conical blooms develop into racemes of shiny red berries that are poisonous. The creek banks nurture **blue columbine, cinquefoil,** and yellowish **bracted lousewort.** The shady periphery of aspen and spruce are preferred by bracted or **fernleaf lousewort** (wort or *wyrt* is Old English for plant).

The trail now crosses a plank bridge and climbs a rough section heading for open glades of aspen virtually carpeted with wildflowers. Gold **blanket-flowers,** white, pink, and bluish **sego lilies,** lavender **harebells,** and white **yarrow** weave a massive tapestry.

Before long, Horseshoe Trail enters the deep grasses of Frazer Meadow. Anchored by a homesteader's log structure, more species of wildflowers grow in the meadow, such as **sandwort, bistort, tall polemonium** or **leafy Jacob's ladder,** and lots of **shrubby cinquefoil.**

Looking north from an open spot in Frazer Meadow, the peak straight ahead is 10,200 foot Mount Tremont. From here, retrace your steps back down to the parking area.

A picnic at one of the 275 sites throughout Golden Gate Canyon State Park would be an appropriate reward upon completion of the hike. Some of the tables are literally surrounded by wildflowers, such as those up Mountain Base Road at Ole Barn Knoll and Bootleg Bottom. A drive up Mountain Base Road invites onlookers to enjoy a colorful corridor of wildflowers while heading to Panorama Point, an overlook featuring the peaks of the Continental Divide to the west.

Golden Gate Canyon State Park is one of the top wildflower viewing destinations close to the Denver metro area. Its well-maintained trails, such as the Horseshoe Trail leading to Frazer Meadow, are clearly signed and a joy to hike amidst a bounty of natural beauty.

HORSESHOE TO FRAZER MEADOW

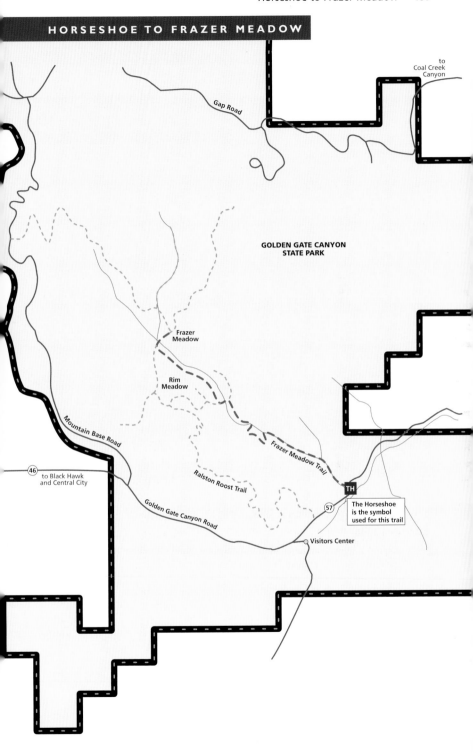

to
Coal Creek
Canyon

Gap Road

GOLDEN GATE CANYON
STATE PARK

Frazer
Meadow

Rim
Meadow

Mountain Base Road

Frazer Meadow Trail

46 to Black Hawk
and Central City

Ralston Roost Trail

Golden Gate Canyon Road

TH

57

The Horseshoe
is the symbol
used for this trail

Visitors Center

Wildflower Hike 29

Hornbek Wildlife Loop

Wildflower alert: Fields of blue flax and a homestead yard of silverweed.

The Hornbek Homestead sits amid a grassy meadow dotted with wallflowers on this loop trail west of Colorado Springs.

Trail Rating	easy to moderate
Trail Length	4.0-mile loop
Location	Florissant National Monument
Elevation	8,260 to 8,560 feet
Bloom Season	June to August
Peak Bloom	mid-June to mid-July
Directions	From Colorado Springs, take U.S. 24 west to Florissant. Turn south on County Road 1 and go 2 miles. Turn right at the entrance to Florissant National Monument. Be prepared to pay the fee.

In French, *florissant* means "flourishing" or "flowering." Indeed, nearly 70 wildflower species flourish along Florissant National Monument's Hornbek Wildlife Loop. The Hornbek name honors a plucky pioneer woman who raised four children in the historic 1878 log house that hikers discover about halfway into the loop. The circuit contains few ascending sections, making the loop a relaxing trail with less traffic than most in the monument.

But the monument's main claim to fame lies trapped in preserved volcanic ash—fossils embedded in the shale of an ancient lake. Giant redwoods and hardwoods rimmed the lake where a warm climate supported all kinds of life some 35 million years ago. Violent eruptions to the southwest trapped living tissue in the powder-fine lake sediments, creating a permanent record. A few of more than 60,000 collected fossil specimens preserved in shale are on display in the visitor center museum.

Some of today's wildflowers harken back to those 35-million-year-old fossils, including the wild rose found along the four-mile Hornbek Wildlife Loop.

The Hornbek Loop and Petrified Forest Loop share a trailhead leading northeast from the parking area. From the start, interpretive signs discuss the park's geologic timeframe.

Straight ahead on this first flat section, on the north skyline, stands the rocky cone of Signal Butte. Off to the side, **orange paintbrush** and **wild geranium** provide color, while **wild buckwheat**, lacking color, compensates in height.

Wild iris blooms early in the season where Hornbek Loop takes a right near some petrified Sequoia tree trunks that anchored the lakeshore in epochs past. Plants contemporary to

WILD BLUE FLAX
Adenolinum lewisii

Five fragile sky-blue petals suspended on long, arched, sinewy stems loaded with pointy buds mark this member of the flax family. To discover the manganese blue of wild blue flax, it is best to look for the silky-flowered plants in the morning. By afternoon, the petals have fallen to earth, only to be replaced by myriad buds opening each in their turn for many mornings to come. Clay-tolerant and drought- and deer-resistant, blue flax makes a superior garden plant.

The portion of the genus name, *linon,* is Greek for "thread;" *lewisii* credits Merriwether Lewis of Lewis and Clark Expedition fame. Resourceful Native Americans made cord and fishing line from the tough fibers of wild blue flax, in addition to using the plant as a laxative and a remedy for sore eyes.

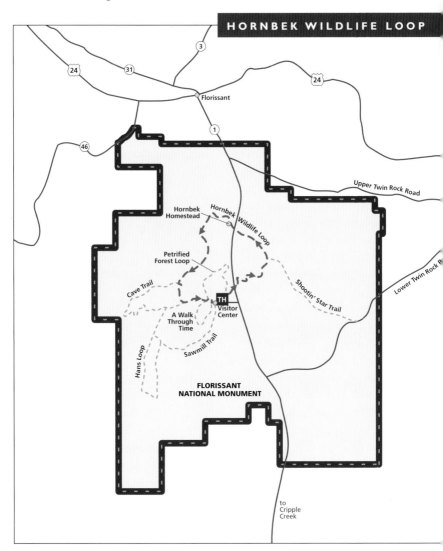

them still exist today in the monument, including **boulder raspberry, waxflower,** and **whiskbroom parsley.**

A short rise brings the trail up on a flat section where, among the earliest bloomers, **pasqueflower** grows among the pines. Now, **kittentails, many-flowered puccoon, little cryptantha**—its flower resembling white **forget-me-nots**—dot the gravelly ground. Tight gray mats of **pussytoes** spread toward the conical nests of thatch ants. Follow the hiker silhouette on a brown post to cross a road into a moist habitat.

The footbridge crossing Grape Creek signals the appearance of **silverweed,** a yellow-flowered, ground-hugging member of the rose family. Nearby,

tall chiming bells and **tall penstemon** tower, and floating in the slow-moving stream, **white water crowfoot** survives. On the far side of the railed span around the base of a worn outcrop, look for pale blue **false forget-me-not**, **few-flowered false Solomon's seal**, and a sprinkling of **bistort** and **shooting stars** among **shrubby cinquefoil** bushes. Those millions-of-years-old relict shrubs, **boulder raspberry** and **waxflower**, cling to the rough monolith.

The trail eases up to a rocky section where **many-flowered puccoon** precedes a copse of white-barked aspen. The incline increases and, marked by a split pine, a small specimen of rosy **Crandall penstemon** presses against a rock in the middle of the trail. A few more may be scattered in the exposed rocky areas near the top of the outcrop where pink-flowered **mountain ball cactus** shares the terrain.

A ravine on the left yields white-flowering **tufted evening primrose** and **yucca**. At the point where the ascent contours up to a promontory with a view to the west, Douglas firs shade the level route before it descends, passing **blue columbine** and **tall scarlet paintbrush.**

A trail direction sign turns the loop left and heads it 0.6 miles to the Hornbek Homestead visible to the northwest. A wide grassland features **shrubby cinquefoil, pink plumes, blue columbine,** red **paintbrush,** and white **northern bedstraw.** Pea family cousins grab your attention here: magenta **Lambert loco** and the short fuchsia-beaked **woolly loco** (a.k.a. **showy loco**).

Narrowing, the trail eases down through **rabbitbrush** and **snakeweed,** both with yellow heads in late summer. More gold-blossomed **shrubby cinquefoil** bushes cloak a swale and accompany the trail down to a slight rise of stony soil that is a home for small pines and violet-pink **tall penstemon.** Then the trail features grassy footing and **blue flax** on the approach to the paved road.

Across the road, the trail continues in view of the Hornbek Homestead, and tall **blue flax** sway in morning breezes. Hikers enter the homestead through a ranch-style gateway and fence. The enclosed yard is carpeted with **silverweed,** which not only survives overgrazing, but has roots once used as food and a remedy for sore throats. The substantial log house, built by Mrs. Hornbek, contains six rooms on two floors—quite sizable for its day. Grape Creek was the family's water supply and a hillside root cellar—still holding up—served as their refrigerator. Three outbuildings complete the well-preserved homestead, testimony to a very successful lady pioneer.

Leaving the house and passing through the north fence, a spur takes the visitor up to the root cellar, while the left fork continues the Hornbek Wildlife Loop. Crossing Grape Creek and skirting the meadow, the trail climbs up to drier ground passing earth-hugging **ground plum,** a milkvetch with distinctive plump pods, to overlook the ancient bed of Lake Florissant.

Circling a reservoir, and passing more of the wandlike **tall penstemon** and equally tall **wild buckwheat,** the loop skirts a meadow that stretches west into a verdant valley. A pair of information signs, guarded by a lone blue spruce, says the elevation here is 8,350 feet and the distance from the visitor center is 0.6 mile. Crossing a drainage nurturing **false forget-me-not** or **stickseed,** the track ascends a quick pitch to level out under ponderosas. The soft, silver, ladder leaves and piquant blooms of **showy** or **woolly loco** appear profusely along the wide graveled path here.

Soon, the visitor center comes into view and with it, wooden walkways.

A day spent among the 6,000 acres of the Florissant National Monument reveals insights into the workings of the earth (and more than 70 species of wildflowers on the Hornbek Wildlife Loop alone). A helpful staff enhances these insights with walks, talks, and reading material, all backed up by the detailed evidence of its outstanding fossils.

Mount Herman

Wildflower alert: An endemic saxifrage, Hall's alumroot, grows in the pink Pikes Peak granite.

The Mount Herman Trail, west of Monument, climbs past bluemist penstemon and other wild-flowers in the thinning forest.

The trail to Mount Herman is one of those semi-secret hikes that conceals a number of wildflower surprises, including an endemic coralbell relative, Hall's alumroot.

For much of the way, the two-mile trek to the summit is shaded. The flower count, in accordance with fickle Rocky Mountain springs, varies widely each year. When spring is warm and early, the same week in June may yield twice the wildflower species as the following year, when a late snowpack and cold temperatures could delay flowering.

Mount Herman

Trail Rating	moderate
Trail Length	4.0 miles out and back
Location	Monument
Elevation	8,200 to 9,063 feet
Bloom Season	June to August
Peak Bloom	late June to early July
Directions	From Colorado Springs, go north on I-25 to the Monument exit. Go west to 3rd Street, left on Front Street, right on 2nd, and left on Mitchell. Turn right at the sign for Mount Herman Road (#320), bearing left at the fork. The trailhead is 4.3 miles past the Pike National Forest boundary sign.

Located northwest of Colorado Springs near Monument in Pike National Forest, the Mount Herman trail begins in a small shady ravine with a tiny creek. It climbs to a pocket meadow and then rises steeply, topping out at an impressive view of Pikes Peak and the vast High Plains.

On weekends, plan to arrive early as parking is challenging after about six vehicles arrive.

Forming the limited parking area and the road cutbanks, decomposed Pikes Peak granite is home to **tufted evening primrose, boulder raspberry,** and shocking-blue **mountain** or, misleadingly named, **alpine penstemon.**

Near the beginning, a small creek accompanies the Mount Herman trail, yielding **tall chiming bells, white geranium,** and shocking-pink **shooting stars.** Many common names, such as **Indian chiefs, roosterheads,** and **birds-bills,** apply to moisture-loving shooting star, a member of the primrose family. High on a straight stalk above smooth basal leaves, the arrow-shaped flowers point earthward prior to pollination, upward after becoming pollinated. In dry years they may not flower at all. In compatible places, **spotted coralroot** shoots up its purple-brown stalk of small orchid flowers. In the same vicinity, **wild rose**—shade-tolerant here—perfumes the sheltered air of the ravine.

The narrow trail rises steadily before widening to arrive at a glade highlighted with clumps of **blue columbine.** Columbine's long spurs are well designed for the long-tongued hummingbirds or coil-tongued hawkmoths. Not far away, **western valerian** may be in bloom, its white heads full of stamens resembling mini-pin cushions.

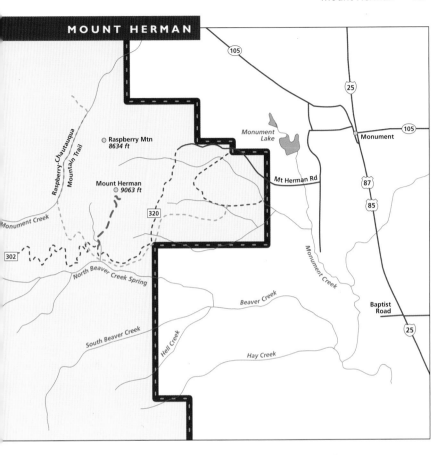

The path becomes more steep after it leaves the stream drainage and traverses an open area of evergreens. Pikes Peak granite boulders stud the landscape. Often found in rocky places, pink-budded, white-flowered **waxflower** shrubs appreciate the gravelly soil here. Small flowers, such as ground-hugging pink **tufted locoweed** and yellow **draba** (a small mustard), thrive in the same mineral ground. Along the way watch for the splayed purple bells of **dainty western clematis**. Picky about its soil, this clematis is partial to decomposed granite, such as that of Pikes Peak.

A steady climb takes the trail to where Pikes Peak occasionally appears through forest openings. Great views of this landmark fourteener emerge farther on from rock outcrops near the summit of Mount Herman. About halfway to the top, as the dark conifers give way to aspens, a delightful pocket meadow appears. Sharing the grassy opening are **cow parsnip, white geranium, valerian,** and **wild iris.**

The route edges up a steep, rocky pitch where footing is a bit precarious. The rough, narrow trail continues up. As the incline eases, pause to check boulder crevices for a **saxifrage** endemic to this region, **Hall's alumroot**—its ivory bells swaying above clumped basal leaves.

As the trail levels somewhat, look for a rock on which to enjoy the marvelous view of Pikes Peak. The top, with yet a different view, is not far. To reach it, hikers walk through a rock garden full of **bluemist penstemon** and yellow **leafy cinquefoil.** In early summer, big white blossoms of **boulder raspberry** decorate the rock-dominated landscape.

The summit of Mount Herman, nearly 3,000 feet above the plains, is almost perfectly flat. If your timing is right, Mount Herman's level top may have colonies of ladybugs, typically in mid-June, crawling out of needle-sharp common juniper bushes. These creatures consume copious numbers of aphids—that mega-multiplying pest that produces offspring without mating.

Conveniently situated on the leading edge of the Front Range between Denver and Colorado Springs, Mount Herman is a fine wildflower hike experience, complete with spectacular views of 14,110-foot Pikes Peak.

HALL'S ALUMROOT

Heuchera hallii

With a fondness for pink Pikes Peak granite, Hall's alumroot is a cousin of red coralbells, which is native to the American southwest. It resembles a compact white version of its famed perennial border relative. Rounded bells cling to bare stems rising from a collection of toothed basal leaves.

Both species are in the Latin genus *Heuchera,* which honors Johann von Heucher, a professor of medicine born in 1677; the species name *hallii* recognizes American botanist Elihu Hall, a Civil War-era collector in Colorado. Hall's alumroot is locally abundant on the upper reaches of the Mount Herman trail.

Once used for curing sores on both horse and man, alumroot also found favor with Native Americans as an eyewash.

Other *Heuchera* in the region include bracted alumroot (*Heuchera bracteata),* common or small-leaved alumroot (*Heuchera parvifolia),* and alpine alumroot (*Heuchera parvifolia ssp. nivalis).* Juices of the alumroot clan, it seems, can be made into invisible ink. Seventeenth-century Britons wrote about *Heuchera's* application in "secret writing." By smashing alumroot in a small amount of water, the liquid becomes invisible ink. Correspondents could pen letters to be read only when held under running water.

Elk/Coyote

(from Ole Barn Knoll to Bootleg Bottom)

Wildflower alert: Colorful sections of trail dominated by penstemons, sulphurflower, bright Lambert, and pastel Rocky Mountain locoweeds.

Hikers can count 70 different wildflowers—including many in the dappled shade of aspen trees—along the Elk/Coyote trails.

easy	**Trail Rating**
2.2 miles out and back	**Trail Length**
Golden Gate Canyon State Park/Golden	**Location**
8,160 to 8,800 feet	**Elevation**
June to September	**Bloom Season**
July	**Peak Bloom**
From Golden, take highway 93 north for 2 miles. Turn left on Golden Gate Canyon Road and go 15 miles to the visitor center. Be prepared to pay the fee. From the center, continue up the highway to Mountain Base Road.	**Directions**

The Front Range is rich in natural treasures. One such paragon is Golden Gate Canyon State Park, less than an hour's drive from the Denver metro area. With 14,000 acres to explore, this state park offers ample opportunities for the outdoor enthusiast. Pick up a map and purchase a pass at the visitor center.

Wildflower enthusiasts can find a trove of calypso orchids in early June on little-used Beaver Trail, accessible via Slough Pond. By July, six dozen flower species spill out along the Elk and Coyote trails.

The mile-long segment of Elk Trail described here begins at the aspen-studded picnic area off Mountain Base Road, called Ole Barn Knoll. Park in the lot farthest to the south at Ole Barn Knoll and look for the access trail just beyond the restrooms. Follow it south to Elk Trail, which heads northwest until it meets Coyote Trail. A right on Coyote leads back to the road at Bootleg Bottom Picnic Area. At this point, choose between retracing steps or following Mountain Base Road back down to Ole Barn Knoll.

Travel down the access path's south-facing slope through **locoweed, sulphur-flower, butter 'n eggs, wallflower** (typically yellow, but also a burnt copper), and **shrubby cinquefoil** or **potentilla**, which blooms all summer.

As the path winds down between picnic benches, look for white **yarrow, standing milkvetch,** and **sandwort.** Appearing from the foothills to the fourteeners, **sandwort** looks like a handful of stars sprinkled on clumps of fine, stiff-bladed grass. **Bluemist penstemon,** magenta **Lambert locoweed,** and bright yellow **stonecrop**

MONKSHOOD

Aconitum columbianum

The evocative name monkshood fits the pointed cowl formed by the top sepal, one of five making up the monkshood flower. Five insignificant petals are concealed under the curved hood, all of which may be responsible for the moniker, friar's cap. This tall, purple member of the hellebore family sometimes creates white mutants.

Though handsome, monkshood is deadly poisonous. Legend has it that werewolves are driven off by it, earning the name wolfbane.

Hellebore family members tend to be toxic, especially to livestock. Among them are early larkspur (*Delphinium nuttallianum*) and white plains larkspur (*Delphinium carolinianum ssp. virescens*). A less formidable relative is blue columbine (*Aquilegia coerulea*), also once in the buttercup family.

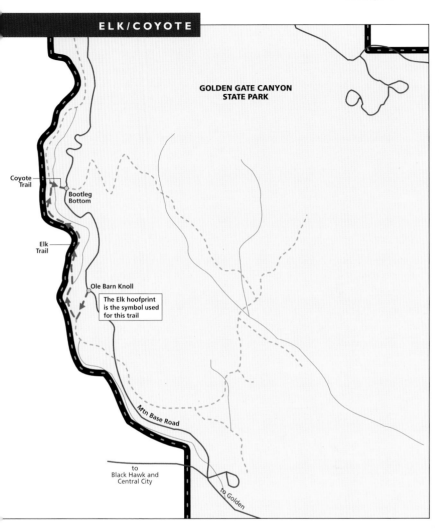

ELK/COYOTE

GOLDEN GATE CANYON
STATE PARK

Coyote
Trail

Bootleg
Bottom

Elk
Trail

Ole Barn Knoll

The Elk hoofprint
is the symbol used
for this trail

Mtn Base Road

to
Black Hawk and
Central City

to Golden

add color. Moving on down the trail may bring the wildflower count to around
70 species at peak bloom.

After passing the remains of some old log structures, the trail turns north
along a riparian habitat. Soon, a natural rock garden on the right includes
pink **wild geranium**, **tall scarlet paintbrush**, lavender **harebells**, and blue-
violet **penstemons**.

Look for tall clumps of **leafy Jacob's ladder** along the more damp left side
of the trail. Also along here, find **black-eyed Susans** and **blanketflower**, with large
red disks and muted yellow ray flowers. Farther up the trail in the filtered shade
of aspens, the midnight-blue spires of **tall larkspur** attain the height of five feet.
In the same area, **nodding onion** hides in a nook among lichen-covered rocks. A
rounded umbel of pink bells bends over distinctively onion-odored foliage.

Elk Trail soon crosses a small footbridge where the keen eye might spot the pale stars of **water spring beauty** tucked under the willows. In the same moist area, look for the vivid pink **shooting stars** during their brief bloom. Just up from the wood bridge, **blue-eyed grass,** an iris relative, may be hidden in the meadow grasses. Nearby, look for **locoweed,** which attracts tiger swallowtail butterflies.

Wildflowers continue to color the next portion of trail at peak bloom. Following some open grassy spaces, a willow-filled boggy area hosts a colony of white **meadow anemone.** Collared by a whorl of deep-green toothed leaves, the five opaque-white sepals—not petals—contain lots of long-stalked yellow stamens. Also known as **windflower,** this plant's roots were considered strong medicine for wounds and lockjaw by Native Americans.

Next along the gently advancing path, white **monkshood** shows up in the damp rich soil under some aspens. Aspens also provide a home for the seemingly dainty **harebell.** Long-blooming, these "**bluebells of Scotland**" are really quite tough and drought-resistant, making them a fine addition to the home garden. Earlier in the season, **wild iris** unfurls here. The aspens grow in number now, and a pair of tall cousins appear in the thick shade: **tall larkspur** and purple **monkshood.**

Continuing, the trail climbs briefly, then levels amidst a colorful display of more than two dozen different kinds of wildflowers. Dominated by **penstemons, sulphurflower,** and both bright **Lambert** and pastel **Rocky Mountain locoweeds,** white **sego lily** adds an accent to this cheerful landscape.

Elk Trail now reaches a junction where Coyote Trail heads right. Before Coyote Trail enters the shade of some sizable aspens, look for pale-blue **false forget-me-nots** growing waist-high.

Cross a small stream where **shooting stars** may be blooming beside **tall chiming bells** and more **monkshood.** Rising out of the plush riparian area, Coyote Trail then traverses a long dry slope under ponderosa pines where **Fendler senecio** grows with small, gold-rayed flowers above lobed grayish leaves. Nearby, **sandwort's** suspended stars reel on wiry stems.

Coyote Trail arrives at Mountain Base Road where you'll find restrooms across the way at Bootleg Bottom. On weekdays, a cautious return by road is possible, or return back down Elk Trail. The picnic area at Ole Barn Knoll is surrounded by more kinds of wildflowers, such as **tall scarlet paintbrush, red globe anenome,** and **pink gilia.** Pastel-tinted hybrids of **locoweeds** are especially beautiful along the paths connecting the widely spread picnic tables.

Golden Gate Canyon State Park is a floristic wonder close enough to go for an evening rendezvous or, better yet, overnight to better explore its some 35 miles of terrific trails. Also along Mountain Base Road is an overlook called Panorama Point with a sweeping view of stunning peaks on the Continental Divide.

Mill Creek Basin

Wildflower alert: Plenty of penstemons and other wildflowers of the montane zone.

The Mill Creek Trail passes aspen sunflowers and some six dozen other species of wildflowers.

easy	*Trail Rating*
3.7-mile keyhole loop	*Trail Length*
Hollowell Park/Rocky Mountain National Park	*Location*
8,400 to 9,860 feet	*Elevation*
June to August	*Bloom Season*
late June to early July	*Peak Bloom*
From Estes Park, take U.S. 36 through the Beaver Meadows entrance station, and go left on Bear Lake Road. Turn right at the Hollowell Park sign and proceed to the trailhead. Be prepared to pay the fee or show your park pass.	*Directions*

Rocky Mountain National Park has so much incredible hiking, it would take weeks to exhaust all the possibilities. Nestled in the montane zone, Mill Creek Basin loop is accessible early in the season. It travels through several habitats and has a number of species of wildflowers to search out.

Where Mill Creek Trail travels beside its namesake stream, it appears to be used more by horseback riders than hikers. By the "keyhole" portion of the loop, the equestrians have veered off, and the remainder of the route is tranquil underfoot. The aspen-studded basin of Mill Creek is a pleasant goal with more than six dozen species of wildflowers awaiting discovery along the way.

Hollowell Park is the jumping-off place, especially for those using the shuttle bus. Parking is not usually a problem, though a picnic area shares the trailhead.

The Mill Creek Basin Trail is illustrated on a kiosk sign under a big ponderosa. To the south is 14,255-foot Longs Peak with its sheer 1,000-foot diamond face showing on the upper half. Sandwiched in a gap to the right is sharp-prowed 12,713-foot Hallet Peak. Even without taking another step, you'll witness more than a dozen wildflower species, including **tall penstemon, sulphurflower, blanketflower, bush sunflower, wild geranium,** and **locoweed.**

Along the wide, flat trail, you'll pass the South Lateral Moraine—the debris of an ancient glacier—and continue through dry, stony soil to meet cool white-to-lavender **sego lily** mixed with **shrubby, silvery,** and **leafy cinque-foils** in varying shades of yellow. Growing in direct sun, these flowers are all drought-tolerant. Just off to the left where thick stands of willow grow, Mill Creek falls over a beaver dam.

Sagebrush and other xeric shrubs, such as the **antelope brush** or **bitter-brush** favored by mule deer, indicate well-drained soil along the next part of the trail. Among them, look for red bracts and lime-green flowers characterizing **narrow-leaved paintbrush,** Wyoming's state flower. Pines appear, and with them **black-eyed Susan** and **mountain parsley.**

The trail winds around the south base of 9,538-foot Steep Mountain. Then it begins to rise on a rocky bed shaded by aspen, Rocky Mountain maple, and some evergreens. Lined with **tall chiming bells** and **cow parsnip,** Mill Creek widens its banks and spreads into the wide meadow below.

The skyline closes in and craggy granite outcrops dominate the north side of the climbing trail. Back in the open, on a dry south-facing slope above the creek, the trail follows a level section before the route narrows and climbs again.

Where the trail comes to a sandy section with aspens and a small waterfall, look for **tall chiming bells, arrowleaf senecio,** and white **monkshood.** Among the trees are **aspen sunflowers** with some **brackenfern** dominating the understory.

In filtered sun on the right of the path, both **white** and **northern green bog orchids** thrive under **tall coneflower.** In the open once more, **wild roses**

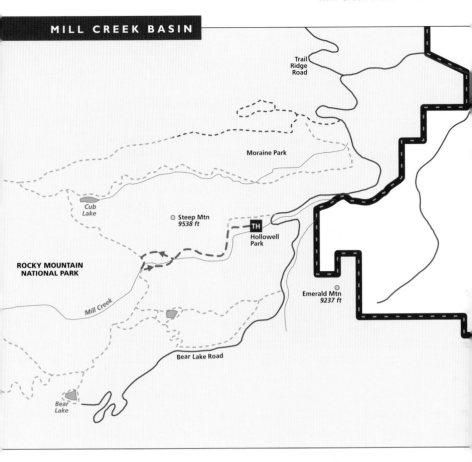

MILL CREEK BASIN

Trail Ridge Road

Moraine Park

Cub Lake

○ Steep Mtn
9538 ft

TH

Hollowell Park

**ROCKY MOUNTAIN
NATIONAL PARK**

Mill Creek

Emerald Mtn
9237 ft

Bear Lake Road

Bear Lake

are responsible for the trail's fragrant scent. A junction introduces the keyhole loop portion of Mill Creek Basin Trail. This heads up to the right on the Cub Lake connection, passing **locoweed** and **blanketflower.** Mature aspens, scarred black where elk have peeled the bark away, shelter **fernleaf** or **bracted louse-wort,** some waist-high.

The trail rises more steeply without the benefit of switchbacks, making it a short but serious workout. Where it levels at last, the trail reveals the tip of Longs Peak above an evergreen-covered hill on the left. Delighting in the mineral soil here is blue **mountain penstemon.** Another blue penstemon, **bluemist,** blooms earlier on this decomposing granite ridge.

Descending through stunted pines, the trail opens to catch a glimpse of the tips of peaks before reaching a sign directing the keyhole loop left to Hollowell Park. In the meadow here, which makes up part of Mill Creek Basin, a flowery hillside and floor line the sandy path as it passes a pair of hitching racks. A bit farther, a sign among lush meadow grasses and **wild strawberries** indicates the location of Mill Creek backcountry campsites.

The **sego lilies** are a luminescent lavender-blue here, amid **beauty cinquefoil** and **rayless arnica**.

The path goes down to the considerable width of Mill Creek where a split-log bridge with a single rail spans the stream. Along the banks look for **cow parsnip**, delicate **cowbane**, and lavender **daisies**. In damp areas across the creek, **pink willowherb**, blue **speedwell**, and the tiny green **mitrewort** grow together.

WILD GERANIUM
Geranium caespitosum

One of the most prolific and showiest pink wildflowers of the foothills and montane zones, wild geranium serves as a food source for wildlife—elk relish the flowers. Ranging from pale to vivid pink, each blossom consists of five petals and sepals, 10 stamens, and a pistil. The pistil elongates into a beak resembling that of a crane (hence, the moniker "cranesbill"). Also, geranium comes from the Greek *geranos,* meaning "crane."

Historical uses of long-blooming wild geranium range from eating the new leaves to concocting a birth control agent from the roots.

White geranium *(Geranium richardsonii)* prefers shade and more moisture than the drought-tolerant wild geranium, though they appear together in some places.

A sign then sends the loop left 1.7 miles back to Hollowell Park. Along the descending road-wide trail, **mountain penstemon** and **Rocky Mountain locoweed** thrive in the disturbed mineral soil. Early in the season, hikers find **purple rock clematis** off to the left. On the right, look closely for the uncommon **rattlesnake plantain** with its flowerstalk over a rosette of white-veined leaves. This inconspicuous orchid contains a substance to conteract rattlesnake venom; however, it does not grow where rattlesnakes live. Also at home on the north-facing cutbank is **green-flowered** and **one-sided wintergreen**.

Flowers are few here in the forest, but occasionally the yellow petals of **heartleaf arnica** stand out. Vegetation thickens as more sunlight penetrates the mixed forest before the loop again crosses Mill Creek and rejoins the trail back to Hollowell Park.

Though horseback riders frequent part of this trail more than hikers, most of the Mill Creek Basin loop offers a modicum of solitude. Add to that the flowery ecosystems along the way and it becomes a fine hike for exploring the lower elevations of Rocky Mountain National Park.

Ouzel Falls

Wildflower alert: Deep shade and forest duff provide ideal habitat for alluring calypso orchids.

Whitewater cascades and wildflowers are in abundance on the Ouzel Falls Trail in Wild Basin west of Allenspark.

moderate	**Trail Rating**
5.4 miles out and back	**Trail Length**
Wild Basin/Rocky Mountain National Park	**Location**
8,500 to 9,450 feet	**Elevation**
June to August	**Bloom Season**
early July to mid-July	**Peak Bloom**
From Lyons, take highway 7 north past Allenspark to the Wild Basin sign. Turn left, pass Copeland Lake, and continue to the parking lot at the Wild Basin Ranger Station.	**Directions**

Wild Basin is the headwaters for the North St. Vrain River, and water is in abundance along the trail. Wildflowers are prolific as well.

A flowery start leads toward a chain of whitewater cascades—from close-in Copeland Falls to shadowy Calypso Cascades and magnificent Ouzel Falls. Roughly 70 kinds of wildflowers represent several ecosystems at peak bloom, typically in July. If you're looking for the exquisite calypso or fairy slipper orchid, June is your best bet.

The uphill trek to Calypso Cascades (1.8 miles) and Ouzel Falls (2.7 miles) should not be missed. Wild Basin's dirt access road leads to a sizable parking area that fills by mid-morning on weekends.

CALYPSO ORCHID
Calypso bulbosa

Calypso means "she who conceals" in Greek. The Queen of Ogygia—better known as Calypso, the alluring sea nymph—cloistered Odysseus for seven years on his homeward journey from the Trojan Wars. The exquisite calypso orchid, too, is covert in deep forest duff under sheltering conifers. Orchid aficionados, however, know that concealment is a trait of orchids, including the pink-pigmented calypso. The colloquial name, fairy slipper, further shapes a mental image. Still, once seen, the alluring calypso is sought again and again, etched in the memory.

The trail for Calypso Cascades and Ouzel Falls begins quietly through mixed forest and wildflowers. Early along the wide pathway, lodgepole pines harbor **wild roses** and **spotted coralroot orchid,** and aspens shelter cool yellow **western paintbrush, tall scarlet paintbrush, blue columbine,** and **aspen sunflower.** Slender **white hawkweed** probably wouldn't be notable except for its color; its close relations, sunflowers, are mostly yellow. Damper conditions suit **pink pyrola,** growing up to 18 inches tall. Also called **bog** or **swamp pyrola,** as well as **bog** or **pink wintergreen,** this plant grows all along this moist section of the trail.

Clear water trickles across the trail set with convenient stones. Growing on the upstream side are **yellow monkey-flowers,** with their red-dotted throats, **monkshood,** and **tall coneflower.** Another rivulet, this one shaded by aspen, alder, and willow, features more **monkeyflower, water spring beauty,** and **twisted stalk.** Yet another sustains **white bog orchid, Richardson's** or **white geranium,** and lacy **cowbane.**

A plank bridge spans the next water-crossing, followed by sheeting granite outcrops where a spur on the left leads to Copeland Falls, just 0.3 mile from the trailhead.

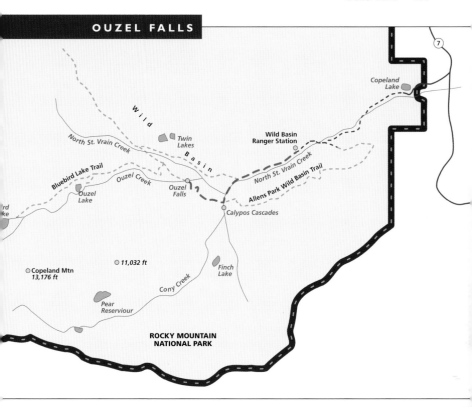

OUZEL FALLS

Drier ground produces **sego lily, northern bedstraw, sulphurflower,** and **harebell.** The whitewater of the rambunctious North St. Vrain River sounds off where granite guards a meadow of **aspen sunflowers, bedstraw,** and lower growing **Geyer onion** in rosy pink.

The shaded, easy-going trail follows alongside the river, and another Copeland Falls sign appears, followed by waterside **wild roses.** The rising, narrowing track reveals **green-flowered pyrola,** as well as **least pyrola.**

Until this point the trail has eased uphill gently; now log risers and granite steps signal the start of a steeper section. Calypso Cascades is just 0.4 mile ahead; Ouzel Falls is 1.3 miles. The route crosses the boulder-lined river and becomes increasingly rugged, ascending on log risers and stone walls. More **green-flowered pyrola** and a wintergreen cousin, **prince's pine** or **pipsissewa,** stand out above glossy evergreen foliage. Along here, look for the paired bells of **twinflower** swinging above round-leaved mats.

Stone risers lead up to meet a damp spot filled with **tall chiming bells, arrowleaf senecio, brookcress, brook saxifrage,** and **cow parsnip.**

As the trail rises so does the sound of gravity-fed water: Calypso Cascades announces itself. The wide cascade takes three bridges to span its divided falls. The deep forest duff in the general vicinity of the cascades is ideal habitat for calypso or **fairy slipper orchids** in late June or early July (depending on snow-pack conditions).

Another 250 feet in elevation gain and 0.9 mile takes the trail up to the spectacular Ouzel Falls. After crossing Calypso's third bridge, check the mossy seep on the left for **mitrewort;** a rotting log by the seep nurtures the wonderfully fragrant **shy wood nymph.**

The forest thins until it exposes the charred trees left standing from the 1978 Ouzel Fire. **Fireweed,** a pioneer in burned areas, is prolific here. Small creeks lead toward a big outcrop shielding a display of white **pearly everlasting, blue columbine,** and **scarlet paintbrush.**

Past the burned area, where the trail starts ascending, look for **dusky** or **Whipple penstemon,** a wildflower said to woo flies with its off-odor.

Not far ahead, a sign stating "privy" signals the trek to Ouzel Falls is almost completed. A bridge across the falls doesn't offer a very satisfying view. But on the near side of the bridge is a suspiciously trampled route up over tree roots and rock. Clamber up this impromptu approach for a stunning frontal view of Ouzel Falls. Footing can be treacherous on the slickened ground.

The scenic combination of waterfalls and wildflowers make this Wild Basin hike to Ouzel Falls an intriguing one.

TWINFLOWER

Linnaea borealis

Twinflower was beloved of Carolus Linnaeus of Sweden, the person who created the Latin binomial system used worldwide for naming plants and animals. The genus name, *Linnaea,* honors this innovative Swedish botanist.

Fragrant and narrow, the pink and white bells hang on forked stems above mats of rounded, polished, evergreen foliage. With a fondness for moist shady forests, this creeping honeysuckle family member is a summer-blooming delight.

Lovell Gulch

Wildflower alert: Hikers discover the "blues:" wild iris, blue-eyed grass, mountain penstemon, and columbine.

Tall, blue wild iris grace a grass meadow along the Lovell Gulch Loop trail just north of Woodland Park.

easy	*Trail Rating*
5.5-mile loop	*Trail Length*
Woodland Park	*Location*
8,600 to 9,240 feet	*Elevation*
June to August	*Bloom Season*
late June	*Peak Bloom*
From Colorado Springs, take U.S. 24 west to Woodland Park and turn right on Baldwin Avenue, which becomes Rampart Range Road. Look for the Woodland Park dog pound, about 2 miles north, adjacent to the trailhead.	*Directions*

Lovell Gulch offers stimulating diversity on its 5.5-mile loop, including varied terrain, interesting ecosystems, and a wealth of wildflowers. Typically, late June is the best time to catch peak bloom.

The trail begins as an easy-going connection to the loop, which at first follows a creek but then climbs to an overlook featuring Pikes Peak. The trail then undulates toward a sharp rise, crests, and drops back to the connection.

Parking is limited adjacent to the dog pound where the trailhead for popular Lovell Gulch is situated.

Pass a steel gate where a sign states: "Trail" to reach another sign stating: "Lovell Gulch." Starting over decomposed granite, the road-wide path travels above a drainage and turns right, up to a gravelly flat. Along here, early-season hikers enjoy **pasqueflowers**; later in the season, several **penstemons** bloom, including **bluemist**, one-sided **alpine** or **mountain penstemon** in saturated ultramarine, and rose-violet **tall penstemon**. Small for its kind, **Parry sunflower** blooms nearby in late June. Ponderosas and aspen anchor the grassy parkland, which is highlighted with golden **wallflower** and **Rocky Mountain locoweed** in tints of lavender, rose, and purple. The trail dips into an aspen-shaded drainage where rosy-violet **American vetch** and **wild iris** thrive. The **wild iris** roots were once used as an ingredient in arrow poison.

ALPINE OR MOUNTAIN PENSTEMON

Penstemon glaber

Listed in some sources as *Penstemon alpinus,* the Latin species name was confusing since this glorious blue pen-stemon thrives down to the foothills along the Front Range rather than at alpine elevation. Therefore, the name mountain penstemon is more apropos. This stunning species is partial to well-drained mineral soil, preferably in a disturbed state. The saturated blues of the stocky floral tubes of mountain penstemon are often tinged with violet. The fifth stamen, called a staminode, is the yellow-haired sterile one.

Penta, meaning "five," and *stemon,* meaning "stamen," reinforces the Latin genus name. The second part of the Latin scientific name, *glaber,* translates as "smooth," which fits the dark leaves that begin broadly at the base of the stout stalk and continue right up into the one-sided flower raceme, tapering as they go.

Gardens with penstemons are hummingbird havens. You can find numerous penstemons in the region. Among them are tall penstemon *(Penstemon virgatus ssp. asagrayi),* white penstemon *(Penstemon albidus),* and scarlet bugler *(Penstemon barbatus).*

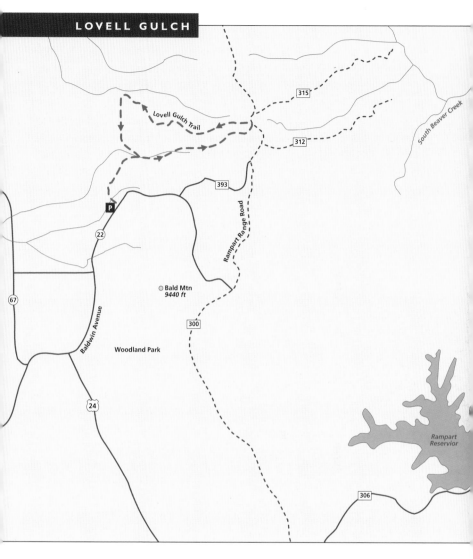

An "S" curve takes the trail west into more ponderosa pines; keep an eye out here for the dark Abert squirrel with its tufted ears. Forest Service trail posts direct hikers along the main route where confusing social trails lure everyone off-track.

The parkland's elegant **wild iris** and quaking aspens are amplified by **tall scarlet paintbrush** and **American vetch** of the prolific pea family. Pines tower over another member of the pea family, **golden banner.** Tree roots wander across the gently ascending trail, which then descends a bit before encountering the pale-purple split bells of **dainty western clematis** and long-spurred **blue columbine.**

At a split in the trail, hikers head down through summer-blooming **fireweed** to cross a little creek. There a sign states: "Lovell Gulch Loop 3.75 miles." A turn to the right is the best direction to hike the loop. It ascends into an open area before easing into a riparian zone shaded by dark-barked river birch and a cadre of **white geranium.** From here, the route crosses through both forest and open spaces. Both mid-sized **fernleaf** and short **Parry louseworts** appear along with **blue-eyed grass** (which is really a member of the iris family) as the path meets the creek amidst gold **shrubby cinquefoil,** fuchsia **shooting stars,** and **wild iris. Rocky Mountain** or **silky locoweed,** in pink and lavender pastels, guide you into aspens where the trail rises.

A flowery vale flanks the single track with **silky loco, wild geranium, chiming bells,** and **mouse-ear chickweed.** Curving, the creekbed presents more **shooting stars.** Aspens, increasing in girth, line the ascending trail with **tall larkspur** and **wild rose** blooming below. On level terrain, the trail passes through Colorado blue spruce studded with **fireweed** in midsummer.

Climbing again, the trail traverses an example of erosion at work. It pulls up into ponderosas where a hefty gate blocks vehicular entry from Rampart Range Road. Turn left under the powerlines and find patches of blue **alpine** or **mountain penstemon** set off by pale mineral soil. Down the wide track, with a dramatic vista of Pikes Peak, showy **silky loco** appears on the foreground.

Following the ridgeline on which the flower-lined service road undulates, look for more signs aiming the gravelly track up steep, but brief, pitches to attain a sweeping hilltop panorama. At this point, take the right fork; the left fork drops precariously and heads away from the loop. Even on the right fork, a careful descent is advised.

Stay right and head down at the next trail sign, traveling through mixed forest to arrive under open skies at a spectacular display of **golden banner, paintbrush, locoweed,** and countless other colorful compatriots. Continue the shady descent to reach a level two-track road that winds through a parkland. Here, the pines and aspen spaces are dotted with **scarlet paintbrush** and **wild iris.** The road contours into a drier area where **perky Sues** add their sunny daisies to the red of **paintbrush,** and Pikes Peak fills the southeastern skyline.

The spur portion of the loop closes on a downhill pitch, arriving at the creek once again to retrace the way back to the trailhead. The 5.5 miles that comprise Lovell Gulch Loop trail are full of changing scenery to motivate hikers. And the wildflowers are spectacular. An easy drive and access makes this flowery foray an ideal day hike.

Lost Lake

Wildflower alert: Dogwood-related bunchberry poses on the lake's northeast shore.

Tall chiming bells thrive along Middle Boulder Creek on the Lost Lake Trail west of Eldora.

moderate	**Trail Rating**
3.0 miles out and back	**Trail Length**
Nederland/Hessie	**Location**
8,750 to 9,780 feet	**Elevation**
June to August	**Bloom Season**
mid-July to mid-August	**Peak Bloom**
From Boulder, take Boulder Canyon (highway 119) west to Nederland, continuing south on 119 to County Road 130, turn right. Continue through the town of Eldora, and go another 2 miles before taking a left to the trailhead. (The road travels in the bed of a shallow rocky stream just before the trailhead. Park on the main road and scout if in doubt.)	**Directions**

The Rocky Mountains are home to several lakes named "Lost Lake." This one, west of Nederland, is hardly lost, but it makes a great wildflowering destination. Though this Lost Lake is fairly low in altitude, it has a more subalpine than montane feeling to it. The trail is a bit steep in its last half mile, but is otherwise fairly easy-going. It takes the hiker to a serene lake nestled in a scenic mountain setting. About six dozen wildflower species color the way.

Even the drive on the Eldora Road to the trailhead may feature a blanket of blooming flowers in midsummer. Some of the restored log cabins in the old mining town of Eldora have whimsical flowerbeds in their front yards.

Nearing the approach road to the trailhead, check the water level before you descend to the creek. The "road" runs right up the creekbed for much of the way to the Hessie trailhead. Nonetheless, this is a wonderfully floristic hike once you solve the parking quandary. (It's not far to the trailhead from the fork in the road, but parking is judiciously limited here.) Hessie is the trailhead for a number of trails, all very popular, so arrive early.

BUNCHBERRY
Chamaepericlymenum canadensis

A dwarf subshrub member of the dogwood family, bunchberry's blooms consist of opaque white bracts that visually serve as petals surrounding minuscule dark purple centers (which are the actual flowers). A hand lens reveals each tiny flower, which will develop into an edible berry-like fruit.

Dwarf Cornel is another common name attached to this lover of moist woodlands, often found in ground-covering patches. The first part of its genus name, *chamae*, is Latin for "on the ground."

Native Americans boiled the dried root and bark of bunchberry as a remedy for fevers, in addition to eating the fruit clusters. The pioneers called it puddingberry. More commonly found in the region is the crimson-barked shrub, red-osier dogwood (*Swida sericea*).

The main parking area for Lost Lake Trail is located next to a fenced meadow full of wildflowers. A rainbow of purple **daisies**, yellow **blanketflowers**, golden **arnica**, magenta **fireweed**, morning-blooming **blue flax**, white **sego lilies**, and lavender **harebells** color the grasses.

A shaded, stony road leads the hiker to a sturdy bridge crossing Middle Boulder Creek. This is the actual trailhead that starts a journey through woods, along streams, and up past flowery hillsides. Along here, as well as many parts of the trail near waterways, lush clumps of **tall chiming bells** thrive. Also called **mountain bluebells**, the lush plants are favored by hungry elk.

Where the rugged roadway is shaded, look for the large leaves of **bush** or **twinberry honeysuckle**. Cupped by bracts that

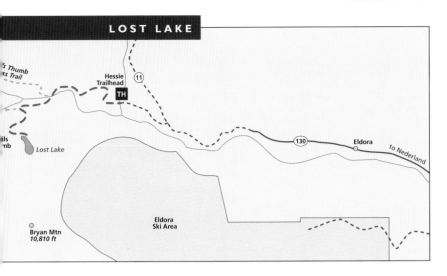

turn red, pale yellow identical-twin flower tubes develop into matched shiny black berries. In the same shady environs, look for the rosy-pink heads of **Geyer onion.**

The broad track levels out at the sound of rushing water. Decorating the trail edges are clumps of **pearly everlasting.** In the same terrain, some tubular flowers in dusty wine and off-white are color variations of **Whipple penstemon.**

The trail travels through substantial conifers that shelter shallow seeps offering **buttercups, brookcress, tall chiming bells,** and lacy white **cowbane.** In the forest shade nearby is **sickletop lousewort.** Its other name, **parrot's beak,** describes the ivory bloom's curved upper lip, which arcs down over a double-lobed lower lip.

The trail crosses a torrent on a hefty bridge where a sign indicates Lost Lake is still ahead. More road than path, the broad track soon offers a good rest stop at the base of a cascading waterfall where clumps of **blue columbine** decorate the rocky incline leading to the water.

Continuing up the trail, a rotting corduroy road leads up to a small trailside seep featuring a colony of **white bog orchids** and **little pink elephants.** On the trail's right, by a granite slab, a sign points left to Lost Lake, 0.5 mile up through the forest. While the trail steepens now, it is not far to the lake.

As the trail finally levels at the lake, dusty-wine specimens of **Whipple penstemon** dot the grasses. Follow the path left around Lost Lake to the north shore. You can see old mining sites on the rugged mountainsides above the eastern end of the lake where a fine colony of **bunchberry** gathers. Other flowers to search for near the water are: **king's crown, brook saxifrage,** and an occasional **least wintergreen.**

Lost Lake offers a world away from the metro area while remaining close in miles. It is a worthy midsummer hike for wildflowers and varied scenery. Watch out for developing afternoon thunderstorms.

Wildflower Hike

36

Three Mile Creek

Wildflower alert: A "century" trail with more than 100 wildflower species at peak bloom, highlighted by fabulously fragrant shy wood nymph.

At a grassy meadow, shrubby cinquefoil joins the parade of more than 100 wildflowers on this trail.

Trail Rating	moderate
Trail Length	6.0 miles out and back
Location	Grant
Elevation	8,980 to 10,680 feet
Bloom Season	June to September
Peak Bloom	mid-July
Directions	From southwest Denver, take U.S. 285 southwest. Drive 11 miles west of Bailey to Grant. Turn right on County Road 62 and go 2.9 miles to the trailhead on the right.

Three Mile Creek Trail in the Mount Evans Wilderness Area features more than 100 kinds of wildflowers along the way. Always within sound of rushing water, the trail travels in a northeasterly direction, steadily gaining elevation. Three miles and 1,700 feet up a creek-accompanied trail, a colorful meadow signals arrival at Three Mile Meadow. Parking at the signed trailhead is limited.

The route for Three Mile Creek Trail slopes up through a hillside stand of small aspens sprinkled with **black-eyed Susan, sego lily, harebell, aspen daisy,** and **wild geranium,** all routinely found at this elevation. A less familiar resident is the uniquely named **dusty maiden.** Its pinkish, curved, button-like heads consist of disk flowers; the rays are absent. Another name is **pincushion.**

After passing a Mount Evans Wilderness Area sign, early-season hikers might note **Rocky Mountain locoweed** and **dainty purple rock clematis** in the vicinity of white-flecked bristlecone pines. The elevated trail overlooks the historical buildings of Tumbling River Ranch, and after following a lodgepole-pine-lined stretch of trail, the path crosses an intersection with the well-traveled guest ranch track. Horse hooves have created muddy stretches requiring some fancy footwork ahead.

One-half mile from the trailhead, a stream follows the trail toward a sunny opening strewn with cool pink **nodding onion** and **golden aster.** Back into the trees, rocks isolated in the damp peaty soil lead up to a creek spanned by a hewn half-log bridge with **wild roses** in the vicinity. A bit farther, wintergreen family members **pink pyrola** and **one-sided wintergreen** dot the mosses and lichens carpeting steep trailside banks. Here, an occasional round-leaved mat of dainty-belled **twinflower** creeps over rocks or mossy hummocks. On this north-facing slope, wintergreen family member **shy wood nymph** thrives with a white head that holds enchanting fragrance often compared to lily-of-the-valley.

Horses ford the stream just down from a sheer outcrop, and foot traffic goes up and around to rejoin the pathway on the other side of the boulder pile. From this point, the canyon tightens and the trail winds up to find more perfumed **shy wood nymphs.**

Waxflower fills the crevices of a towering pale-salmon granite outcrop where the trail cruises for a while before crossing (as it will many times) the creek on a split-log bridge. It can take a bit of scouting to find these wood spans when distracted by obvious fords used by horseback riders. At this particular creek crossing, vibrant pink **shooting stars** embellish the far side shoulder. Up a bit farther where it's drier, look for **Parry harebell** in a particularly luminescent shade of warm purple. Unlike its common cousin, the familiar harebell with its nodding bells, **Parry harebell** blossoms face up, sometimes more than an inch across.

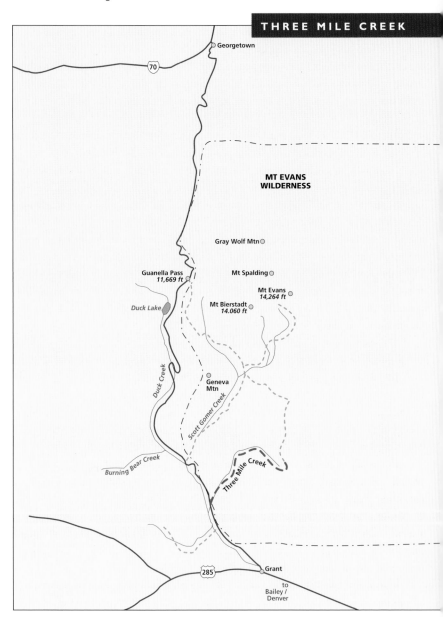

Georgetown

70

MT EVANS
WILDERNESS

Gray Wolf Mtn

Guanella Pass
11,669 ft

Mt Spalding

Mt Evans
14,264 ft

Duck Lake

Mt Bierstadt
14.060 ft

Duck Creek

Geneva
Mtn

Scott Gomer Creek

Burning Bear Creek

Three Mile Creek

285

Grant

to
Bailey /
Denver

Under open skies now, the level trail crosses a grassy meadow where **tall false dandelion, sego lilies,** violet-blue **mountain penstemon,** magenta **woolly or showy locoweed,** and sassy spikes of **yellow owl clover** are joined by **prairie cinquefoil** and light-blue **false forget-me-not.**

Well over half the wildflowers to be counted on Three Mile Creek Trail have appeared by this point. For those not wishing to continue the ascent, this is a logical spot to relax and enjoy the surroundings before turning back.

Taking on a more riparian lushness, the trail edges nearer the stream to exhibit **cow parsnip** and **monkshood.** You can hear spilling water off to the right; the left is virtually covered with glossy mats of evergreen **kinnikinnick.**

Rising up a rooty section, the route navigates past bristlecone pines to reach a small, still pool. A gentle segment meanders through plush stands of **clover.** The next span over Three Mile Creek is a motley trio of logs. Ever rising, the track passes more plush **Rocky Mountain loco** and smaller **showy** or **woolly loco** together.

The path weaves in and out of flowery pocket meadows populated by **wild roses,** purplish **tall larkspur, lupine,** and bright **fireweed.** Peeled log risers climb onto a fairly smooth gradient to an area of pink **wild** and **white geraniums** and lavender-blue **aspen daisy** shielded by aspen.

Three Mile Creek Trail continues its steady incline past the ruins of an old log structure guarded by quaking aspens. Following this, the trail climbs to a stony footbed flanked by gold-trunked aspens to more creek crossings, one with **tall chiming bells** and **tall scarlet paintbrush** alongside.

The waterway pools and drops in its tight canyon where it narrows to expose a great monolith. Nearby grows another nodding member of the wintergreen family, **green-flowered wintergreen.** Early-season hikers might view hot pink **Parry primrose** near here; later in the season, **arrowleaf senecio** and airy **brook saxifrage** carry on the perennial procession.

The rocky track climbs through primal wilderness to reach a log bridge. A ragged outcrop on the north side of the tumbling creek heralds **blue columbine** and **scarlet paintbrush.** Another creek crossing steers the path toward cool yellow **northern paintbrush**

SHY WOOD NYMPH OR SINGLE DELIGHT
Moneses uniflora

Reflecting its Latin scientific name literally—from the Greek *monos,* meaning "one," and *hesis,* meaning "delight"— the common name "single delight" makes perfect sense, particularly if one gets a whiff of this bowed white flower. Another label, one-flowered (*uniflora*) wintergreen, is also logical. Found in damp mossy forests, its single round seedpod was once a food source, raw or roasted, for Native Americans.

Other wintergreens found in shady forests are pink pyrola (*Pyrola rotundifolia ssp. asarifolia*), an erect stalk of scalloped bells ranging in color from blushed to rose; green-flowered wintergreen (*Pyrola chlorantha*), a straight stalk of greenish pendant parasols; and, one-sided wintergreen (*Orthilla secunda*), whose arched stalk holds dangling rounded pale flowers.

and midnight-hued **subalpine larkspur.** Back in the open, find throngs of **fireweed.**

Through aspens, the trail leads into open skies and a mountain appears ahead. A wet passage, diverted by **queen's crown** and **little pink elephants,** discloses an unexpected bridgeless crossing. Here, Three Mile Creek Trail reaches Three Mile Meadow where **shrubby cinquefoil** and clumps of purple and white **columbine** bloom. And in August, the deep blue chalices of **Parry gentian** bloom on the heels of the columbine bloom season.

Three Mile Creek Trail is a wonderful way to view more than 100 wild-flower species. Shade-loving, dry meadow, and wetfeet species abound along the flowery way. Just an hour from the Denver metro area, this trail can be included in a spectacular loop drive up and over Guanella Pass.

Dream and Emerald Lakes

Wildflower alert: A good summer trail to view marsh marigold, globeflower and pink bog laurel.

Bog laurel can be found along the mossy shoreline of Dream Lake.

easy to moderate	*Trail Rating*
3.6 miles out and back	*Trail Length*
Bear Lake/Rocky Mountain National Park	*Location*
9,520 to 10,080 feet	*Elevation*
July to August	*Bloom Season*
mid-July	*Peak Bloom*
From Estes Park, take U.S. 36 through the Beaver Meadows entrance station in Rocky Mountain National Park. Go left on Bear Lake Road to the shuttle parking lot, or continue to the Bear Lake parking lot. Be prepared to pay the fee or show your park pass.	*Directions*

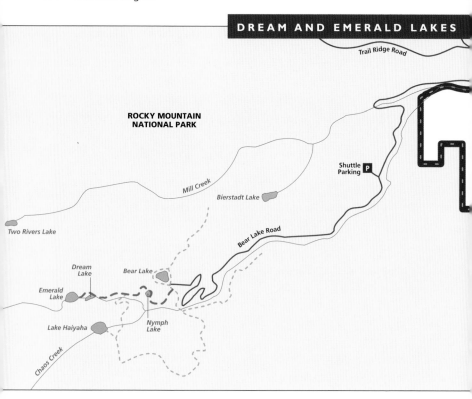

DREAM AND EMERALD LAKES

Of the many lovely lakes in the 415-square-mile Rocky Mountain National Park, you'll rarely find three in a row, especially so close together. Nymph, Dream, and Emerald lakes are varied in settings, each more stunning than the last. About 40 kinds of wildflowers contribute colorful accents, including some spring bloomers coming out in summer where snow lingers late.

To insure a quick start on a hike to the three lakes, hop the shuttle. The busy Bear Lake parking lot is nearly always full. The trail begins between the Bear Lake information booths and rises to Nymph Lake, followed soon by well-named Dream Lake. The last pitch to reach Emerald Lake is steep and rugged, but worth the effort.

The most popular jumping off place for hikers along Bear Lake Road is Bear Lake itself. A number of trails emanate from its scenic shores, one the popular 1.8-mile route to Emerald Lake.

A trail kiosk starts the Emerald, Dream, and Nymph Lakes trail up a well-trod path through a forest that, like most coniferous habitats, is parsimonious with its wildflower production. Some **sickletop lousewort**, its off-white coiled blossoms cocked like parrots' beaks, adds interest under the evergreens. Pink parasoled **prince's pine** and rusty red **pinedrops** may also peek out.

It is only 0.5 mile and 225 feet in elevation gain to Nymph Lake. Benches placed on the shores of the serene lake invite visitors to enjoy **yellow pond lilies** in July. Dream Lake is just another 0.6 mile and 200 vertical feet up the trail. Ascend the paved pathway and look for a seep with **tall chiming bells** and **arrowleaf senecio** or **groundsel**. A turn of the trail rises to cross an outcrop-protected creeklet where **subalpine daisy** and **green-flowered northern bog orchid** and **little pink elephants** bask in the sun.

Constructed around unyielding granite, the track opens up a grand view of the Keyboard of the Winds on the southern skyline. The ascending trail passes **Whipple** or **dusky penstemon** with its wine-colored tubes.

Another granite-dominated turn reveals rushing Glacier Creek. A sign marks where the trail heads right. **Tall scarlet paintbrush** and **blue columbine** grow near a bridge leading toward the junction with the Lake Haiyaha Trail. Turn right here—Dream Lake is just ahead. A small meadow sports **marsh marigold** and **globeflower**—spring flowers, but snow stays late here— while its creekbanks yield **white violets** and **buttercups.**

The entry into the fabulous Dream Lake basin is bedded by natural stone steps. Head left and find a perfect curve of rock on which to relax above the jade waters.

Leaving Dream Lake, continue on to Emerald Lake 0.7 mile farther, following the trail paralleling the north shore of the sparkling waters. Damp areas along the way encourage **mountain blue violets,** while nearby, conifers shelter **spotted coralroot.**

Where the trail passes into evergreens, a side trip to the lake may turn up **pink bog laurel**, particularly on the mossy shoreline. A rock footbed precedes a pocket meadow of **little pink elephants.** The trail then clambers up a rugged segment over rock and logs, again meeting the creek where it pushes out from under a boulder. This section quickly tops

MARSH MARIGOLD
Psychrophila leptosepala

Marsh marigold's genus name, *psychros,* meaning "frigid," and *philein,* meaning "to love" in Greek, gives away its favorite habitat. This member of the hellebore family craves cold wet feet. In fact, it often blooms right after snowbanks recede. You can find the flowers in icy runoff and sodden meadows.

Several white sepals, their undersides a steel blue, surround a number of pistils and stamens, perhaps accounting for the nickname, meadowbright. Its thick dark leaves inspired other common names, such as elk's lip and cowslip. Marsh marigold was formerly in the buttercup family.

out, and roots polished by countless feet heading up to Emerald Lake join rocks underfoot.

The trail crosses bedrock toward cascades racing past a towering outcrop where flowers bloom and falling waters squeeze between plump green banks. Ahead, a jagged mountain escarpment stretches across the skyline.

A plank bridge spans the stream and a seep, revealing a stand of **subalpine** or **delicate Jacob's ladder.** Passing a worn granite face, the route climbs to a lush riparian area with more **little pink elephants,** and then it continues up onto granite polished to a slippery sheen. **Blueleaf cinquefoil** accompanies the easing trail passing **marsh marigolds** and **little pink elephants,** followed by **white bog orchid** and, a bit farther on, the tiny green spiderwebs of **mitrewort** (use a hand lens to examine the snowflake-like blooms that contain a tracery of maroon webbing). A natural trough carries a rivulet leading the hiker up to a fine display of **globeflower** and related **marsh marigold.**

A quick last pull draws Emerald Lake into sight. The jutting prow of 12,713-foot Hallett Peak on the left, the eternal snow of Tyndall Glacier in the center, and ragged spires on the right frame the dark lake waters. A slab of granite slanting from the shore invites the hiker to enjoy the magnificence of the landscape.

The trail to Nymph, Dream, and Emerald lakes is a sublime example of the montane life zone edging into subalpine within Rocky Mountain National Park. A hike here enhances the experience for each visitor to this treasured park.

GLOBEFLOWER
Trollius albiflorus

Often found growing with marsh marigold, globeflower likes the same soil conditions: wet and cold. Five ivory sepals cup three or more green pistils and many stamens of this hellebore family member that loves melting snow near treeline. The light leaves are toothed and deeply divided.

Early spring-blooming globeflower is sometimes confused with narcissus anemone, which is a summer bloomer and is typically multi-flowered. And, like marsh marigold, globeflower was once in the buttercup family.

Cahill Pond

Wildflower alert: Dark blue mountain or alpine penstemon and lots of Rocky Mountain locoweed.

Aspen trees along this trail in Mueller State Park are heavily scarred by elk feeding on their bark. Scarlet paintbrush and golden banner grow at their base.

easy	**Trail Rating**
2.5-mile loop	**Trail Length**
Mueller State Park/Divide	**Location**
9,400 to 9,600 feet	**Elevation**
June to August	**Bloom Season**
mid-June to early July	**Peak Bloom**
	Directions

From Colorado Springs, take U.S. 24 west to Divide. Then turn south on highway 67 to Mueller State Park on the right. Be prepared to pay the fee.

In Mueller State Park and Wildlife Area, more than 40 trails offer plenty of variety to choose from. In fact, choosing a hike can be more difficult than the hiking itself. One excellent choice for a rewarding short trail is the 2.5-mile loop that features Cahill Pond and about 60 kinds of wildflowers.

Armed with a trail map available from the entrance station or the spacious visitor center, you can use the named and numbered trails to take in every corner of the 12,000-acre, sprawling park; most shorter hikes are concentrated in the northern half of the park. The Cahill Pond Loop involves segments of trails with names such as Cheesman, Cahill Pond, Moonshine, and Lost Still (the last referring to bygone alcohol production, not to hikers unable to find their way back).

The parking lot farthest north up Wapiti Road launches the Grouse Mountain/Cheesman Ranch trailhead. The loop segment numbers, in order, are as follows: 17, 35, 34, 36, and 17. (This is the best direction for hiking the Cahill Pond Loop).

The trail starts up an old road bordered by starry **sandwort** and **early blue daisy** where you can see the west flank of Pikes Peak beyond a white and yellow slope of **mouse-ear chickweed, cinquefoil, senecio,** and **golden banner.**

A three-way junction sends the loop right on number 17 (Cheesman Ranch Trail) to curve through aspen and pine. Underfoot, the decomposed Pikes Peak granite shows off the stunning dark blue violet of **mountain penstemon,** which thrives in the roadway. Where the trail forks, continue straight ahead on the right fork.

GEYER ONION

Allium geyeri

Thriving from the foothills to the tundra, rosy-pink Geyer onion spices up the landscape. A compact umbel of upfacing, pointed tepals sits atop a round hollow stem—long at lower elevations and short on the tundra. (Tepals are petals and sepals undistinguishable from each other.)

Colonizing in well-drained soil, Geyer onion and other *Alliums* served as a rudimentary insect repellent as well as a food source for early Native Americans. Edible onions always smell oniony. (Their poisonous look-alikes, death camas, don't.) Additionally, the onion family was used to relieve flatulence, as a diuretic, and as a natural remedy for fighting pneumonia. Onions are also rich in salts and minerals. Carl Geyer, the species honoree, collected plants along the Oregon Trail in 1844 with the Nicollet expedition.

Wild onions widely spread in the region include sand onion (*Allium textile*) and nodding onion (*Allium cernuum*).

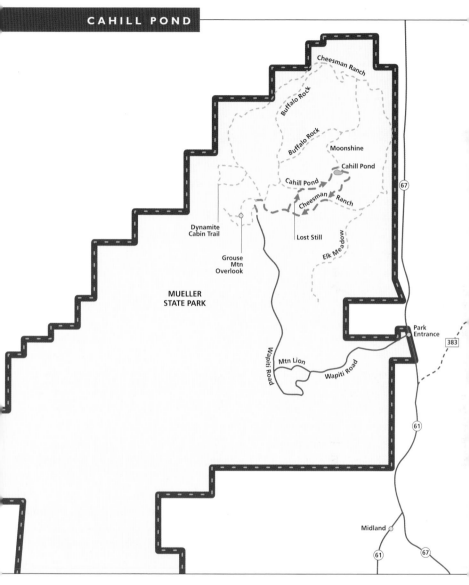

Winding through a mixed forest, the route sweeps into the open at a meadowed slope framing the 14,110-foot peak commemorating the early 19th-century explorer Zebulon Pike. Treeline is well-defined on this fourteener rising approximately 4,500 feet higher than the elevation of the upcoming junction where the loop takes a left on number 35 (Lost Still). In the vicinity, look for **tall scarlet paintbrush**, **Rocky Mountain** or **silky locoweed**, and pink-headed **Geyer onion**. Wild onions were relished for more than their role in flavoring the foods of Native Americans and pioneers; they furnished juice to fight pneumonia, were a handy diuretic source, served as a primitive insect repellent, and, when chewed, relieved flatulence.

Lost Still Trail curves down through conifers into mixed woods, opening to the red and gold of **paintbrush** and **golden banner.** Next along the way, an elderly aspen grove shelters a stand of purple **wild iris. Pink pussytoes** line the trail up a grassy slope to a road where a sign indicates number 34 (Cahill Pond) to the right, down the roadcut.

Sizable aspens tower over **shrubby cinquefoil** and **wild iris** before giving way to sun-loving **scarlet gilia** along the right cutbank. The aspens are heavily scarred by elk scraping the bark in long upward strips (Wapiti have no upper front teeth). Not only is Mueller State Park a recreational area, but it's also a sanctuary established by the ranching Mueller family as a game preserve for elk, bighorn sheep, and bear. The left side of the trail is covered with prolific but non-native **butter 'n eggs.**

Curving gently down, the overgrown ranch road heads right to the dark waters of Cahill Pond. On the way, two members of the iris family, **blue-eyed grass** and **wild iris**, commune with **shooting stars** and **pink plumes** along the drainage leading into the still pond.

In front of the old earthen dam holding back the pond's waters, hikers wade through a swale of grass to reach a trail sign on the far side. The loop now takes off right onto number 36 (Moonshine) and immediately enters aspens.

The long skyline of Pikes Peak slips into view to the east while you pass rolling meadows with the pink sweet-pea-like flowers of **American vetch.** In the vicinity, a bounty of pink **Geyer onion** honors a man who collected plants along the Oregon Trail in 1844.

While found mostly west of the Continental Divide, **orange sneezeweed** does grow in the Pikes Peak region. Cattle know to ignore this robust hip-high plant with its lazy, daisy-like flowers and pale-green foliage—probably because it is poisonous. Its yard-high size among the benign aspens catches the attention of hikers passing by.

Vestiges of a long gone ranch make terraced ripples in the wide grasses leading the trail past clumps of **Rocky Mountain locoweed.** A signed junction returns the trail to number 17, Cheesman Ranch (there really is a ranch on the far end), where a right turn heads the hiker back to close the loop. On the way, a single big spruce interrupts the flow of aspen; it shelters **Parry sunflower.**

Mueller State Park, an easy drive from metro areas, provides the adventuring wildflower lover with 85 miles of trails to explore.

Diamond Lake

Wildflower alert: A "century" trail with more than 100 species of wildflowers at peak bloom.

The trail to Diamond Lake is popular with Front Range hikers, but wildflower and scenery enthusiasts are heavily rewarded.

One of the top high-country wildflower hikes on the Front Range, Diamond Lake Trail has in excess of 100 different kinds of wildflowers coloring sweeping slopes and intimate glens, as well as plenty of crystalline waterfalls along the way.

Initially, the trail follows the same path as that of Arapaho Pass and Fourth of July Mine. After 1 mile of steady climbing, Diamond Lake Trail branches off left and drops a few hundred feet before rising again to the lake. Both coming and going, hikers accumulate altitude losses and gains.

Diamond Lake

Trail Rating	moderate
Trail Length	5.0 miles out and back
Location	Nederland/Eldora
Elevation	10,160 to 10,950 feet
Bloom Season	July to August
Peak Bloom	mid-July to early August
Directions	From Boulder, take Boulder Canyon (highway 119) west to Nederland, continue south to County Road #130 (Eldora Ski Area Road), and go right. (The pavement ends after 4 miles.) Continue through the town of Eldora, and go about 5 miles on rough road to the Fourth of July Trailhead.

Located on the south end of the Indian Peaks Wilderness Area at the Fourth of July Trailhead, Diamond Lake Trail is extremely popular. High-season weekend parking is creative after 9 a.m.

The trail begins in a northwesterly direction behind the campground restrooms. Soon, hikers pass a sign displaying destinations, including Diamond Lake. Within sight of the sign, many flowers stand out, most notably **tall chiming bells, bracted lousewort, white geranium,** and **fireweed.** Peeled log risers then lead the hiker onto a trail accompanied all the way by wildflowers.

Small pocket meadows in the forested stretch are subtly populated with **Whipple** or **dusky penstemon, sickletop lousewort,** and **rayless** or **Parry arnica.** The trail levels to present glades nurturing **monkshood, subalpine larkspur,** and **arrowleaf senecio** in complementary purple and gold.

A small bridge crosses a creeklet introducing a verdant meadowful of blooming beauties. Look for **false Solomon's seal** and **twisted stalk** at the next creeklet. Yet another rivulet crosses the trail, this one spanned by a short boardwalk that enters spruce forest.

Uneven and rooty, but not too taxing, the trail then narrows as it rises. Along the way in openings, look for tall woolly-budded **pink-headed daisy** and **mountain death camas.** A solid white torrent rushes off a cliff across the valley to the south. An upcoming sign indicates you've reached the Indian Peaks Wilderness Area boundary.

Switchbacks soon carry the hiker higher, passing a small seep at trail level that features **brook saxifrage, subalpine larkspur, bistort,** and lots of **scarlet paintbrush** and **blue columbine** upslope. Slopes swathed in pink-budded,

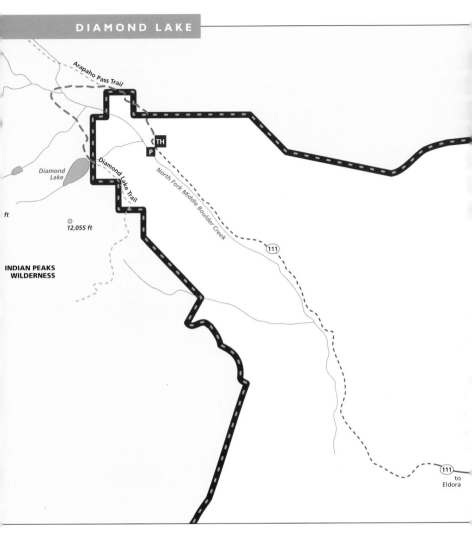

blue-blossomed **tall chiming bells,** golden **senecio,** purple **monkshood,** white **cow parsnip,** and magenta **fireweed** fill in the foreground.

Next, peeled-log channels divert runoff, and the footing becomes rocky. A tiny rivulet curls down on the right, bright with **yellow monkeyflower.** The trail enters a dark spruce forest where roots rule a gentle segment, after which, in the open once again, you step on stones to cross a waterway lined with white **brookcress.**

The next water-crossing requires a bit of fancy footwork as the path approaches a stand of **aspen sunflowers,** each turned to receive morning sun. More roots and rocks claim the level forest trail ahead. Color reigns on a wide-open steep slope beside a broad cascade with a tricky crossing. A seep filled with fragrant **white bog orchid** and green, snowflake-like **mitrewort** is followed by yet another seep featuring **yellow monkeyflowers.** Look for **Parry primrose** nearby early in the season.

After one mile and several dozen wildflower species, Diamond Lake Trail takes off left from the Arapaho Pass Trail. Within 10 feet of the junction is a seep sporting the unusual **fringed Grass-of-Parnassus** and airy **brook saxifrage.** Clumps of **blue columbine** overlook the scene.

Down the trail past a tract of evergreens take in a view of towering mountains with snowfields furrowing their sides. A meadow full of strong color furnishes the perfect foreground. Now the track drops to a boggy area spanned by half logs.

Where the trail turns rocky, it passes a draw studded with **little pink elephants.** Farther down the trail when snowbanks recede, a rockfall courses down. Early in the season, **glacier lilies** adorn the newly exposed earth; later their distinctively paneled pods point skyward.

Switchbacks take the trail past outcrops and flower-filled glades before dropping to bridged bogs. At the bottom, a social trail off to the right leads to a big slab of rock fronting a noisy cascade—a good spot for a snack. Back on the main trail, a sturdy, one-railed split-log bridge crosses rushing Boulder Creek.

The pathway then enters shade interspersed with damp areas of wildflowers. Rocky and criss-crossed with roots, the route

YELLOW MONKEYFLOWER
Mimulus guttatus

Seep-spring monkeyflower is another name for this beguiling member of the figwort family, which you'll find in places with a constant water source. Bright yellow snapdragon-like blossoms with a sprinkling of red dots could, with a little imagination, resemble laughing monkeys. The genus name, *Mimulus,* is derived from the Latin for "buffoon," while the species name, *guttatus,* means "speckled."

The green, toothed leaves were used raw in salads and smashed to relieve the pain of rope burns by Native Americans. Monkeyflower roots made an effective astringent.

Some very showy cherry-red monkeyflowers (*Mimulus lewisii*) inhabit east-facing slopes along Colorado's North Park. Another, *Mimulus gemmiparus,* grows in Rocky Mountain National Park where water seeps continuously over slabs of tilted granite.

uses log water bars to take the hiker up past a small stream with an early display of **Parry primrose.**

Switchbacks carry the trail east toward Diamond Lake. At one zigzag, an opening reveals a sharp peak cradling a snow-filled couloir. Afterward, the track pulls up over rock and big log risers to level out in a wildflower meadow of several acres. On the far side of this colorful area a sign indicates Diamond Lake is to the right. This is also the place to search the ground for lots of starred **pygmy bitterroot,** both pink and white.

Wind your way through some stones and soon Diamond Lake appears in a setting of rugged Continental Divide peaks rising to nearly 13,000 feet. To the south, the lake meets a talus slope sliding down more than 1,000 feet.

Along the shallow north shore, look for pink **bog laurel** in mossbound huddles. **Paintbrushes** (in rose, white, yellow, and red) are scattered through the grasses across the lake. Follow the northshore track to the west end where a cascade empties into Diamond Lake. Continue up to where the cascade evens out by a small meadow to view **blueleaf cinquefoil, star gentian, Parry clover,** and **marsh marigolds.**

By all counts, especially the floristic, Diamond Lake and its approach trail is one of the greatest wildflower hikes around. It should be high on the summer list of wildflowering destinations.

Wildflower Hike 40

Herman Gulch

Wildflower alert: A "century" trail with more than 100 wildflower species at peak bloom, plus an abundance of blue columbine in June.

The meadows along the popular Herman Gulch Trail are awash in up to 100 different kinds of wildflowers including rosy paintbrush and bistort.

Trail Rating	moderate to strenuous
Trail Length	6.8 miles out and back
Location	Off I-70 just west of the Bakerville Exit
Elevation	10,400 to 11,900 feet
Bloom Season	mid-June to late August
Peak Bloom	late June to early August
Directions	From Denver, take I-70 west past Silverplume to exit 218 (unmarked), just past the Bakerville Exit. Turn right into the parking area.

The Herman Gulch Trail is heavily traveled due to its generous wildflower displays and its close proximity to the Front Range. Highlighted by a bounty of blue columbine in mid- to late June, the trail draws wildflower aficionados who can find roughly 100 wildflower species at peak bloom (late July). Add mountain-girt vistas and an alpine lake, and the hike, though a bit strenuous at the start and on the final pitch, is one of the best around.

Though the parking area is sizable, the popularity of this trail fills the lot on peak season weekends. An early arrival not only secures a spot but helps you avoid summer thunderstorms that often build up by early afternoon.

The forested trail begins gently on a path of crusher-fines (minced rock). Soon it reaches a fork, where the Herman Gulch Trail turns left and the Watrous Gulch Trail bears right. Here, the Herman Gulch Trail begins a steady incline. Early in the season, **wild rose** perfumes the ascent. A tiny seep on the right supports **green bog orchid** along this steep stretch.

The sound of whitewater signals the end of the first pitch as the hiker reaches a small lush area sheltered by willows and punctuated by **monkshood, white geranium, arrowleaf senecio, little pink elephants,** and **cinquefoil.**

As summer progresses, look for **fringed gentian** in the thick grasses beyond the willows—a stunning annual whose blooms twist closed on cloudy days and at nightfall. Two more gentians found in the vicinity are small, satin-starred **rose gentian** and the cobalt blue **Parry gentian.** The gentian family honors King Gentius of Ancient Illyria—today's Albania. This monarch is said to have discovered important medicinal properties in the gentian family.

Before entering more forest, the pathway is flanked by composites such as **asters,** daisy-like **fleabanes,** and **aspen sunflowers,** which, like other sunflowers, face east. A chemical in their stems constricts with the heat of the sun, allowing the heads maximum exposure to morning rays.

Continuing in deep shade, the track passes a spring on the right sheltering pink **queen's crown,** purple **monkshood,** scented **white bog orchid,** and **fringed Grass-of-Parnassus.**

Moving up the trail, evergreens give way to open skies, and another streamlet boasts more white **fringed Grass-of-Parnassus,** deserving of a close look. Ahead in the distance is the rugged face of 13,553-foot Pettingell Peak; wildflowers fill a broad meadow in the foreground.

In the latter half of June, this verdant meadow comes alive with an extravaganza of long-spurred **blue columbine.** Although many spots in Colorado boast large amounts of this lovely wildflower—chosen for the state's flower in 1899—the show in Herman Gulch is exceptional at peak bloom.

Adding bright touches to the dense shade along this stretch of trail, early-blooming hot-pink **Parry primrose** flourishes by a split-log bridge. Along here, watch for roots and rocks underfoot. The trail becomes more demanding; look for small patches of flower-filled meadows. As switchbacks take the hiker higher, peak-ringed views call for appreciation pauses. Along this challenging section of trail, **arnica** grows in spongy seeps alongside **little pink elephants** and **white bog orchids.** In cold, damp areas, the early-season hiker may encounter creamy **globeflower** and white **marsh marigold.** The petal reverses of marsh marigold are a cool steel blue.

Rougher underfoot, the track heaves up a final pitch. At last, the trail levels out and passes patches of stunted Engelmann spruce, commonly known as "krummholz" (German for crooked wood). **Black-headed daisies** abound in the gravelly soil. These daisies are the most common fleabane—or *erigeron*—found in the high country. Wool-like fuzz under this fleabane's head accounts for the name, while in fact, the ray petals are a clear white.

At a small pond on the right, look for the ivory-tubed **snowlover,** resembling an unfinished penstemon. The presence of snowlover indicates a deep-drift zone. Near receding snowfields, look around recently exposed areas for **snow buttercup,** sometimes blooming right through lingering snowbanks.

Set in a mountain-girt bowl, Herman Lake glistens with a celadon green color. Find a boulder, relax, and enjoy the scenery. Several 13,000-foot peaks of the Continental Divide tower immediately above. Herman Gulch is a grand place to experience what the Rockies have to offer in scenery, wildflower gardens, and exhilarating hiking.

FRINGED GRASS-OF-PARNASSUS

Parnassia fimbriata

Popularly associated with the saxifrage family, Grass-of-Parnassus actually is the sole genus in its own family. The fanciful white flowers consist of five petals finely-fringed on their inner edges on top of long, slender stems. There are two sets of five stamens—one set is sterile and has pinkish balls on the ends. Alternating with the showy stamens is a fertile set with fat yellow glands tucked in at the base of each petal. This inch-wide wildflower is centered with a pear-shaped ovary. Glossy, rounded, heart-shaped basal leaves complete this very ungrasslike plant.

Look for fringed Grass-of-Parnassus in its favored habitats: subalpine bogs and stream edges.

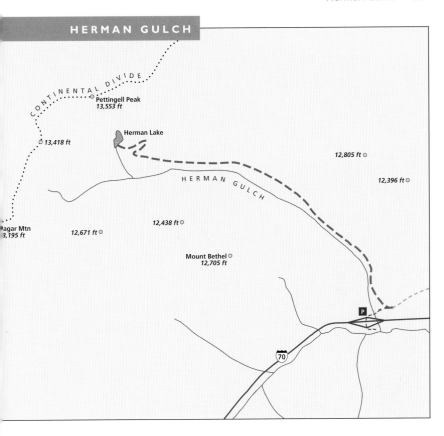

HERMAN GULCH

CONTINENTAL DIVIDE

◎ Pettingell Peak
13,553 ft

◊ 13,418 ft

Herman Lake

12,805 ft ◎

12,396 ft ◎

H E R M A N   G U L C H

12,438 ft ◎

agar Mtn
3,195 ft

12,671 ft ◎

Mount Bethel ◎
12,705 ft

P

70

Wildflower Hike 41

Butler Gulch

Wildflower alert: A superb "century" hike with more than 100 wildflower species at peak bloom.

The Butler Gulch Trail climbs through moist seeps and stream crossings to arrive in a high basin studded with rosy paintbrush and other wildflowers.

Trail Rating	moderate to strenuous
Trail Length	5.0 miles out and back
Location	Jones Pass/Empire
Elevation	10,400 to 11,640 feet
Bloom Season	July to early September
Peak Bloom	late July to mid-August
Directions	From the Front Range, take I-70 west to U.S. 40 and go northwest through Empire to the Henderson Mine turnoff at Big Bend Picnic Area. Drive 2.5 miles to Jones Pass Road, and turn right at a fork by Henderson Mine. The trailhead is 0.5 mile at a gate on the left.

At peak bloom, Butler Gulch is a wildflower viewer's dream. More than 100 species live near the cascades, seeps, and meadows. Consider carrying an extra pair of socks in your pack as you trod through sodden zones where plenty of water washes the steadily rising route. Butler Gulch Trail requires aerobic effort, but with considerable wildflower rewards.

Parking is limited at the gated trailhead, so early arrivals get the choice spots. As with other trails that travel above treeline, an early start helps you avoid afternoon thunderstorms.

Pass around the gate and check the trenches alongside the old mine road for **rose gentian** and **milky willowherb.** Cross the dam-sized fill elevating the roadway over rushing Clear Creek; on the steep banks grow **fireweed, asters, harebell, aspen sunflower,** and **subalpine** or **creamy buckwheat.** Nearly 30 kinds of flowers appear before the trail enters a drooping forest.

The rocky road leads into close-ranked conifers where **shy wood nymph** grows amid green mosses. Another white bloomer fond of shade is **sickle-top lousewort,** its arced blossoms resembling the hooked beaks of parrots —hence another common name, **parrot's beak.**

Watch for a short social trail on the left leading to a meadow sporting every sort of wet-root wildflower, from **rosy paintbrush** to **little pink elephants** and from **monkshood** to **cow parsnip.** Pocket meadows hide in many forest openings. The next one is full of **subalpine larkspur, monkshood,** and lacy, white **cowbane.**

Just up the rutted track, the next opening adds yellow **arnica** and **senecio** to the purples of **monkshood** and **larkspur.** On the left, by an old snag, a soft cushion of mosses features the uncommon **side-flowered mitrewort.** A hand lens reveals the intricacy of the minute white snowflake-like petals lining a straight stem. Here, too, is **delicate Jacob's ladder.**

BROOKCRESS
Cardamine cordifolia

A member of the prolific mustard clan, brookcress (a.k.a. bittercress) favors the habitat along mountain waterways where it can spread underground with abandon. The typical mustard flowers with four petals in a cross shape are white and develop into erect seedpods. These are said to once have been used to remedy heart problems. Before brookcress blooms, its leaves are peppery; after bloom the name bittercress is more fitting.

Peppery leafed cousins are wintercress (*Barbarea orthoceras*) and watercress (*Nasturtium officinale*).

When the trail reaches a wide creek, walk upstream to a fallen tree to cross. (Test the tree for stability before crossing.) Step across the next stream, and look for pink **alpine willowherb** paralleling the trail. In the soggy trail that follows, pass **little pink elephants.**

Butler Gulch Trail turns to the left and spans a lively creek over fallen logs to a flowery meadow of woolly-budded **pink-headed daisy**, **tall chiming bells**, and pale yellow **western** or **northern paintbrush.** A few steps farther introduces **blue columbine.**

The next meadowscape along the ascending trail is dominated by **rosy paintbrush.** From here, a brief but arduous pitch passes vibrant **Parry primrose** and white **brook saxifrage** beside a creek. The trail eases, passing a small creek flanked by snowy **brookcress, marsh marigold, arrowleaf senecio, subalpine larkspur,** and a host of other wildflowers.

Water, water everywhere... Still climbing up, the next saturated stretch of trail is covered by rows of logs set on their sides. Up ahead, a cascade tumbles down the hillside.

Switchbacks then pass another colorful meadow, followed by another cascade of water and flowers. Here, **rosy paintbrush** sets off Vasquez Peak in the background.

BROOK SAXIFRAGE

Micranthes odontoloma

Dainty white stars swinging on reddish wiry stems distinguish brook saxifrage. The quarter-inch flowers grow in panicles branching from long, sticky stems— later developing into dark red seedpods. The rounded basal leaves are smooth and toothed.

Fond of rocks and moving water, brook saxifrage is a summertime bloomer in the upper montane and subalpine zones. A close relative is snowball saxifrage (*Micranthes rhomboidea*).

Just ahead, a brook courses down through tussocks of emerald moss and flat rocks. More floriferous glades border the ascending trail until it breaks out of the trees into the open meadow of Butler Gulch. Curving around the basin are peaks that form a stretch of the Continental Divide, some still carrying the white snowfields of winter on their shoulders.

Black-headed daisies and subtle **bog saxifrage**, mixed with the flamboyant throngs of **rosy** and **scarlet paintbrushes**, fill the meadow. In August, royal blue **Parry gentian** bloom near a lone square boulder anchoring the left side of the track.

The trail continues to climb, and the going is slow at 11,500 feet. **Kings crown, pygmy bitterroot, alpine avens,** and both **snow** and **subalpine butter-**

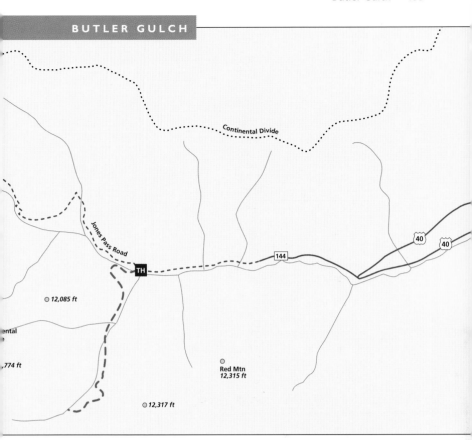

cup, along with a few small buns of **moss campion** and **alpine sandwort,** enter the picture. Great talus slopes tumble down from the left, supporting showy clumps of **blue columbine.** The raw rock is also home to the gerbil-sized pika.

Up ahead, Butler Gulch Creek rushes down through brilliant **Parry primrose** and white **brookcress.** Although you have the option to cross the creek and continue climbing up to the cirque to see occasional tumbledown mining cabins, the near side of Butler Gulch Creek is the turn-around point.

Seeking peak bloom along the 2.5-mile length of Butler Gulch Trail makes a trip flower aficionados will not want to miss.

Wildflower Hike

42

Blue Lake

Wildflower alert: Pockets of subalpine flowers, including little pink elephants, asters, and blueleaf cinquefoil.

The busy Blue Lake Trail climbs past little pink elephants and other wildflowers indicative of the trail's subalpine elevation.

Trail Rating	moderate
Trail Length	5.0 miles out and back (trailhead sign: 6.0 miles)
Location	Brainard Lake/Ward
Elevation	10,480 to 11,440 feet
Bloom Season	July to September
Peak Bloom	mid-July to mid-August
Directions	From Boulder, take highway 119 up Boulder Canyon to Nederland. Turn north on highway 72, and just past Ward, turn left on County Road 102 (Brainard Lake Road). At Brainard Lake, follow the lake around to the right, and turn right to the Mitchell Lake trailhead. Be prepared to pay the fee.

Surrounded by 12,446-foot Little Pawnee Peak on the south, 13,223-foot Mount Audubon on the north, and majestic Mount Toll rising due west, Blue Lake sits in a magnificent setting.

To reach Blue Lake, the trail travels nearly 2.5 miles through terrain filled with nook-and-cranny meadows of subalpine wildflowers. Water is a near-constant companion, whether confined as a pond or lake, or running in streams. The first trail segment, which takes the hiker to Mitchell Lake, gains only about 300 feet in elevation; continuing on to Blue Lake adds another 700 vertical feet.

The Indian Peaks Wilderness Area tends to be very busy on summer weekends. Early arrivals fill the parking lot quickly.

Flanked by subalpine fir (with flat, blunt-needles) and Engelmann spruce (with square, pointed needles), the Blue Lake Trail starts out level and heads west. Soon, the trail grows rockier and begins rising. **Paintbrush, asters,** and both ferny-leafed **bracted** and smooth-leafed **sickletop lousewort** line the trail to a footbridge spanning a small creek. Another bridged stream, Mitchell Creek, follows, where lush clumps of **tall chiming bells** and taller **arrowleaf senecio** are dominant.

Continuing on, the trail arrives at a sign for Indian Peaks Wilderness Area. Rockier underfoot, the trail now proceeds through the forest to Mitchell Lake at the foot of Mount Audubon. As the trail continues above the lake's south shore, meadowed swales provide the boggy soil for **little pink elephants.** Also along here, **marsh marigolds** and **globeflower** begin the subalpine blooming season.

Rude log bridges cross the inlet flowing down from Blue Lake, offering a vantage point for spotting **Parry primrose** and **tall chiming bells**. Nearby, **subalpine** or **woolly-leaved arnica** accent the landscape, as does **fireweed** later in the season.

Along a stretch of granite-covered hillside, look for the yellow-colored **dwarf goldenrod, western paintbrush,** and **alpine avens. Arctic gentian,** a white wildflower that appears striped when closed, appears about six weeks before snowfall. On a warm, late-summer day, the thought of winter can be a bit disconcerting.

Climbing an eroded section of mineral soil, the trail crests a ridge with a sprinkling of **black-headed daisies** near the top. On the next ridge, the view expands to encompass ragged peaks before the route reaches a rust-colored pond. Further on, a boardwalk crosses a wetland, and more pocket ponds lead up to an even finer view.

On the climb up, note the "flagged" spruces. Strong prevailing winds from the west nip the growth buds on the windward side, creating one-sided evergreens.

A cascade bordered by hot-pink **Parry primrose** and **little pink elephant** heads is later trimmed with lavender **subalpine daisies, blueleaf cinquefoil,** and long-blooming **bistort.**

LITTLE PINK ELEPHANTS

Pedicularis groenlandica

This lover of moist meadows is a clever mimic of its namesake. Tiny flower heads, composed of a slim twisting upper petal, form the waving trunk, and lower lip petals stand out from the "elephant's head" as flapping ears. Typically found in large "herds," it is clear little pink elephants are fond of their own kind. Other common names are: elephantella, elephant heads, and little red elephants.

Long-blooming, these plants have fern-like, reddish-purple leaves up to six inches long, and the upright stems grow up to two feet high. They provide summer food for elk.

Other *Pedicularis* species found in the region include several louseworts (*Pediculus,* meaning "louse," came from an old belief that lice could be eliminated with this plant); sickletop or parrot's beak louse-wort (*Pedicularis racemosa ssp. alba*); bracted or fernleaf lousewort (*Pedicularis bracteosa ssp. paysoniana*); and alpine or Rocky Mountain lousewort (*Pedicularis scopulorum*), a rather uncommon pink alpine and subalpine dweller.

Cairns guide the hiker as the rocky trail narrows, passing thick tufts of vegetation, including **queen's crown, alpine avens,** and **arctic gentian.** The trail levels and crosses a boardwalk covering soggy ground. Soon, a cascade flows down into a flower-bedecked pool. The trail then tackles a rough incline near treeline, passing "krummholz" patches of stunted spruce. After the next rise, the trail is at treeline. The rugged landscape now travels through pocket meadows and hanging gardens. More cairns mark the way over barren rock, where broad slabs of granite are interspersed with wildflowers, such as lavender **asters,** sour **alpine sorrel,** and **Parry lousewort.**

When the trail tops out, Blue Lake comes into view, along with its rock-bound feeder stream coursing down from Mount Toll.

With subalpine and alpine destinations so close to the Denver metro area, it is no wonder the Indian Peaks Wilderness Area is wildly popular. Blue Lake is a satisfying destination for a high-level summer hike in the Rockies.

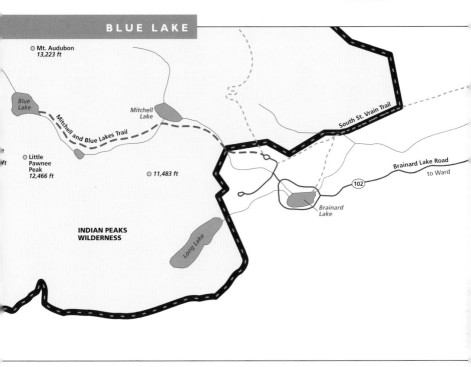

Lake Isabelle

Wildflower alert: Cascades filled with Parry primrose, queen's crown, tall chiming bells, and subalpine larkspur.

Flourishing subalpine wildflowers, including marsh marigold and Parry primrose, follow the hillside streams on the popular hike to Lake Isabelle.

Trail Rating	easy
Trail Length	4.0 miles out and back
Location	Brainard Lake/Ward
Elevation	10,500 to 10,870 feet
Bloom Season	July to August
Peak Bloom	mid-July to mid-August
Directions	From Boulder, take highway 119 up Boulder Canyon to Nederland. Turn north on highway 72, and just past Ward, turn left on County Road 102 (Brainard Lake Road). At Brainard Lake, turn right at the second trailhead road. Be prepared to pay the fee.

The trail to scenic Lake Isabelle rises less than 400 feet in its 2-mile length. Several dozen species of subalpine wildflowers add to the trek. Due to lingering snowbanks near the lake, even a late summer hike yields fresh flowers. For people who love mountain-girt lakes and crystalline cascades bright with flowers reached by congenial trail, Lake Isabelle is a great destination.

Located in the popular Indian Peaks Wilderness Area west of Boulder, Lake Isabelle can be crowded on summer weekends. The parking lot at the trailhead, which serves several trails, fills quickly with early risers. Casual arrivals may be directed to park at the side of the road (only where parking is permitted).

The trail to Lake Isabelle begins as a wide, level path through a forest of smooth-barked subalpine fir and scaly-barked Engelmann spruce. In the sheltered undergrowth, **delicate Jacob's ladder**, **Whipple** or **dusky penstemon**, **sickletop lousewort**, and **heartleaf arnica** bloom amidst **broom huckleberry**.

The broad pathway, amenable to the occasional **many-rayed goldenrod,** soon crosses South St. Vrain Creek. From here, three signs appear in succession: the first announces entrance into Indian Peaks Wilderness Area; the next says to head left on the Jean Lunning and Isabelle Glacier/Lake trail; the third points to the Lake Isabelle trail (which continues to Isabelle Glacier) along the right fork.

Once headed right, the trail parallels Long Lake for about 0.7 mile. Along the way, meadows and inlet streams provide damp habitats for early blooming **marsh marigold, globeflower,** and **Parry primrose. Queen's crown, senecios, arnicas,** and **little pink elephants** appear slightly later in the season.

PARRY PRIMROSE
Primula parryi

Also called alpine or brook primrose, Parry primrose's saturated-pink color enlivens the edges of high country streams. Too bad its aroma doesn't match; one sniff never calls for a second.

Tall (up to 18 inches) with long, thick leaves and five magenta petals centered with a bright yellow eye, Parry primrose is hard to miss. Parry primrose was named for Dr. Charles C. Parry of Iowa, an ardent 19th-century plant collector of east slope species—a number of which carry his surname.

An early-blooming cousin, alpine or fairy primrose *(Primula angustifolia)* has the sweet scent gene its cousin didn't genetically inherit. Small and bright pink, fairy primrose tucks itself into sheltered spots in the tundra's rocky landscape.

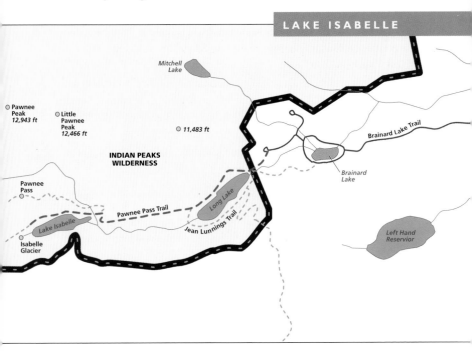

The trail begins rising near a view of Long Lake and becomes rocky as it leads away from the lake and curves up where tall **twisted stalk,** with white bells in its summer bloom, later develops orange-scarlet berries. The forest here is a good place to watch for a robin-sized bird with touches of red in its plumage: the pine grosbeak.

A sign at the western end of Long Lake directs the Isabelle Glacier/Lake hiker to the right. The trail drops slightly and crosses a plank bridge where pink **Parry primrose** blooms early. The rocky trail begins to climb and passes glades of wildflowers before arriving at an open view of the rugged peaks and cascading South St. Vrain Creek.

As the trail leaves the forest, **alpine clover** (a.k.a. **whiproot clover**) hugs the exposed mineral soil. Soon, the trail crosses a meadow on flat stones where hikers may encounter **little pink elephants,** white-headed **bistort,** and rosy-globed **Parry clover.**

Continuing west, you'll pass a colorful, boulder-studded glade full of starry **sandwort, paintbrushes, orange agoseris,** and **rayless arnica** thriving in the well-drained soil. The narrowing trail increases its incline and switchbacks over a cascade —a choice habitat for **brook saxifrage.** As the trail continues, rising toward some conifers, the route eases. A hillside on the right is bright with flowers.

Though brief, the next section of trail climbs roughly over granite and tops out by a rushing cascade where lingering snowbanks may allow **Parry**

primrose and **marsh marigold** to bloom late in the season. The view grows expansive now, encompassing some of the jagged Indian Peaks: Navajo, Apache, Shoshoni, and Pawnee.

A sharp pitch primes the hiker for the first glimpse of Lake Isabelle. **Paintbrush** in red, white, and yellow, **alpine avens, black-headed daisies, Parry clover,** and both tall **American bistort** and its short cousin **alpine bistort**—also called **serpentgrass**—celebrate high-country summer.

The trail forks just before Lake Isabelle. Continue straight ahead parallel to the lake toward Isabelle Glacier. The right fork climbs to Pawnee Pass— also rich in wildflowers. Straight ahead is a wide sheet of icy water lined with **tall chiming bells, queen's crown,** and **subalpine larkspur.** You can cross the sparkling, flower-lined cascade by stepping carefully across the rocks and avoiding those coated with slippery algae. Once past the water obstacle, the shores of Lake Isabelle offer a number of places to relax and soak up the scenery.

Lake Isabelle's lush wildflowers, clear waters, and towering peaks make for a grand subalpine destination.

Hassell Lake

Wildflower alert: A diversity of habitats and wildflowers.

A short but steep trail leads to glimmering Hassell Lake in the Henderson Mine area off Berthoud Pass.

Trail Rating	moderate to strenuous, but short
Trail Length	2.0 miles out and back
Location	Empire
Elevation	10,500 to 11,335 feet
Bloom Season	late June to August
Peak Bloom	mid-July to mid-August
Directions	From the Front Range, take I-70 west to U.S. 40. Go through the town of Empire, and continue on to the Big Bend Picnic Area/Henderson Mine turnoff. Turn left and continue on to Wood's Creek/Urad Road #146, and go left. Continue for 1.3 miles. Then take the left fork and go 2.5 miles, passing Urad Lake to the trailhead.

Guarded on the west by the Continental Divide, pretty Hassell Lake is a short but somewhat arduous hike. En route to the scenic lake, the one-mile trail gains more than 800 vertical feet; fortunately most of that gain is in the first half of the trail when the hiker is fresh and eager.

More than five dozen wildflower species appear along the way, the most interesting of which grow around the shores of the lake. The trailhead is only an hour or so from the Denver metro area. Parking is at road's end where Hassell Lake Trail begins.

Walk up the berm-blocked road at the west end of Urad Lake, and then continue down toward the lake's inlet. Along the way, in late summer look for **dwarf goldenrod, arnicas** (including **rayless arnica**), **cinquefoils,** several **senecios, alpine kittentails,** and a bit later, **fireweed.**

The track eases down past a seep to a sign on the left that states "Trail." (It should say "muddy trail.") To avoid muddy feet, take the spur path before the seep and enter a stand of conifers. There, a wide-planked footbridge crosses a creek where **brookcress** and **alpine willowherb** grow. In late summer, the inky berries of **subalpine** or **Colorado black currant** ripen here in the shade.

The trail quickly arrives in the open to traverse a dry south slope above Urad Lake. **Many-rayed goldenrod,** scarlet and yellow **paintbrush,** and **pink pussytoes** fare well on this warm exposure. Around mid-August, the deep, royal blue **Parry** or **Rocky Mountain gentian,** accompanied by **creamy** or **subalpine buckwheat** and **harebell,** command attention.

While it is apparent here that many previous hikers have taken shortcuts, stay on the main trail. Not only is short-cutting unnecessary, but it causes unsightly tracks and exacerbates erosion. Small aspens and bristlecone pines join the switchbacking trail up through a challenging section.

PARRY OR ROCKY MOUNTAIN GENTIAN
Pneumonanthe parryi

Stunning in royal blue, the generous chalices of Parry gentian are frequently found in the landscape of late summer. Among the 20 species in the Rockies, this one, named after 19th century physician and botanist Charles Parry, is up to one foot high and always catches hikers' eyes.

Around the world, 1,000 species of gentian grow from New Guinea to the Alps, and from Eurasia to the Rockies. These memorable wildflowers honor King Gentius of ancient Illyria—today's Albania—who is said to have discovered the medicinal value of gentians. Native Americans routinely ate the fleshy root of Parry gentian.

Urad Lake sparkles far below as the slope gets steeper and mats of early bloom-ing **alpine clover** (a.k.a. **whiproot clover**), creeping **kinnikinnick**, and needle-sharp common juniper fill in the eroding cutbank soil.

Along with **yellow stonecrop** and **golden aster**, height-challenged trees cling to the precipitous trail sides. After the climb, level means anything short of perpendicular. Finally the trail levels and passes through a rock-studded landscape—the strenuous part of Hassell Lake Trail is now behind.

STAR GENTIAN
Swertia perennis

Bog swertia, star swertia, and fel-wort (although this latter common name also belongs to a related but different species in the gentian family) are also applied to dusky purple star gentian.

Found in damp habitats, the five pointy-petaled, thick-stamened flowers occur in clusters like stars made of mauve-striped silk with dark purple bursts exploding from their cores. Growing up to 18 inches, this basal-leaved lover of moisture occurs from alpine down to mon-tane life zones.

The genus name recognizes a 16th-century herbalist from Holland, Emanuel Sweert. Hikers may also come across other gentians, such as moss or compass (*Chondrophylla prostrata*) and rose or little gentian (*Gentianella acuta*).

The path enters taller evergreens sheltering well-named **daffodil** or **nodding senecio, sickletop,** and **bracted louseworts.** Accompanied by the sound of flowing water, the trail continues into cooling shade where a cascade tumbles down the mountainside through the complementary colors of purple **monkshood** and golden **arrowleaf senecio.** Early in the season, **Parry primrose** and **marsh marigolds** are dominant here.

The route, momentarily cushioned by soft forest duff, relaxes along a clear stream, ideal habitat for moisture-loving flowers such as **rosy paintbrush, queen's crown, bistort,** and the homely **bog saxifrage.** Across the way, stately spires of purple **subalpine larkspur** and **monkshood** stand out.

The trail becomes faint as it nears the gently flowing outlet of Hassell Lake. This well-watered area supports **little pink elephants** and dusky-purple **star gentian.** A bit of determination finds a pair of logs crossing the outlet, after which a turn to the left brings you to the lake's edge. A pathway fol-lows the south shore to a sunny spot rife with **black-headed daisies.** This pic-nic site is worth considering before the bushwhacking begins. The flowers get

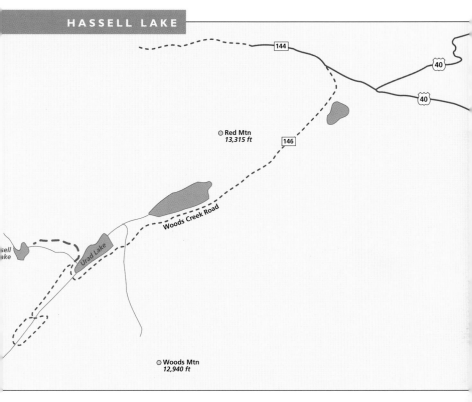

more interesting around the west end of Hassell Lake—well worth trekking through a few bogs to see.

Begin bushwhacking around the lake through waist-high willows where mauve **star gentian, rosy paintbrush, bistort,** lavender **subalpine daisies,** sturdy-stalked, round-umbeled **Gray's angelica**—a member of the celery family—and more **little pink elephants** mingle. With luck and planning, you can keep your feet dry by maintaining a high route on the hummocked side of the boggy areas.

Along the way, miniature landscapes have positioned themselves one after the other: one has a foot-high waterfall; another shows off **fringed Grass-of-Parnassus;** and one more, within the sound of rushing water, is a stony seep shaded by conifers. There, pink-cupped **pink bog laurel** is cradled in cushions of soft moss. Many common names, such as **swamp, alpine, bog kalmia,** and **mountain laurel,** claim this evergreen member of the heath family that has the ability to form running patches. While not frequently found, this bright pink subshrub is booby-trapped for bees. Spring-loaded stamens pop out of tiny pockets in the petals and catapult pollen onto unsuspecting bees when the insects' weight jars the blossom.

Tall willows mark several water-crossings. Head up high to span a small, well-concealed creeklet. Here, clumps of airy **brook saxifrage** sport white stars that later develop into deep red seedpods. Near the exuberant main inlet creek, look for late-blooming **marsh marigolds** and peppery-leafed **brookcress** while searching for a way to cross. Nimble feet are dry feet.

Cross a few easily spanned inlets before arriving on dry land. Campers have created bare spots among the trees and rocks where the trail reappears. It winds around making its way back to the outlet creek where a mile of downhill travel awaits.

Not far off Interstate 70, Hassell Lake Trail is convenient for hikers with limited time and a desire to reach a subalpine lake. Just a few acres in size, the lake and its access trail offer plenty of diverse scenery and a wide variety of wildflowers.

Silver Dollar Lake

Wildflower alert: A moveable feast
of nearly 100 wildflowers species.

The steady—and airy—climb to Silver Dollar Lake passes tall chiming bells, bistort, rosy paintbrush, nodding senecio, and many other wildflowers.

The Front Range of the Rockies contains several great hiking trails, a fair number of which are superb for wildflower viewers. Silver Dollar Lake Trail is one—and it is also short and scenic, culminating at a high-alpine lake. During peak bloom, close to 100 wildflower species grow along the 1.5-mile stretch of trail. Flower displays are usually still glorious well into August. The early-season hiker may encounter lingering snowbanks.

Silver Dollar Lake

Trail Rating	moderate
Trail Length	2.6 miles out and back
Location	Georgetown/Guanella Pass
Elevation	11,200 to 11,950 feet
Bloom Season	July to August
Peak Bloom	mid-July to early August
Directions	From the Front Range, take I-70 west to Georgetown. Follow the signs for Guanella Pass through town. Turn south on Guanella Pass Road, and drive 8.5 miles to the spur road on the right (just past Guanella Campground). Follow the rough road to the trailhead.

The mile-long spur road to the trailhead is rough, but experienced drivers with high-clearance vehicles can make it. You can also choose from plenty of parking where the spur road takes off from Guanella Pass Road; leaving a vehicle there adds two additional miles to the round-trip hike. On weekends, the trail-head parking area fills with early arrivals planning to complete the hike before summer afternoon thunderstorms strike.

The flowers begin right at the trailhead. Long-blooming **pink-headed daisies** and lilac and lavender **asters** color the area in summer. On the left side of the trail, **subalpine larkspur, monkshood,** several kinds of **senecio,** and **arnica** brighten the willow patches. Both **rayless senecio** (sleek and nodding) and **rayless arnica** (hairy and upfacing) bloom here.

The path winds up and approaches a small creek where delicate-looking **brook saxifrage** blooms next to the water. The incline increases on its way through large spruce trees to a small drainage that is home to distinctive **daffodil** or **nodding senecio.** This senecio is easy to spot and quite stately. White-flowering **subalpine valerian, bistort,** and **brookcress**—or **bittercress**—also grow here. **Parry primrose** blooms here early in the season.

The path, still shaded, rises to cross a tiny outlet flowing from a small pond. Encircling it are **tall chiming bells, arrowleaf senecio, brookcress,** and **brook saxifrage.** A closer look may reveal dusky-purple **star gentian** and pastel **queen's crown.**

Continue to a sunlit opening in the forest populated by **harebells, sandwort, stonecrop,** and perhaps hard-to-spot **alpine kittentails.** Creamy or **subalpine buckwheat,** showy in fresh ivory or aging salmon, thrives where the trail begins curving up. Where a social trail meanders, keep to the left.

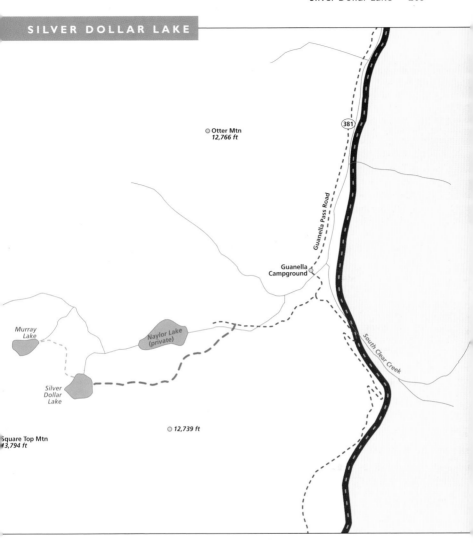

As the track climbs and the trees grow shorter, look for **dwarf goldenrod, western paintbrush,** and just up the trail, a good-sized colony of **alpine avens.** Switchbacks take the trail up past hearty **subalpine daisy** and more **daffodil senecio.** Where the trail opens it passes a slope filled with lavender, yellow, white, and salmony-red wildflowers.

The trail now eases, and clumps of yellow **rock senecio** accent the boulder-scape. Below is private Naylor Lake with a few cabins on its banks. As the trail curves with the contours of the mountainside, look for **shrubby cinquefoil, alpine sorrel,** and **Hooker thistle.** Also called **alpine, woolly,** or **frosty ball thistle,** this tall plant may appear soft, but is actually prickly from its thick stalk to its nodding head.

The trail comes up on a rocky ravine that may harbor a stubborn snow-bank. Above it, a dozen kinds of small wildflowers, such as **alplily, snowball saxifrage, greenleaf chiming bells** and perhaps **snowlover,** bloom where the ground is free of snow.

The trail narrows, passing **alpine avens, spotted** or **moss saxifrage,** and some **alpine** or **whiproot clover.** Willows cover a cut-bank where a mossy seep sports a cluster of **gold-bloom saxifrage.** Next, along a fairly level section, exposed banks are home to pink **Parry clover** and bi-colored **alpine clover.** Dusty-purple **alpine kitten-tails** and creamy **Parry lousewort** like the same lithic soil. August-blooming, white **arctic gentians** are the last wildflower of the season.

Dipping into a ravine, look for **snow buttercup** at the retreating foot of a snow-bank. From the dip, the trail climbs up a rocky slide where cushions of bright pink **moss campion,** mats of white **alpine sandwort,** rosettes of **bigroot spring beauty,** and sprigs of **vivid fairy primrose** grow in this harsh habitat. Just upslope are clumps of **blue columbine.** Downslope and to the right is a steep meadow brimming with yellow **western paintbrush, rosy paint-brush, smooth aster, blue columbine, tall chiming bells,** and **daffodil senecio.**

BIGROOT OR ALPINE SPRING BEAUTY
Claytonia megarhiza

One of the more unique wildflowers of the intimate landscape above treeline is the succulent-leaved, waxy-white flowered alpine (a.k.a. bigroot) spring beauty. Fond of tucking its substantial rosette of dark leaves close to boulders, this plant's common name, bigroot, is appropriate—if not obvious. Its impressive taproot may penetrate gravelly soil for as much as eight feet below the surface. When the unstable slope it grows in moves downhill, the taproot simply elongates to accommodate the change.

The starry, pink-veined blossoms begin as red-dish buds. The plant's thick leaves are edible, as are many species in the purslane family. A purple-red dye can be made by boiling bigroot.

The genus name, *Claytonia,* honors John Clayton, an American botanist who lived from 1686 to 1773. The species name, *megarhiza,* meaning "big root," accounts for one of its common names.

Prolific in the foothills and montane zones, pink-petaled spring beauty (*Claytonia rosea*) is often the earliest wildflower to bloom. Water spring beauty (*Crunocallis chamissoi*) is not as pervasive as its pink-petaled cousin.

As the trail grows rocky, pass **little pink elephants**, yellow **whiplash saxifrage**, and the infrequent **alpine lousewort**, its arced flowers a rich pink. Next, on the right, **tall chiming bells** blooming in both blue and soft violet-pink accent a meadow full of pink, yellow, and white **paintbrush**. Uphill on the left is a cascade of **columbine** interspersed with pink **queen's crown**.

Continuing on, an inspiring view widens to a sweeping panorama of the Continental Divide. Late-blooming **marsh marigolds** and **Parry primrose** arrive on the scene where snowfields dwindle under the summer sun. The path levels for a stretch before it resumes its rocky climb. Knee-high spruce "krummholz" line the trail, along with creeping mats of early-blooming **mountain dryad.** In late summer, its creamy flowers become wispy plumes; the scalloped dark-green leaves turn burgundy in autumn. Ptarmigan love to feast on it in any season.

The trail becomes more path-like as it levels out among thick turf grasses where the small blue **moss gentian** may be found. Cloud cover, or even a hand suspended over this diminutive gentian, causes the flower to close.

The route rises again before dropping to Silver Dollar Lake pressed against the flank of 13,794-foot Square Top Mountain. Hikers may choose to continue on up to Murray Lake where they will find swaths of rosy **paintbrush** and **alpine lousewort.**

So close to the Front Range, yet far from its noise and bustle, Silver Dollar Lake is a must for midsummer wildflowering.

Boreas Pass East

Wildflower alert: Rare and fragrant globe gilia
is a "find" here.

*Boulders and
flowers cover
the expanses of
tundra along the
Boreas Pass East
hike east of
Breckenridge.*

The ancient Greeks named the god of the north wind Boreas. Colorado's Boreas
Pass, crossing the Continental Divide between South Park and Breckenridge,
withstands blizzards capable of piling up to 10 feet of snow. But in summer,
Boreas Pass offers a fine hike up the east side of the divide where wildflowers
line the trail and the view extends forever. Even late in the season, you can
find as many as seven dozen different species. The route up from Como to the

Trail Rating	moderate
Trail Length	1.5 miles out and back
Location	Como/Breckenridge
Elevation	11,480 to 12,029 feet
Bloom Season	early July to August
Peak Bloom	mid-July to mid-August (early- to mid-July for buns and cushions)
Directions	From southwest Denver, take U.S. 285 to South Park and the turnoff to Como. Turn right on the Boreas Pass Road. Park on the south side of the pass at the trailhead.

pass is scenic and gentle—and generous with wildflowers. In August, a plentiful lavender, yellow, and white floral procession colors the aspen-lined road.

The pass is popular with visitors on weekends, many taking a look at the historic railroad house whose sturdy walls continue to stand. Parking is available on both sides of the road; the trailhead is on the south side.

Near the trailhead, willows shade moisture-loving **little pink elephants**. Moving away from the parking lot and heading south, the trail follows the flat railbed. **Bistort**, **cinquefoils** of several kinds, and a patch of **littleflower penstemon** in purplish-blue add dabs of color. **Parry lousewort** and **delicate Jacob's ladder**, midsummer bloomers, pop up among the willows along the wide track's edges. **Sibbaldia**, the color of salmon in the fall, grows in the center of the rising road.

Ahead, conifers spike the wide slopes. Just below a diversion berm that sends the trail southwest, loose mats of **Nuttall's sandwort**, sprinkled with pink seedling stars, skims the disturbed road margins. In the same unsettled soil, **horned dandelion** and its cousin **orange agoseris** (not as burnt-orange or large-headed as it is in the foothills) poke up here and there. Short, but brilliant **leafy aster**, a yellow-centered, violet daisy-like flower also grows along here.

The trail climbs up another berm with clumps of **aspen sunflowers**, **subalpine larkspur**, **Whipple** or **dusky penstemon**, **pink-headed daisies**, and golden **woolly arnica**.

Where the trail turns southeast, the triple summits of Bald Mountain—all exceeding 13,600 feet—command the view to the northwest (of the 15 mountains named Bald in Colorado, this is the highest). Supplying the photogenic foreground are **pink-headed daisies, rosy** and **western paintbrushes, tall chiming bells,** and **subalpine larkspur.**

A steeper pitch passes a slanting meadow of purple and gold. On the sides are **one-headed daisies, angelica,** and both **rayless senecio** and **rayless arnica.** Cadres of pale yellow **western paintbrush** spatter the hillside. The evergreens retain a good size right up to treeline. On the left, a few frame a view of South Park, while tall, late-blooming **daffodil senecio** leans over a patch of rosy **Parry's clover.**

Willows follow Boreas Pass' sweeping expanse of meadowed slopes up the old jeep road, turning west to expose the boulders that mark the trail's end. Look for blue-purple **subalpine larkspur,** golden **senecio,** and soft-pink **fleabane daisies** here at the top of the hike.

NARCISSUS ANEMONE

Anemonastrum narcissiflorum ssp. zepyhrum

Of all the anemones in the region, narcissus anemone is larger-flowered—with several to a stalk—and it is the showiest. Resembling the old-fashioned poeticus narcissus with its distinctive eye, creamy-cupped sepals surround a number of showy pistils and curved stamens. Each pistil develops into a flattish black seed, called an "achene" in the buttercup family. Striking narcissus anemone favors the upper subalpine zone, often above treeline.

The anemone of legend is said to have sprung from tears shed by a grieving Venus for her lost Adonis. Close to 100 anemone species have been found worldwide. In England the flower has some very colorful names, such as granny's nightcap, ladies shimmy, and shame-faced maiden. Here, it's sometimes called windflower, which explains its subspecies *(ssp.)* name: *zephyrum.*

Other windflowers commonly found in the region include red globe anemone *(Anemone multifida ssp. globosa),* meadow anemone *(Anemonidium canadense),* and candle anemone or thimbleweed *(Anemone cylindrica).*

On the northeast side of the Continental Divide, towering over the pass is 13,082-foot Boreas Mountain. Gracing the long view east down Tarryall Creek—where gold was found in 1859 and a town of the same name was founded—is South Park. Drifts of **scarlet paintbrush** color the foreground of this view. **Alpine milkvetch,** with its lavender pea-type flowers, line the trail cutbanks. Among the thick grasses and sedges, an occasional **arctic gentian** blooms, announcing that snow is six weeks away.

In the stunted willows, look for red **kings crown, little pink elephants,** and lovely **narcissus-flowered anemone,** a creamy, multi-flowered anemone of the high country.

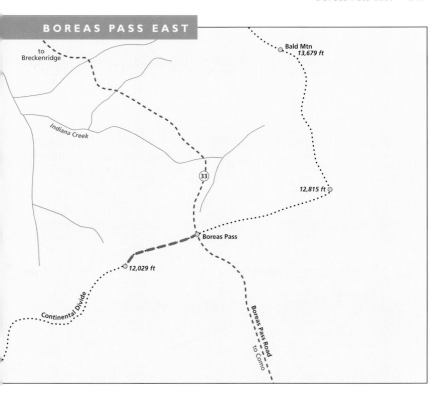

In the open meadows above treeline are **harebell** and **bistort,** and the flower with the largest bloom above treeline: **old-man-of-the-mountains.** Among the rocks in this area, the rare **globe gilia** blooms in midsummer. Its pale lavender-blue flowers have a wonderful fragrance.

The path curves back toward the boulders at 12,029 feet, which is the high point of the trail. Around the heaped limestone, lavender **pinnate-leaved daisy, blue columbine,** and long-blooming **sandwort** add to the floristic count. Bright pink **moss campion** and **alpine sandwort** still bloom at the end of the flowering season in a variety of mats, buns, and cushions. Perfected for the severe environment they inhabit, these tundra flowers make up the floral tapestry along the Continental Divide.

The 360-degree view from the top of Boreas Pass is stunning. You'll never forget the panorama ringed by peaks. The wildflowers only enhance the view. Two visits (early July, if road conditions allow, and another later in midsummer) would broaden your scope of Boreas Pass wildflowers at their best.

Wildflower Hike
47

Mount Goliath/ M. Walter Pesman Alpine Garden Loop

Wildflower alert: Alpine rock gardens displaying dozens of colorful tundra and subalpine species.

Hikers pass scarlet paintbrush and other alpine wildflowers as they climb the Mount Goliath/Pesman Trail, east of the Mount Evans Road.

Trail Rating	moderate
Trail Length	3.0 miles out and back with keyhole loop
Location	Mount Evans/Idaho Springs
Elevation	11,540 to 12,150 feet
Bloom Season	late June to mid-August
Peak Bloom	early to late July
Directions	From the Front Range, take I-70 west to highway 103 (exit 240). Go south 14 miles to Echo Lake. Then turn right on highway 5 (Mount Evans Road). Go 2.9 miles to the parking lot on the left at the lower trailhead.

En route along the highest paved road in North America, the Mount Evans Road, is a great wildflower hike that encompasses both tundra and forest. In this case, much of the forest is an incredible collection of picturesque, ancient bristlecone pine trees interspersed with colorful flowers.

Mount Goliath is a sub-peak of 14,280-foot Mount Evans. The Mount Goliath Natural Area, in which the M. Walter Pesman Trail travels, is on a south-facing slope. If you use two vehicles, this trail can be a one-way downhill trek of 1.5 miles. It is treated here as a climb from the lower parking area through conifers, into the bristlecone area, and then more steeply up across alpine terrain until it joins the 0.5-mile Alpine Garden Loop trail.

Even the drive to the lower trailhead from the Echo Lake turnoff is trimmed with flowers, dominated by paintbrushes and fireweed. Farther up, rock senecio, sky pilot, and old-man-of-the-mountains decorate the roadsides.

At 12,150 feet—the elevation of the upper end of the trail—you'll breathe about one-third less oxygen, but you'll absorb about one-third more solar radiation than at sea level.

From the large, paved parking area at the lower end of the Mount Goliath Natural Area, the trail immediately enters a world of high-altitude wildflowers. A sign stating "Trail" takes the route up where, even late in the season, **dwarf goldenrod, sandwort,** and **pinnate-leaf daisy** bloom among rough-surfaced rocks. Draping itself over the granite, **whiproot** or **alpine clover** offers contrasting textures.

The decomposed granite trail brushes through stunted willows and **shrubby cinquefoil** sheltering **Parry lousewort, king's crown, tall chiming bells,** and cool yellow **northern** or **western paintbrush.** Rising, the trail meets **redstem cinquefoil** and **scarlet paintbrush,** along with **creamy** or **subalpine buckwheat.** The **Whipple penstemon** here tends more toward white than its usual dusky wine.

Contorted bristlecone pines are adorned with **delicate Jacob's ladder** at their bases. Violet-hued **leafy aster** chooses to inhabit sunny spots along the leveling trail. More creeping mats of **whiproot clover** define the trail margins as the path heads up over rocks and roots. Showy

DWARF OR DEER CLOVER
Trifolium nanum

Unlike most other high-altitude clovers, dwarf (*nanum*, meaning dwarf) clover blossoms are sparingly produced and huddle tightly on a dark-leaved mat. The slim, heart-shaped pink flowers resemble a miniaturized doe's hoofprint. Only a few blooms and leaves are produced each season. In harsh tundra habitat, a handspan-wide mat may be a half-century old.

M. Walter Pesman Alpine Trail
and Trailhead Parking

Mt. Goliath
12,216 ft

Mt. Goliath Natural
Area and Lower
Trailhead Parking

Mt. Evans Road

5

Echo
Lake

103

to Idaho Springs

to Bergen Park

bracts of **scarlet paintbrush,** mounds of **dwarf golden aster,** and clumps of **bistort** grow near curves of alpine driftwood.

Where the trail switchbacks up, spikes of **purple fringe** thrive in the disturbed trailside soil. A member of the waterleaf family, **purple fringe** or **silky phacelia** earns recognition for its protruding gold stamens and deeply cut gray-green leaves.

Sentinel snags filter the view down a meadowed valley to the east and the broad tundra sloping up toward Mount Evans to the south. One such trunk, sandblasted smooth, stands next to the trail and rubs its millennium-old shoulder with the hiker's.

Next along the way, ivory **mountain death camas** and pink **Geyer onion** lead to a climb up and over granite rock. On the way up, look for mats of **alpine sandwort** as the sculpted pines thin. The granite—some pale salmon now—creates miniature rock gardens occupied by gray-leaved mounds of **dwarf sulphurflower, paintbrush, asters,** and **harebells.** Note the declining height of the harebells compared to those nearer the base of the trail: the lavender bells remain disproportionately large, though the stem may be just inches tall.

Dominated by great chunks of granite on the skyline to the north and sweeping alpine slopes to the south, the trail climbs steeply, using raw rocks as steps. Pause near a scattering of young pines and **frosty ball** or **alpine thistle** to view a series of Front Range mountains.

Tall valerian, quite delicate up here, and chalky deep-blue **greenleaf chiming bells** accompany the trail as its ascent eases. **Shrubby cinquefoil** grows more prostrate.

Sedges, grasses, and long-blooming **alpine avens**—its yellow flowers lifted above ferny leaves—fill in the landscape as Pesman Trail reaches the Alpine Garden Loop. Turn right and enter a sheltered tundra zone. Wildflowers, such as **fireweed** and **harebell**, flourish in the lee of granite outcrops. The granular path winds up to a gap where a fine view of Mount Evans, Mount Bierstadt, and Grays and Torreys Peaks on the Continental Divide sweep the horizon.

Here, in this intimate rock garden where tumbled boulders dictate the path's curvature, **kings crown, alpine** or **bigroot spring beauty,** and **greenleaf chiming bells** flourish. Long-blooming **bistort** and masses of **alpine avens**—a favorite of pikas and marmots—flank the descending trail. You might spot brown-coated bighorn sheep from this vantage point. White mountain goats are also residents of Mount Evans.

As you circumnavigate the outcrop area, you'll spot **sulphur paintbrush, old-man-of-the-mountains, senecio, pygmy tonestus,** and **dwarf sulphurflower.** A week in early July produces a cornucopia of color in **paintbrush, alplily, blue columbine, sky pilot,** and vivid but covert **fairy primrose. Alpine pussytoes'** ground-hugging bluish foliage and hummocky hairgrass complement a trio of high-country clovers: rosy-headed **Parry clover,** bi-colored **whiproot clover,** and pink **dwarf clover.** As you approach the upper parking area, the trail winds its way to an information sign.

While easing back down the segment of the Alpine Garden Loop and Mount Goliath/Pesman Trail, you'll notice how the mineral soil

PARRY OR ROSE CLOVER
Trifolium parryi

Found in the subalpine as well as the alpine zones, Parry clover's rosy-pink heads are held fairly high above pointed three-part leaves (*tres,* meaning "three," and *folium,* meaning "leaves"). To further identify it, look for papery white bracts that cup the fragrant rounded heads.

Dr. Charles C. Parry of Iowa, an ardent 19th-century plant collector, surveyed east slope species—a number of which carry his name.

is rife with mats and buns of early-blooming white **alpine phlox**, blue **alpine forget-me-not**, and pink **moss campion**, among others. The trail forks right to retrace the steps back to the lower parking area.

Less than 40 miles from Denver, the Mount Goliath Natural Area of Mount Evans provides a wonderful window into both tundra and treeline realms. A hike here can be an interesting uphill exercise or, with two vehicles, a rugged descent. Either way, the trail is memorable.

ALPINE OR WHIPROOT CLOVER
Trifolium dasyphyllum

Bi-colored, in both flowers (white and reddish) and bracts (white and green), alpine clover spreads its mat-like clumps over mineral soils in tundra and subalpine areas. While not wide, the pointed leaves sport hairs on the undersides and are fairly substantial (*dasy,* meaning "thick, rough," and *phyllum,* meaning "leaves").

King Lake Trail

Wildflower alert: Early tundra flowers and, within six weeks of autumn snowfall, a bounty of arctic gentians.

King Lake's flower-filled bowl comes alive in midsummer. The lake is less than one mile off the Rollins Pass Road.

easy to moderate	*Trail Rating*
1.8 miles out and back	*Trail Length*
Rollins-Corona Pass/Winter Park	*Location*
11,200 to 11,666 feet	*Elevation*
July to August	*Bloom Season*
late July to August (tundra bloom in July)	*Peak Bloom*
From the Front Range, take I-70 west to highway 40. Go north over Berthoud Pass. Just past the Winter Park Ski Area, turn right on Rollins Pass Road (halfway between mileposts 231 and 232). The trailhead is 15 miles up a good dirt road at a sign for The Moffat Road Hill Route.	*Directions*

The sweeping landscape on the way to King Lake and its satellite lake, calls for separate spring and summer visits to explore two distinct plant communities. Corona Pass, called Rollins Pass on the east side, is an expansive and level stretch on the Continental Divide. Tundra wildflowers first appear in late spring, while later in the summer, the flower-lined bowl sloping down to King Lake is in full bloom. An even more flowery smaller lake to the east is also in full bloom at this time of year. Snow lingers in these protected bowls so the bloom season lasts far into summer. In late summer, an impressive number of arctic gentian fill the basin and signal that snow is not far off.

Parking is generous at the Corona Pass trailhead, where a kiosk contains information on a number of hikes radiating from the pass. Even the 15-mile drive to the trailhead is interesting, featuring wonderful panoramas, views of alpine lakes, and remnants of local railroad history. Corona-Rollins Pass was once home to one of the world's most dangerous lengths of rail, the Moffat Road Hill Route.

QUEEN'S CROWN
Clementsia rhodantha

A rounded head of warm-pink pointed florets and thick succulent leaves are features that help identify queen's crown. Another clue is its preference for wet places where its shallow roots can easily draw water. A less obvious hint is the midrib under the leaves.

The plant's roots are said to be rose-scented, hence the alternate name, roseroot. The leaves turn almost neon red in the fall. Native Americans ate the young leaves raw or boiled.

The stonecrop family, of which queen's crown is a member, also includes burnt-red king's crown (*Rhodiola integrifolia*) and yellow stonecrop (*Amerosedum lanceolatum*).

Sitting above treeline along a portion of the Continental Divide Trail at 11,666 feet, Corona Pass is a great place to wander among myriad early-blooming alpine mats, buns, and cushions. Later in the season, **western paintbrush, bistort, Parry clover,** and long-blooming **alpine avens, pinnate-leaved daisy, and alpine sandwort** extend north toward the boundary of the Indian Peaks Wilderness Area. Grazing on the flora, mountain goats are at home on the exposed granite ridge.

Late summer brings out lots of small **rose gentian,** deeper in color here than is common. The vegetation thickens as the trail eases down past still pools where you can find **alpine avens** and pink **queen's crown**—whose foliage turns neon red in the fall.

King Lake Trail takes off to the right at the junction with the High Lonesome Trail. Steep snowbanks on the west end of the lake's deeply

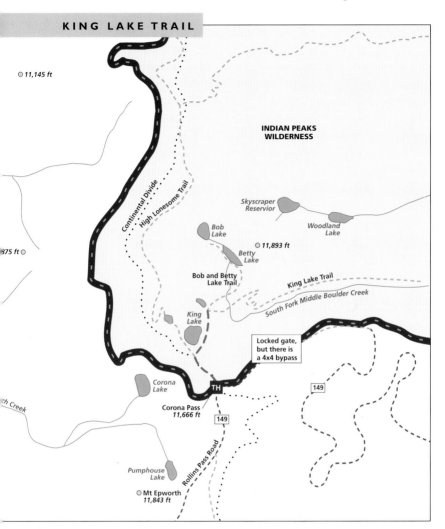

KING LAKE TRAIL

○ 11,145 ft

INDIAN PEAKS
WILDERNESS

*Skyscraper
Reservoir*

*Woodland
Lake*

*Bob
Lake*

○ 11,893 ft

*Betty
Lake*

Continental Divide

High Lonesome Trail

*Bob and Betty
Lake Trail*

King Lake Trail

South Fork Middle Boulder Creek

875 ft ○

*King
Lake*

Locked gate,
but there is
a 4x4 bypass

*Corona
Lake*

TH

149

ch Creek

*Corona Pass
11,666 ft*

149

Rollins Pass Road

*Pumphouse
Lake*

○ Mt Epworth
11,843 ft

---

cut banks are covered with reddish-pink algae called "watermelon snow." It is said to smell like the ripe melon, but ingesting it can be disastrous. The trail descends and passes yellow **paintbrush**, both **western** and **sulphur**, and both white **black-headed daisy** and lavender **one-headed daisy**. Where the snow has recently receded, look for **snow buttercup.**

Deep drifts make for condensed bloom times at the emerald lake and its rugged cliffs, so a single trip to the lake likely includes sightings of pink **moss campion** (a spring bloomer); creamy **mountain dryad,** (another spring bloomer that is a ground-hugging subshrub in the rose family); **dwarf golden aster** (a summer bloomer) and **arctic gentians** (a late-summer bloomer).

At the base of a picturesque lichened outcrop, look for the blue **delicate Jacob's ladder** and **greenleaf chiming bells** mingling with the yellow **alpine** avens and buttery **paintbrush.** Granite crevices shelter thick rosettes of **bigroot spring beauty** and **moss campion.**

The descending track becomes more rocky and steep before leveling by stunted spruce and willow where **whiproot clover, alpine sandwort, spotted saxifrage, bracted alumroot,** and bright **moss campion** grow among the rocks. Drop toward a ridge saddle to view a cascade rushing into the drainage of the South Fork of Middle Boulder Creek.

The trail snakes down, arriving at an unmarked point where it is easiest to push through low willows to the inviting shore of King Lake. Along its margins, patches of eye-catching **rosy paintbrush** and lavender **subalpine daisies** grow are among the grasses. **Queen's crown** and **star gentian** thrive in moist depressions. The lakeshore meadow is also home to cold-soil plants, **marsh marigold,** and **little pink elephants.**

Returning to the trail, a flowery passage reveals a well-watered glade of **tall chiming bells, blue columbine, senecios, arnicas,** and **angelica.** Set off in a northeast direction to King's satellite lake, passing a braided cascade lined with clumps of **Parry primrose** and **marsh marigold.** Even more flowers flourish alongside King Lake's cascading outlet, which feeds into a glistening teardrop-shaped lake. Great chunks of granite are cushioned in grassy hummocks beside the tumbling waters flowing below the small lake.

Before climbing back out of the King Lake basin, look around the lower lake and its environs for **pink bog laurel, mountain blue violets,** and **white paintbrush.**

King Lake makes a satisfying hike, both above and at treeline. Add the adjacent satellite lake and its flowery glades, and you could wile away a whole day in this colorful alpine basin.

Square Top Lakes

Wildflower alert: Fields of scarlet paintbrush.

The trail to Square Top Lakes off Guanella Pass provides one of the closest tundra-viewing excursions to metro-Denver.

moderate	**Trail Rating**
3.0 miles out and back (to lower lake)	**Trail Length**
Guanella Pass/Georgetown	**Location**
11,700 to 12,050 feet	**Elevation**
late June to August	**Bloom Season**
late-July	**Peak Bloom**
From the Front Range, take I-70 west to Georgetown. Drive into town and follow the signs to Guanella Pass. Follow the pass road to the trailhead on the west side of the pass.	**Directions**

Guanella Pass is famous for its high-alpine scenery. But also at the pass, on the opposite side of the road from the Mount Bierstadt trailhead, lies the trailhead for scenic Square Top Lakes. The trail shares parking with several other routes, including the popular fourteener, Mount Bierstadt (Geneva Mountain Trailhead). An early start ensures not only convenient parking, but a hike that can be completed before summer afternoon thunderstorms strike.

Square Top Lakes Trail (sometimes called South Park Trail) starts on a level trail through tundra flowers and drops into a rich boggy area prior to rising gently across a floristic south-facing slope. It then turns west to reach the lower of the two Square Top Lakes. More than six dozen wildflower species enliven this 1.5-mile alpine hike.

Setting out across alpine tundra, hike through **alplilies, alpine avens, sky pilot,** and electric blue **alpine forget-me-nots** blooming early in the season. The rutted trail soon descends and crosses a boggy area rife with **little pink elephants.** A close look at this unique plant shows how well it is named and how well it likes its own company. The curved heads of pink **queen's crown** are made up of individual florets. **Rose crown** is another common name stemming from the plant's root, which is said to smell likes roses. This stonecrop's foliage turns vibrant red with the onset of autumn. Here and there, alongside the willow flanking the path, are colorful clumps of yellow **western** and **rosy paintbrush.**

The path ascends gently along a south-facing slope where legions of **subalpine valerian** bloom early in the season. With protruding stamens resembling pins in a cushion, the curved clusters of blushed white-to-pink flowers contrast with the nondescript bloom of a less vibrant nearby cousin, **tall** or **edible valerian.** In ancient times, valerians were considered strong medicine, espe-

ALPINE BLADDER CAMPION

Gastrolychnis apetala

The alpine bladder campion, a high-altitude native, is also known by a descriptively clever name, alpine lanterns. The balloon-like, dark-striped calyxes of this rather rare alpine resident do indeed resemble Japanese lanterns. Or, visualize the flower using the Greek word *gastridos,* meaning "pot-bellied."

The dusty-pink, cleft-petaled blossoms are diminished by its showier, early-blooming cousin moss campion (*Silene acaulis ssp. subacaulescens*). Both are members of the pink family famed for such garden favorites as carnations and baby's breath.

SQUARE TOP LAKES

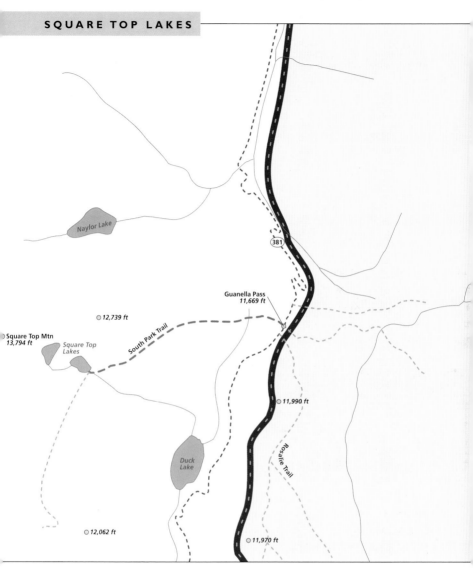

Naylor Lake

381

Guanella Pass
11,669 ft

○ *12,739 ft*

○ **Square Top Mtn**
13,794 ft

*Square Top
Lakes*

South Park Trail

○ *11,990 ft*

*Duck
Lake*

Royalle Trail

○ *12,062 ft*

○ *11,970 ft*

cially as nerve tonics, and even as an antidote for poison. In late summer, this slope is studded with **sandwort**, its clumps of stiff grasslike leaves dotted with white star-shaped flowers (take a look at the stamens with a hand lens). Adding more white stars to the tundra are **alpine mouse-ear** and mat-forming **alpine sandwort**—also called **sandywinks.**

Continuing up the double-tracked trail (remnants of an old road once used to stock Square Top Lakes with trout), pass along a slope of vibrant **scarlet paintbrush.** In the same vicinity, **old-man-of-the-mountains,** with its over-sized yellow heads, is on the wane late in the season. Earlier, this conspicuous composite commands attention; its sunflower heads face east, turning their fuzzy backs to the prevailing winds. A smattering of **sky pilot** lights up the surrounding landscape with bluish-purple trumpets and neon orange anthers. Its other common name, **skunkweed**, describes the odor the fern-like leaves emit when rubbed. Pure white **sky pilot** mutants are sometimes present.

Farther on, the track levels briefly by a small pond on the right. Here, watch for small, alpine-dwelling pika and the white-crowned sparrow recognized for its black-and-white-striped cap. The pika is a member of a ancient order that includes rabbits and hares.

The track wanders up past the white heads of **American bistort**, which grow from the upper foothills to the alpine zones. **Bistort** is relished by ptarmigan, believed to be more plentiful on Guanella Pass than elsewhere in the region.

Ahead, look for the burnt-red heads of **king's crown** in a steep ravine filled with sharp-edged boulders. Clumps of **blue columbine**, Colorado's state flower, also grow among the rugged rocks. Continuing on, the path becomes boggy and more **little pink elephants**, white **marsh marigolds**, and the uncommon **alpine lousewort**—which is related to little pink elephants—grow in the cold, spongy ground. Look around for dusky-purple **star gentian**—or **bog swertia**.

Back on open rocky ground, look for the yellow up-facing blooms of **woolly actinella**. At a cascading falls on the left is the eye-catching hot-pink **Parry primrose**. Check next to the trail for uncommon **alpine bladder campion**—also called **alpine lanterns**—its soft-pink petals surrounding the plump, striped calyxes. Close by, pink-family cousin **moss campion's** tight buns are covered with bright pink flowers early in the season.

The track is rougher now, but the first lake is just ahead. In its willow-lined bowl, Lower Square Top Lake sits at 12,050 feet. In the background, tipped on edge, is 13,794-foot Square Top Mountain. Among the dense grasses and short willows near the water grow more **star gentian, queen's crown,** and, late in the season, **arctic gentian**, a harbinger that winter is approaching. Marmots romp in the rocks above the lake.

A brewing afternoon thunderstorm may precipitate a quick return to the trailhead. Clear skies may allow for the 250-vertical-foot climb to Upper Square Top Lake. On the return trip, the grandeur of Mount Evans—also a fourteener—and its connecting "sawtooth" ridge to Mount Bierstadt, is an inspiring sight.

One of the closest trailheads to metro-Denver that directly accesses the tundra, South Park Trail to Square Top Lakes is floristically endowed and offers sensational scenery. You can enjoy a fine, scenic-loop drive by continuing south on Guanella Pass Road as it leads down to a flat, lush valley before dropping once again to meet highway 285 and the return route to the Front Range.

Tundra World/ Toll Memorial

Wildflower alert: Blooming tundra on every side.

A short, one-mile hike out and back—but at 12,000 feet in elevation—the Tundra World/Toll Memorial Trail offers sweeping vistas.

easy	*Trail Rating*
1.0 mile out and back	*Trail Length*
Rock Cut/Rocky Mountain National Park	*Location*
12,110 to 12,310 feet	*Elevation*
late June to July	*Bloom Season*
typically early to mid-July	*Peak Bloom*
From Estes Park, take U.S. 34 west into Rocky Mountain National Park (becoming Trail Ridge Road) to the Rock Cut/Tundra World parking lot, approximately 6 miles east of the Alpine Visitor Center. Be prepared to pay the fee or present your park pass.	*Directions*

Rocky Mountain National Park is such a treasured resource that it has been designated an International Biosphere Reserve. The park is visited by more than 3 million people every year. Famed Trail Ridge Road, the highest continuous highway in the nation, reaches heights of 12,183 feet.

ALPINE FORGET-ME-NOT
Eritrichum aretioides

One of the early-blooming tundra wildflowers is also one of the most striking in color. The electric blue alpine forget-me-not is a sweetly scented member of the borage family (which includes chiming bells and miner's candle). It can sometimes produce pure white flowers instead of the typical blue. The five-lobed flowers sport a yellow eye and grow close to the hairy silverish foliage of the thick tiny leaves which form tight mats. Its growth habit helps alpine forget-me-not to survive frigid temperatures and desiccating winds in its favored gravelly ridge-top terrain.

To see these startlingly blue tundra forget-me-nots at their best means a late June or early July hike to their chilly alpine habitats.

The genus name *Eritrichum* is descriptive of forget-me-not foliage and comes from the Greek *erion,* meaning "wool," and *trichos,* meaning "hair."

Six miles east of the Alpine Visitor Center is the site of the Tundra World Trail—a window into an ecosystem equivalent to going to the Arctic Circle. Hiking at this altitude is not for everyone. But for those who choose to trek here, a unique half-mile paved walk starts from the parking lot at Rock Cut. Without harming the fragile, slow-to-recover tundra, you can admire several dozen miniature wildflowers along the short Tundra World Trail. Since the growing season high above treeline here is short, a mid-July visit is your best bet.

Although a lengthy chunk of tundra was carved out to accommodate several vehicles, Rock Cut's popularity sometimes fills all the parking slots.

In just one-half mile, the blacktop trail provides a look at several dozen high-altitude flowers ready to set seed in a brief six- to eight-week time frame. A buck-and-rail fence protects the fragile tundra next to the parking spaces. Along its length, on the adjacent sidewalk's ragged edge, look for **bigroot spring beauty, alpine sorrel,** and **alpine paintbrush.**

Find the opening in the ranch-style fence. Here, the tundra is sheltered enough to produce ideal examples of yellow **alpine avens** (whose foliage turns wine-red in the fall), the intense

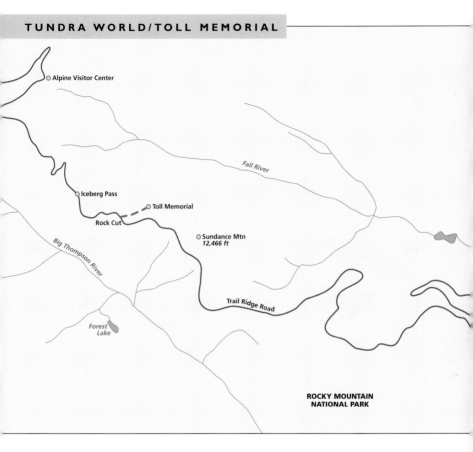

cobalt blue **greenleaf chiming bells,** the warm blue **sky pilot,** and the pale yellow **western paintbrush.** Yellows and blues, touched with the pink of **clovers** and the white of the delicate **alplily,** paint the summer tundra in this rock garden.

You might find all three kinds of high-altitude clovers here. Tight mats of **dwarf clover,** also called **deer clover,** hug the gravelly earth (its sparingly produced flowers resemble the hoofprints of a doe). Pointed leaves arc up to provide a cozy bed for the reddish-tinged white flowers. Bi-colored pink and white **alpine** or **whiproot clover's** slim leaves sport hairs on their undersides; the sepals are also hairy. Growing either in spreading mats or rounded clumps, this clover likes the stony soil of the high country. While all clovers are fragrant, the big, round, rosy heads of **Parry clover** are the sweetest-smelling among the tundra clovers, and they are certainly the bravest in height.

The tallest bloomer in sight along the trail, **American bistort** waves white bottlebrush heads in this windy landscape where gusts can reach 100 miles per hour. The myriad flowers making up the inflorescence deserve a closer look.

The ptarmigan, a tundra dwelling grouse that is snow-white in winter and mottled gray and brown in summer, is partial to bistort.

With Mummy Range in the background, an interpretive sign about the alpine tundra excerpts Ann Zwinger's *Land Above the Trees*, "...a land of contrasts and incredible intensity...the sky is the size of forever and the flowers the size of a millisecond."

The largest flower on the alpine tundra is **old-man-of-the-mountains,** a sunflower family member that faces each day's rising sun. It spends years gathering energy to present its showy gold head once before dying.

Moss campion, with bright pink blossoms, is the most noticeable among buns and cushions. A pioneer plant designed to anchor the granular tundra soil, it may spend a decade mounding up tight foliage before blooming. Mat-forming **alpine sandwort** adds a touch of white in the vicinity. Another ground hugger, **alpine phlox,** presents fragrant flat flowers ranging from pale lavender-blue to white. You'll also notice **alpine wallflower's** clear yellow blossoms.

Another interpretive sign overlooking the Continental Divide and glacier-carved Forest Canyon mentions, "...rivers of ice were a thousand feet thick..." (though the ice rivers didn't come up this high). Soon after, watch for yellow-eyed, pink **alpine** or **fairy primrose** tucked in the rocks. This is another delicately perfumed tundra plant aiming to entice pollinators. The electric blue **alpine forget-me-not** blooms nearby on fuzzy gray-green mats.

Decorating the almost barren soil coming up on the right, blue **alpine forget-me-not** coexist with white **alplily** and **fernleaf candytuft.** A bit farther, **dwarf** and **Parry clovers** grow among the frost-heaved rocks. Lichens glued to these rocks may live to be thousands of years old; they are among the first to occupy areas exposed by retreating glaciers and have been assigned a taxonomic kingdom of their own.

Take a moment to complete a 360-degree sweeping look at the stunning scenery, including the jagged heights of the Keyboard of the Winds, Longs Peak's 14,255-foot summit, and the glacier-gouged depths of Forest Canyon. The pavement levels as mushroom-shaped outcroppings—white quartzite capped by resistant gray schist—rise against the prevailing winds. Here, spot the fetching pink **fairy primrose** in the rock-studded grasses.

A bit of a scramble up dark rock attains the last few feet of elevation to the Toll Memorial. A bronze plaque commemorates Roger W. Toll, the man who was superintendent of Rocky Mountain National Park from 1921 to 1928. At the top is a bronze disk listing the landscape features of the panoramic view. From here, canyon after canyon and range after range appear from the rooftop of the tundra world.

Tundra World specializes in the miniature flowers of the windswept, high-altitude landscape, where each plant is specially adapted to its harsh environment.

Lovely stands of midsummer-blooming fireweed line the trails along many Colorado hikes. Here, it is found along the Gem Lake Trail in Rocky Mountain National Park.

Index

Pamela Dearborn Irwin and David Harlan Irwin

Pamela has been a volunteer naturalist at Roxborough State Park southwest of Denver since the early 1980s, and was introduced to wildflower identification as a volunteer at the Denver Botanic Alpine Gardens. She has participated in many wildflower identification hikes from the plains to the tundra with such experts as Andrew Pierce, formerly senior horticulture advisor at the Denver Botanic Gardens and now executive director of the Hudson Gardens.

Pamela is a member of the Rocky Mountain Nature Association, the Rocky Mountain Chapter of the American Rock Garden Society, the Windflowers Garden Club, the Colorado Mountain Club, and the Audubon Society.

David purchased his first 35mm SLR camera as a teenager and has been behind a lens ever since. His favorite subjects are people of foreign lands, the remnants of past civilizations, and the textures of western terrain.

The two maintain an extensive slide library, and have given slide-illustrated talks for various organizations. Additionally, many of David's photographs and Pamela's watercolors are now in private collections.